T0238570

Future Generation Information Technology

First International Conference, FGIT 2009
Jeju Island, Korea, December 10-12, 2009
Proceedings

Tai-hoon Kim
Hannam University
Daejeon, South Korea
E-mail: taihoonn@hnu.kr

Wai-chi Fang
National Chiao Tung University
Hsinchu, Taiwan
E-mail: wfang@mail.nctu.edu.tw

Dominik Ślęzak
University of Warsaw & Infobright Inc.
Warsaw, Poland
E-mail: slezak@infobright.com

Library of Congress Control Number: 2009939138

CR Subject Classification (1998): C.2, G.2.2, H.3.4, B.8, C.4, D.2.8, D.4.8

LNCS Sublibrary: SL 5 – Computer Communication Networks and Telecommunications

ISSN   0302-9743
ISBN-10   3-642-10508-4 Springer Berlin Heidelberg New York
ISBN-13   978-3-642-10508-1 Springer Berlin Heidelberg New York

As future generation information technology (FGIT) becomes specialized and fragmented, it is easy to lose sight that many topics in FGIT have common threads and, because of this, advances in one discipline may be transmitted to others. Presentation of recent results obtained in different disciplines encourages this interchange for the advancement of FGIT as a whole. Of particular interest are hybrid solutions that combine ideas taken from multiple disciplines in order to achieve something more significant than the sum of the individual parts. Through such hybrid philosophy, a new principle can be discovered, which has the propensity to propagate throughout multifaceted disciplines.

FGIT 2009 was the first mega-conference that attempted to follow the above idea of hybridization in FGIT in a form of multiple events related to particular disciplines of IT, conducted by separate scientific committees, but coordinated in order to expose the most important contributions. It included the following international conferences: Advanced Software Engineering and Its Applications (ASEA), Bio-Science and Bio-Technology (BSBT), Control and Automation (CA), Database Theory and Application (DTA), Disaster Recovery and Business Continuity (DRBC; published independently), Future Generation Communication and Networking (FGCN) that was combined with Advanced Communication and Networking (ACN), Grid and Distributed Computing (GDC), Multimedia, Computer Graphics and Broadcasting (MulGraB), Security Technology (SecTech), Signal Processing, Image Processing and Pattern Recognition (SIP), and u- and e-Service, Science and Technology (UNESST).

We acknowledge the great effort of all the Chairs and the members of the advisory boards and Program Committees of the above-listed events, who selected 28% of over 1,050 submissions, following a rigorous peer-review process. Special thanks go to the following organizations supporting FGIT 2009: ECSIS, Korean Institute of Information Technology, Australian Computer Society, SERSC, Springer LNCS/CCIS, COEIA, ICC Jeju, ISEP/IPP, GECAD, PoDIT, Business Community Partnership, Brno University of Technology, KISA, K-NBTC and National Taipei University of Education.

We are very grateful to the following speakers who accepted our invitation and helped to meet the objectives of FGIT 2009: Ruay-Shiung Chang (National Dong Hwa University, Taiwan), Jack Dongarra (University of Tennessee, USA), Xiaohua (Tony) Hu (Drexel University, USA), Irwin King (Chinese University of Hong Kong,

Tai-hoon Kim
Wai-chi Fang
Dominik Ślęzak

the events organized as parts of the First International Mega-Conference on Future Generation Information Technology (FGIT 2009), held during December 10–12, 2009, at the International Convention Center Jeju, Jeju Island, South Korea. Out of approximately 300 papers accepted for 10 out of 11 FGIT 2009 conferences, (i.e., ASEA, BSBT, CA, DTA, FGCN/ACN, GDC, MulGraB, SecTech, SIP, and UNESST), we chose 10%. The remaining accepted papers were included in the proceedings of particular events, published by Springer in the CCIS series (respective volume numbers: 59, 57, 65, 64, 56, 63, 60, 58, 61, 62).

The papers in this volume were recommended based on their scores obtained from the independent reviewing processes at particular conferences, and their relevance to the idea of constructing hybrid solutions to address the real-world challenges of IT. The final selection was also based on the attempt to make this volume as representative of the current trends in IT as possible. The papers were then split into two sections on: "Data Analysis, Data Processing, and Advanced Computation Models," and "Security, Software Engineering, and Communication and Networking." Moreover, the volume begins with two papers prepared by the FGIT 2009 keynote speakers: "Computer Science: Where Is the Next Frontier?" by Ruay-Shiung Chang, and "Video Forgery" by Timothy K. Shih et al. We would like to acknowledge all the authors of keynote and regular papers for their extremely interesting and valuable contributions.

We realize that the idea of preparing this volume, with the papers corresponding to such diverse aspects of future generation information technology, may need further, perhaps critical, analysis. FGIT 2009 is not the first attempt to grasp the concept of hybrid solutions in IT (sometimes called h*ybrid information technology*). However, this is the first case wherein the publication process comprises two stages: the review processes related to particular conferences/disciplines, and the recommendation/selection procedure finally resulting in this volume. We are grateful to Springer LNCS, especially to Alfred Hofmann, for their trust in our efforts. We welcome the feedback from everyone who may happen to study the gathered material. We strongly believe that this kind of vision is worth continuing in the future.

Once more, we would like to thank all the organizations and individuals who supported FGIT 2009 and, in particular, helped in the preparation of this volume, with their hard work.

Data Analysis, Data Processing, Advanced Computation Models

Security, Software Engineering, Communication and Networking

Data Analysis, Data Processing, Advanced

National Dong Hwa University, Hualien, Taiwan
rschang@mail.ndhu.edu.tw

Abstract. Enrollments for computer science have dropped in recent years. Why is the trend? Can we do something to stop it? In this talk, we discuss the issues and propose some research directions with the hope that computer science can be revitalized. Coded as ACGT, we identify four interesting areas for computing. Furthermore, we preach for system openness and a simpler programming environment for small and smart devices.

Keywords: Autonomous Computing; Cooperative Computing; Green Computing; Trusted Computing; Open Systems.

1 Introduction

In September 8, 1966, American television company NBC debuted Star Trek TV series (http://www.startrek.com/). At the show's beginning, the following texts were narrated:

"Space... the Final Frontier. These are the voyages of the starship Enterprise. Its five-year mission: to explore strange new worlds, to seek out new life and new civilizations, to boldly go where no man has gone before."

The final frontier for space exploration is so interesting, daunting, and vast that it will keep generations of children intrigued. Remember also that the studies of cosmology dated back to the days before Christ. On the contrary, counting from the ENIAC (Electronic Numerical Integrator and Computer, the first general purpose computer) built in 1946, studies of computer science have only been existed for 63 years. However, we seem to see an alarming decline in the interest of pursuing degrees in computer science around the globe. According to a survey by the Computing Research Association (CRA) [1], the number of computer science majors in US fell 18 percent nationally from 2005 to 2006, continuing the 7-year trend. The results also showed that the number of students enrolled in fall 2007 is half of what it was in fall 2000. The situation is not alone. In Taiwan, the rankings of departments of computer

the recent smart devices are two possible major reasons. In this talk, I will elaborate on these two fronts.

2 In Need of New Fields and Excitements

We now know that ACGT stands for the four nucleic acid bases that make up DNA [6]. I would propose the ACGT for computer sciences. These are Autonomous computing, Cooperative computing, Green computing, and Trusted computing. Interestingly, in DNA, A is bonded only to T and C to G. In computer sciences, autonomous computing should be trusted and cooperative computing should be green.

2.1 Autonomous Computing

When IBM initiated the autonomic computing [7] concept in 2001, it was meant to reduce and solve the system management complexity issues. But I see there is an urgent need for autonomous computing application in one particular field, the robotics [8]. Human beings are autonomous. How to make a robot autonomous enough to mimic humans? It is the task of autonomous computing. In a book by CSIS (Center for Strategic and International Studies) [9], the world population is ageing and it is "certain and lasting. There is almost no chance that it will not happen—or that it will be reversed in our lifetime." Therefore, robots will come in handy in many fields, e.g., in supplying the lacking workers in factories, in taking care of sick and elderly people, and so on. However, before that comes true, many barriers have to be overcome. Mechanics and human ergonomics, though tough, are relatively solvable. The hardest part is the intelligence [10]. That is, can a robot be smart enough to be really able to replace humans in some endeavors? This is where autonomous computing comes in. Autonomous computing in robotics will change our future if it is successfully and well done.

2.2 Cooperative Computing

Interested in Aliens? Download a program from SETI@Home (http://setiathome.ssl. berkeley.edu/) and run it in your computer. You will be contributing to the project of

2.3 Green Computing

When crude oil climbed to more than 140 USD per barrel in 2008, we began to realize how much power computing devices consume and how much computing costs us. Green computing [20,21] tries to reduce the power consumption and reduce the cost of computing. Seen from a grander picture, it consists of a chain of events from manufacturing of computers to the user's habits of using computers. In the first step, we can narrow green computing down to the task of reducing energy consumption in hardware design and software operations. In hardware, low-power design [22] is common now. However, how to make software more energy efficient is an interesting new research. A paper studied the electric prices and concluded that a routing algorithm would be more economical if the algorithm could identify where the electric price is lower and routed around it [23]. Another interesting scenario is shown in Figure 1. I would call it as the *dormant router problem* [24]. In Figure 1, if the network traffic is very light, we don't need all routers to be operational. For example, we can turn off routers B, C, and E for the route from A to G. That leaves only one route, A-D-F-G. It should be fine if the traffic is light.

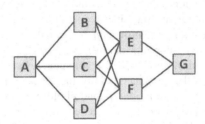

Fig. 1. An example of a routing network

Besides networking algorithms, there are many other places where green computing can be applied, for example, in the operating systems, in the middleware systems, in repetitive applications, etc. What we need is a tool or many tools to help us design and gauge the energy efficiency of a software system, which won't be easy.

3 More Openness in Small and Smart Devices

In the good old days when we only had personal computers, we learned to program it using Basic or Fortran. The grammar is simple and the program is plain and easy to understand. After learning the basic programming skills, we can write programs for various applications run by different PCs. Now most people use handheld devices. We learn how to operate it. Most people don't learn how to program it because it is called an embedded system. Embedded is embittered since not all embedded systems are created equal. Jonathan Zittrain, a Harvard law school professor, recently published an article [27] in New York Times and wrote a book [28] about this topic. He argues that PC and the Internet were originally "generative" platforms, where users can improve the basic function of the platform through easily adding applications. Now we are full of non-generative ones that only the vendor in charge can control. We consumers need to be careful of becoming too star-struck by our smart devices. Not all agree of course. People might prefer a well-designed closed system to a system using other open sources since user experiences are more important than programming experiences. However, as computer scientists, we like to program and we should encourage more openness. Openness may not necessarily bring innovation. Openness may not be omnipotent. But without openness, nothing is possible.

The industry has noted this situation and formed the Open Handset Appliance (OHA) (http://www.openhandsetalliance.com/) in 2007. Its members include mobile operators, software companies, semiconductor companies, handset manufacturers, and so on. At the same time as the announcement of the formation of the alliance, it also unveiled Android, an open source mobile phone platform based on the Linux operating system. Behind the scene, Google is believed to be a big player and the major developer for Android. Android aims to compete against other mobile platforms from Apple, Microsoft, Nokia, Palm, Research In Motion, and Symbian. As a result, none of the above companies joined OHA as of September, 2009.

Even under the OHA, Android is not completely open. The Android Software Development Kit License Agreement [29] states something that seems just like some proprietary software will do. For example, if you want to modify the Android SDK (Software Development Kit), be aware of the following sentence:

"Except to the extent required by applicable third party licenses, you may not copy

Will computer science as a discipline die? The answer is probably not since we are becoming more dependent (if not already) on computers and networks. To keep attracting young talents into our field, we need to keep the subject interesting and simply elegant. From my point of view, ACGT computing is useful and interesting. Its advances will certainly help mankind.

Two things will probably stay forever for computer sciences. One is the Internet and the other is the mobility. The combination is that more and more people are using Internet while they are on the move. What this trend will bring remains to be seen.

When a computer system becomes more complex, we need more intelligent and simple interface. Everyone can learn to drive a car easily. Can everyone learn to write a program as easily? To keep the innovation going, we need mathematicians, physicists, chemists, civil engineers, and so on, to be able to write programs to solve their problems. Making the programming task complex is not the way to go.

Finally, we should endeavor to attract women and minorities [30] into computer science departments. Recently, an interim report [31] from ACM and the WGBH Educational Foundation confirms a significant gender gap among college-bound students in their opinions of computing as a possible college major or career. The research found that 74 percent of boys – regardless of race or ethnicity – considered that a college major in computer science was a "very good" or "good" choice for them, but only 10 percent of girls rated it as "very good" and 22 percent rated it "good." I think this trend is alarming. If half of the populations are left out of computer science, the field will become boring, if not endangered.

Acknowledgments. I thank FGIT organizing committee for giving me this chance to talk. I also thank NSC of Taiwan for financial support in this research.

References

1. Computing Degree and Enrollment Trends: From the 2007-2008 CRA Taulbee Survey,
   `http://www.cra.org/taulbee/`
   `CRATaulbeeReport-StudentEnrollment-07-08.pdf`
2. Commentary: Outsourcing Jobs: Is It Bad? (August 25, 2003), BusinessWeek
3. Friedman, T.L.: The World Is Flat: A Brief History of the Twenty-First Century, Farrar, Straus and Giroux Publisher (April 5, 2005)

Kaufmann, San Francisco (2004)

12. Chang, R.-S., Chang, J.-S., Lin, S.-Y.: Job scheduling and data replication on data grids. Future Generation Computer Systems 23(7), 846–860 (2007)

13. Rittinghouse, J., Ransome, J.: Cloud Computing: Implementation, Management, and Security. CRC Press, Boca Raton (2009)

14. Buyya, R., Yeo, C.S., Venugopal, S.: Market-Oriented Cloud Computing: Vision, Hype, and Reality for Delivering IT Services as Computing Utilities. In: Proceedings of the 10th IEEE International Conference on High Performance Computing and Communications, Dalian, China, September 25-27 (2008)

15. Mendoza, A.: Utility Computing Technologies, Standards, and Strategies. Artech House Publishers (March 2007)

16. Wang, Y., He, H., Wang, Z.: Towards a formal model of volunteer computing systems. In: IEEE International Symposium on Parallel & Distributed Processing, May 2009, pp. 1–5 (2009)

17. Anderson, D.P., Fedak, G.: The Computational and Storage Potential of Volunteer Computing. In: Sixth IEEE International Symposium on Cluster Computing and the Grid, May 16-19, vol. 1, pp. 73–80 (2006)

18. Beckman, P.: Looking toward Exascale Computing. In: Ninth International Conference on Parallel and Distributed Computing, Applications and Technologies, December 1-4, p. 3 (2008)

19. Exascale Computing by 2015? IEEE Spectrum 45(12), 12

20. Wang, D.: Meeting Green Computing Challenges. In: International Symposium on High Density packaging and Microsystem Integration, June 26-28, pp. 1–4 (2007)

21. Harris, J.: Green Computing and Green IT Best Practices on Regulations and Industry Initiatives, Virtualization, Power Management, Materials Recycling and Telecommuting, Emereo Pty Ltd. (August 2008)

22. Rabaey, J.M., Pedram, M.: Low power design methodologies. Kluwer Academic Pub., Dordrecht (1996)

23. Qureshi, A., Weber, R., Balakrishnan, H., Guttag, J., Maggs, B.: Cutting the Electric Bill for Internet-Scale Systems. In: ACM SIGCOMM, Barcelona, Spain (August 2009)

24. Chang, R.-S.: Green Operations in Networks (manuscript in preparation)

25. Mitchell, C.: Trusted Computing, Institution of Electrical Engineers (2005)

26. Schneider, D.: Fresh Phish. IEEE Spectrum 45, 34–38 (2008)

27. Zittrain, J.: Lost in Clouds, New York Times, Opinion Section (July 20, 2009)

28. Zittrain, J.: The Future of the Internet and How to Stop It. Caravan Book (2008)

29. Android Software Development Kit License Agreement,

Asia University, Taiwan
[2] Tamkang University, Taiwan
timothykshih@gmail.com, kkiceman@gmail.com

In this section, we discuss about the technology of video forgery. There are three technologies we will discuss. The first is inpainting, inpainting is an algorithm developed for a long time. It includes image inpainting, video inpainting, and motion inpainting. Exemplar-Based Image Inpainting[1] is a technique which be proposed in 2004. It completes the area of an object which is manually selected and removed by the users. The image inpainting is focused on images computing, when this technique was used in a video sequence, it will produce another problem called "ghost shadow". In order to prevent this phenomenon, we proposed a method to solve in our previous research [2]. We use our proposed algorithm to generate the panorama of our video.

The background of the input videos can be divided into two parts. One is the stick background, in this part; we can do inpainting computing via our proposed video inpainting approach. But the dynamic background like fire, water or smoke can't be computed by our previous approach. So we use another way to make the dynamic background smoother.

The second part is about the object computing. There are many approaches that we can use in our tool. Motion estimation is an approach used in video compression, motion compensation or object tracking. The motion map of the object plays an important role in motion interpolation. In order to generate a new motion between two original motions, the precise motion vectors on object are necessary. Cross-Diamond-Hexagonal Search [3] is a novel algorithm proposed by Chun-Ho Cheung and Lai-Man Po. It composes of three algorithms – cross search, diamond search and hexagonal search, and capture benefits of these three algorithms. The result and performance of this algorithm is better than others proposed previously.

In the third part, we discuss about the forgery of the videos. Alex Rav-Acha et al. [4] proposed a video forgery algorithm focus on the dynamic stereo. They generated dynamic mosaics by sweeping the aligned space-time volume of the input video by a

1. Object tracking
2. Video inpainting
3. Video motion interpolation
4. Motion inpainting of background video
5. Video planning

The first challenge to alter the behavior of actors (or objects) in the original video involves a precise object tracking technique in stationary and non-stationary videos. Precise object tracking obtains the contour of video object by using color and motion information. The precision of tracking may affect the outcome of altering the obtained object, especially for non-stationary video sequences. The second issue is related to removing objects from a video, usually, called video inpainting. The key technology of video inpainting in non-station video is to remove object without leaving a "ghost shadow," which is created if the continuity of video frames were not considered in the inpainting procedure. To avoid ghost shadow, motions of objects need to be calculated to produce references for the video inpainting procedure to predict movements. The third issue in video forgery is to change the behavior of actors. For instance, the outcome of a 100-meter race in the Olympic Game can be falsified. Objects in different layers of a video can be played in different speeds and at different reference points with respect to the original video. In order to obtain a smooth movement of target objects, a motion interpolation mechanism can be used based on reference stick figures (i.e., a structure of human skeleton) and video inpainting mechanism. The fourth challenge issue is to alter the background video. For instance, special effects in the movie industry usually have fire, smoke, and water, etc. To produce a fake but realistic background, the dynamic motions need to be predicted and reproduced in a realistic way. This step of special effect production can be further enhanced with combining natural scenes, to prepare a background video for inserting actors and objects. The last interesting issue is to create a video database with a rich set of video clips, classified according to their scenery and video behavior. An efficient retrieval technique needs to be developed along with a friendly authoring tool for video planning. The optimal goal of video planning is to create new video sequences, based on video clips available in a large video database.

Fig. 1. The Left are the original videos and the right are the falsified videos

Fig. 1. (*continued*)

References

1. Criminisi, A., Perez, P., Toyama, K.: Region Filling and Object Removal by Exemplar-Based Image Inpainting. IEEE Transactions Image Processing 13, 1200–1212 (2004)
2. Shih, T.K., Tang, N.C., Hwang, J.N.: Ghost Shadow Removal in Multi-Layered Video Inpainting. In: Proc. of the IEEE 2007 International Conference on Multimedia & Expo, July 2007, pp. 1471–1474 (2007)
3. Cheung, C.-H., Po, L.-M.: Novel cross-diamond-hexagonal search algorithms for fast block motion estimation. IEEE Trans. on Multimedia 7(1), 16–22 (2005)
4. Rav-Acha, A., Pritch, Y., Lischinski, D., Peleg, S.: Dynamosaics: Video Mosaics with Non-Chronological Time. IEEE Trans. Pattern Analysis and Machine Intelligence 29(10), 1789–1801 (2007)

Banacha 2, 02-097 Warsaw, Poland
Infobright Inc., Poland
Krzywickiego 34 pok. 219, 02-078 Warsaw, Poland
{slezak,mkowalski}@infobright.com

Abstract. One of the major aspects of Infobright's relational database technology is automatic decomposition of each of data tables onto *Rough Rows*, each consisting of 64K of original rows. Rough Rows are automatically annotated by *Knowledge Nodes* that represent compact information about the rows' values. Query performance depends on the *quality* of Knowledge Nodes, i.e., their efficiency in minimizing the access to the compressed portions of data stored on disk, according to the specific query optimization procedures. We show how to implement the mechanism of organizing the incoming data into such Rough Rows that maximize the quality of the corresponding Knowledge Nodes. Given clear business-driven requirements, the implemented mechanism needs to be fully integrated with the data load process, causing no decrease in the data load speed. The performance gain resulting from better data organization is illustrated by some tests over our benchmark data. The differences between the proposed mechanism and some well-known procedures of database clustering or partitioning are discussed. The paper is a continuation of our patent application [22].

1 Introduction

Database systems are used to store and manage increasingly large amounts of data of increasingly different types and complexity. It is a continuing objective to maintain the speed of query-based data analysis in the face of diversified workloads and a need of assuring that newly incoming data portions are immediately ready for efficient querying together with the already stored ones. In [23,26], we reported that our technology – currently available as *Infobright Community Edition* (*ICE*, open source) and *Infobright Enterprise Edition* (*IEE*, commercial subscription) [10] – enables to deal with such challenges. Analytical workload diversity is addressed by *Knowledge Grid* that replaces standard indices with smaller, more flexible structures called *Knowledge Nodes* (*KNs*). The second above requirement is satisfied thanks to ability to quickly recalculate KNs

turbed, i.e., each Rough Row was assembled from 64K of rows incoming to ICE/IEE one by one. On the other hand, it is possible to reorganize the flow of incoming rows on-fly in order to produce Rough Rows with KNs that are of better quality. One might adopt for this purpose some well-known techniques of, e.g., database clustering or partitioning. However, we rather need a simple solution that would be more directly related to maximization of the quality of KNs in terms of their usage in query optimization and execution, and that would not suffer from such problems as, e.g., a lack of flexibility with respect to mixed and dynamically changing query workloads.

We propose an alternative, better-adjusted mechanism of data granulation (i.e., decomposition of the streams of rows into Rough Rows) [22]. The presented approach has analogies to incremental data clustering in the area of data mining [1,5] and may be a good example of how to adopt data mining methods to improve the internals of database and data warehouse technologies. On the other hand, our objectives to group data, including later usage of the obtained groups in practice, remain completely different than in the data mining scenarios. Consequently, the technical details of our approach differ from the incremental clustering methods as well.

The paper is organized as follows. In Section 2, we discuss the basics of our approach in comparison to some other methodologies at the edge of physical database tuning and the above-mentioned data clustering. In Section 3, we recall the foundations of Infobright technology, with additional emphasis on the benefits that may be obtained as a result of better data granulation. In Section 4, we introduce the details of the proposed mechanism and its integration with the Infobright's production software. In Section 5, we report the results of performance tests prior and after application of the proposed mechanism. Section 6 concludes the paper.

2 Related Work and Discussion

2.1 Physical Database Model Tuning

The mechanism that we present in this paper is actually an example of online database self-tuning process. With this respect, a state of the art in database optimization is presented in [6]. The authors emphasize a need for procedures that require less manual effort. They also compare offline and online tuning, wherein, in the first case, the model changes may be more drastic (e.g.: rebuild of some of indices, re-partitioning,

of KNs are fixed and let us focus on tuning at the level of row organization.

A widely-applied approach to improve query efficiency is related to data partitioning/clustering [9]. An example of advanced database clustering can be found in [2], wherein data rows are partitioned with regards to their values on multiple columns. It partially resembles the concept of clustering in data mining, where the idea is to gather together the rows with similar values (see Subsection 2.2). However, in databases, the value-ranges for particular clusters are usually pre-defined. When the database query workload changes and one decides to modify cluster definitions, the data needs to be re-partitioned at once or gradually, although that second option is rather hard to implement. In the next sections, one will be able to realize that our requirements for data granulation that improves the quality of KNs are far less rigorous, with a need of neither pre-defined value-ranges nor – which is the case of classical data clustering approaches in data mining – mutually disjoint value-ranges of the resulting Rough Rows.

Yet another approach is to sort data tables with respect to columns that are most crucial for queries. Actually, in a typical data warehouse scenario, such a kind of data processing can be performed prior to data load or, as proposed e.g. in [20], it can be done automatically as an internal stage of database tuning, with ability to maintain multiple partial data copies sorted in different ways, therefore better prepared for different queries. Analogous approaches have been always popular among database and data warehouse practitioners, although one needs to remember about significant computational cost of sorting, especially if we assume that the newly-inserted rows should be somehow synchronized with the old data. Moreover, in the case of dynamically changing workloads, it may still happen that there are no data copies that would work well for new queries. It is generally not a surprise that sorting with respect to some of data columns may destroy regularities with respect to the others. Hence, in our approach, we again attempt to avoid such rigorous assumptions about data organization, pointing out that the quality of KNs representing multiple subsets of data columns can be optimized with a need of neither sorting nor creating multiple data copies.

2.2 Data Clustering vs. Our Approach

Clustering is understood quite differently in the database and data mining communities. In data mining, it is defined as organization of rows into clusters based on similarity

afford only single pass through incoming data; we can keep only small fraction of data in memory. 2) We know neither the number of incoming rows nor their value-ranges; we can base only on history. 3) Produced Rough Rows are of constant cardinality; there is no need to keep their value-ranges disjoint. 4) The approach should be extendable with regards to arbitrary data types and their corresponding KNs.

The above items illustrate that – given fundamental differences in the high-level objectives of our KNs-related data granulation versus typical database and data mining scenarios – we need to expect significant differences also at the level of algorithmic design. On the other hand, it is still possible to borrow some ideas from research areas of the clustering of data streams or the incremental clustering [1,5,8,27]. For example, let us refer to the approach described in [1], wherein the streams of data are gathered into intermediate blocks that are used at the next stages to build the final knowledge models (e.g., meaningful data clusters according to the above data mining-related definition). Actually, one may say that our Rough Rows play the same role, however, the stage of building a knowledge model – specific for data mining or machine learning – is replaced by a framework for optimizing and executing queries in a relational database.

3   Infobright Technology

3.1   High-Level Architecture

As illustrated by Fig. 1, MySQL code is used for connection pooling, as well as storing table definitions, views and user permissions [17]. We use MySQL query rewriting and parsing. However, the major optimization parts are replaced. MySQL optimizer is kept as a subpart of ours, in connection to MySQL storage engine interface.

Our interpretation of the concept of *Knowledge Grid* is different than in grid computing or semantic web [4], although there are some analogies in a way our Knowledge Grid *mediates* between the query engine and the data. Also, our KNs should not to be confused with any type of *nodes* in grid/distributed/parallel architectures [9].

Data Packs at the bottom of Fig. 1 result from both vertical and horizontal data decomposition. As stated in Section 1, we group rows into Rough Rows. For each Rough Row, we store the values of each of the columns separately. Such obtained packs are compressed and managed as described in [25]. Currently, the rows are not reorganized

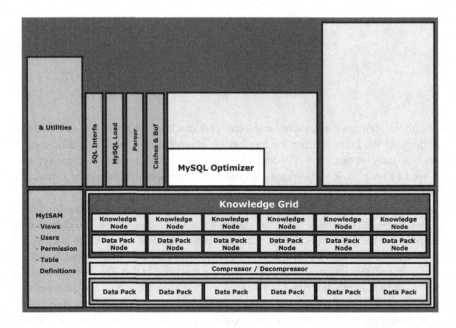

Fig. 1. Infobright's integration with MySQL. Standard MySQL optimizer dedicated to the pluggable storage engines in now a part of more advanced Infobright Optimizer and Executor.

formance because of their size. The size is related to details of design. Efficiency of the whole solution depends on how that design fits the data warehousing applications, in particular, how efficiently the functions using particular KNs while optimizing/executing queries are implemented. With this respect, there are some analogies with the research on standard database indices. However, KNs enable us to switch to *rough indices* defined at the level of Data Packs and Rough Rows. This leads to a number of novel structures aiming at speeding queries up. We are working towards providing the ICE users with ability to contribute with their own KNs to the open source code [21]. Let us present just two examples of KNs that are currently used in production:

- *Data Pack Nodes* (*DPNs*) contain such statistics as the minimum and maximum values (interpreted specifically for different data types), the total of values (for numeric data types), the number of null values, and the number of all elements in the Data Pack. They are automatically created for all columns in all tables. DPNs play an important role of linking Knowledge Grid to Data Packs, including smooth access to Data Packs. Their usage is partially analogous to some other database architectures [7,16], although the example presented in Subsection 3.3 shows that

area covered by 1's in HIST
of rough row X for column A

Fig. 2. HIST for Rough Row X with respect to its Data Pack for numeric column A

Data Pack which drops into the given interval, and 0 otherwise (see Fig. 2). Our HISTs are not so comparable to those widely studied in the literature [11], as they provide binary and very local Data Pack-related information. On the other hand, extensions of the currently implemented HISTs are still possible, while keeping in mind the constraint of a relatively small size of KNs. For analogous structures for alpha-numeric columns and other already used or planned KNs, we refer to [23,26].

3.3 Query Execution – Examples

Infobright optimizer implements a number of estimation methods based on KNs instead of standard indices. Its main advantage, however, is ability to simulate the steps of query execution at the level of Knowledge Grid, with no need to access Data Packs yet. In [21,23,26], we present various examples of using internal interface with KNs to speed up particular data operations. It is important to refer to those methods in order to better understand the results in Section 5. Here, just for illustration, let us recall the most fundamental example of using KNs to classify Data Packs into three categories:

– *Irrelevant Data Packs* with no data elements relevant for further execution
– *Relevant Data Packs* with all data elements relevant for further execution
– *Suspect Data Packs* that cannot be classified as Relevant/Irrelevant ones

Inspiration to consider such three categories grew from the theory of rough sets [18], where data is split onto *positive, negative,* and *boundary regions* with respect to their membership to the analyzed concepts. Algorithms based on rough sets are often used in data mining and KDD to search for meaningful data dependencies [15]. They can be also applied to improve database performance by employing such dependencies to deal with query filters [13]. Our idea is different. We apply Knowledge Grid to calculate *rough approximations* of data needed for resolving queries at the exact level and to assist query execution modules in accessing required Data Packs in an optimal way.

will become Irrelevant or will require exact processing too (Fig. 3d).

Pack A		Pack B		b)			c)		d)	
Pack A1 Min = 3 Max = 25		Pack B1 Min = 10 Max = 30			S	S	S	E		E
Pack A2 Min = 1 Max = 15		Pack B2 Min = 10 Max = 20			S	I	I	I		I
Pack A3 Min = 18 Max = 22		Pack B3 Min = 5 Max = 50			S	S	S	I/E		I/E
Pack A4 Min = 2 Max = 10		Pack B4 Min = 20 Max = 40			R	I	I	I		I
Pack A5 Min = 7 Max = 26		Pack B5 Min = 5 Max = 10			I	I	I	I		I
Pack A6 Min = 1 Max = 8		Pack B6 Min = 10 Max = 20			S	I	I	I		I

a)   b)   c)   d)

Fig. 3. Illustration for Section 3.3: (a) Simplified Knowledge Grid; (b,c,d) Query execution stages. RSI denote Relevant, Suspect and Irrelevant Data Packs. E denotes processing at the exact level.

4   Task Formulation and Solution

4.1   Quality of KNs and Rough Rows

As pointed out in Section 3, KNs should be evaluated with respect to their ability to assist in query optimization and execution. However, regardless of how well a given KN is designed, it may suffer in case data values of a given column behave too *randomly*. For example, imagine a column where the values of consecutive rows look like a "white noise" and, consequently, the min and max values stored in DPNs are distant from each other and HISTs spanned across DPN ranges for particular Data Packs are mostly filled with 1's. Imagine this is the case of column A or B in Table T, Subsection 3.3. Then, our benefit from KNs would be quite limited comparing to Fig. 3.

refer to [22] for more examples of quality function definitions.

We can now formulate the task of optimal granulation of rows into Rough Rows as maximization of qualities of KNs. In order to evaluate which rows should be assigned to which Rough Rows during data load, we need to translate quality functions of KNs to the quality function of Rough Rows. We follow a widely-applied idea to weight columns, indices, execution patterns, etc. according to their frequency of occurrence in the historical (or sampled) query workload [3,20]. In our case, it means measuring the frequency of usage of particular KNs by the Infobright's query optimization/execution modules. Certainly, there are many possibilities how to use such frequencies to weight quality functions of KNs. In this paper, we report the results of experiments for the Rough Row quality function $qual(X)$ that is simply a weighted sum of qualities $qual_{KN}(X)$. We refer again to [22] for more variants.

4.2 Algorithmic Framework

Our approach is illustrated by Fig. 4. Every incoming row is assigned to its *closest container*. Containers collect just-assigned rows. When a container reaches the maximum of 64K rows, its contents are forwarded as a new Rough Row to the next processing stages (partial recalculation of KNs, splitting onto Data Packs, compressing and locating Data Packs on disk). The container gets emptied and it is immediately ready to receive further data. We assume there is $k * 64K * rowSize$ memory available, where $k \in \mathbb{N}$ denotes the number of containers and $rowSize$ is the size of a parsed row.

We assign KN quality functions to containers, as if they were incomplete Rough Rows. Selection of the closest container X for an incoming row x requires fast (in some cases approximate) calculation and comparison of quantities of the form

$$dist(x, X) = qual(X) - qual(X \cup \{x\})$$

In the algorithm shown in Fig. 4, function $getNext(Buf)$ reads row x. Function $closestContainer(x, \mathbb{C})$ is responsible for choosing the best container in $\mathbb{C}$ for x. Function $createRoughRow$ transfers all rows from the container to a new Rough Row, empties the container and restores it.

In such an approach, there is a danger that a container which is (almost) empty will be always preferred over an almost full one. To avoid it, particularly when row x is well-

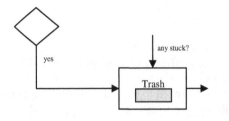

yes

any stuck?

Trash

```
if x = NULL then
    bufNonEmp ← FALSE
else
    closest ← closestContainer(x, ℂ)
    C_closest ← C_closest ∪ {x}
    if IsFull(C_closest) then
        B ≪ createRoughRow(C_closest)
    end if
end if
end while
end while
for each non-empty container:
B ≪ createRoughRow(container)
return B
```

Fig. 4. Top: A high-level diagram of the implemented granulation algorithm with the trash container. **Right:** Pseudocode of the simplified version of the algorithm, with no trash container.

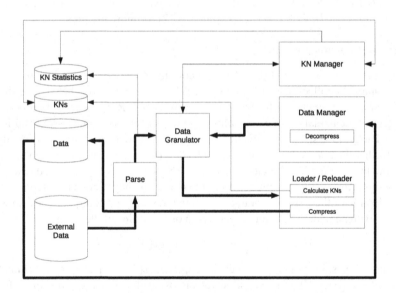

Fig. 5. Interactions between major pieces of ICE/IEE architecture. KN stands for Knowledge Node. Data Granulator, KN Statistics, as well as Reloader functionality are the new components.

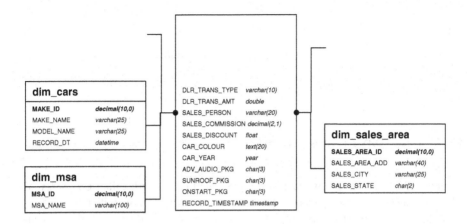

Fig. 6. The database schema for Car Sales data warehouse

Trash container helped us also in solving the problem of data patterns changing rapidly during load. In such cases, there may be some relatively old rows that are stuck in containers, with no ability to get matched with the freshly incoming rows. Accordingly, for each container, we maintain information about its latest modification. If the container is not updated for too long time (which is also expressed in terms of parameter), we liberate it by throwing all of its contents into the trash container.

4.3 Design of Integration

In the experiments presented in the next section, we implemented a partial solution based on reorganizing data prior to their load into Infobright. However, we did it in such a way that the future integration with the production system is fully simulated. The final integration schema is illustrated by Fig. 5. One can see that the proposed mechanism, referred as *Data Granulator* is located between the parsing and the compression stages of loading the data. It should be noted that there are also potential applications of granulation while re-optimizing the data organization (e.g. related to data vacuuming, which is beyond the scope of this particular paper but remains one of important items on our roadmap). Although these aspects are not covered by this paper, let us emphasize that the designed architecture enables us to *reload* data in a way transparent to the queries being run by the end users, with no need of massive calculations at a time. This way, it fully satisfies the assumptions of online tuning, as discussed in Section 2.

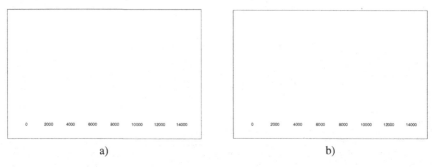

Fig. 7. Weighted DPN's qualities in Rough Rows of fact_sales: (a) without; (b) with granulating

expected. We created our own artificially generated benchmark called *Car Sales*. We adjusted data (Fig. 6) and queries (Appendix) to what we observed with customers.

In the reported experiments, we used a scaling factor yielding 120 GB database size (raw data) during data generation. The resulting fact table fact_sales contains 1 billion rows (15,259 Rough Rows). Dimension tables are relatively small (dim_dealers: 1,000 rows, dim_msa: 371, dim_cars: 400, dim_sales_area: 32,765, dim_dates: 4,017) and each of them corresponds to a single Rough Row. The algorithm discussed in the previous section is tested for fact_sales only. The rows in fact_sales are partially (but not completely) ordered with respect to TRANS_DATE. The remaining columns that are meaningful in queries are more or less uncorrelated to TRANS_DATE.

5.2 Results

We processed fact_sales using the algorithm in Fig. 4 with four containers and trash. We assumed query workload resembling queries in Appendix, as well as other queries being usually tested against Car Sales in Infobright. For simplification, we assigned equal positive weights to DPNs of three columns only: DEALER_ID, MAKE_ID and TRANS_DATE. It means that we do not care for any other types of KNs and any other columns while computing the distances between rows and containers in the algorithm.

Fig. 7 presents the DPN qualities for DEALER_ID, MAKE_ID and TRANS_DATE. The original data is partially organized (but not sorted) with respect to TRANS_DATE. On the other hand, the values of DEALER_ID and MAKE_ID behave quite randomly, resulting in poor qualities of their DPNs. As the result of data granulation, we can obtain even better quality of DPNs of TRANS_DATE (still not sorted but better organized) and far better qualities with respect to DEALER_ID and MAKE_ID. It is quite a different outcome than what we would get after re-sorting data with respect to DEALER_ID or MAKE_ID. In such a case, improvement of DPNs would be observed only for one of

	granules	20.97	0	14637			granules	48.20	0	14624	639
Q3	original	32.60	0	8632	7852	Q7	original	971.98	1	0	15260
	granules	23.87	0	14311	1801		granules	927.50	1	0	15260
Q4	original	189.77	15259	0	15259	Q8	original	532.16	0	0	30520
	granules	108.13	15259	0	15259		granules	34.38	28666	0	1854

well as the number of Rough Rows classified as relevant, irrelevant and suspect during query evaluation. Let us emphasize one more time that such classification is just one of many aspects of using KNs. Therefore, in the case of some queries these statistics are not available. For example, consider Query 5, where the number of distinct values of TRANS_DATE was much easier to be found after granulation, although it is not directly related to the above-mentioned classification.

6 Conclusions

The proposed mechanism of organizing data into such Rough Rows that maximize the quality of KNs turns out to be an efficient complement of so far developed Infobright's database technology. Certainly, there are still lots of open questions related to, e.g., managing small data loads (of less than 64K rows) and insert/update/delete operations, integration with multithread load mechanisms, or efficient acquisition of the weights of KNs. Although a thoughtful pipeline-oriented implementation of data load as composition of parsing, granulating and compressing should prevent the granulation algorithms from becoming a bottleneck, setting up appropriate requirements for the balance between load speed and query speed is necessary. At a more conceptual level, the formulas for Rough Row quality need to be significantly revised in case the KN statistics are not reliable enough. Further, in our experiments, we did not use more advanced types of KNs. Their introduction will require developing more sophisticated formulas for row-container distance calculation or, perhaps, coming up with a completely different decision making procedure. Nevertheless, in spite of all the remaining challenges and simplifications made in the paper, the results convince us to proceed with the final code integration in the nearest future. The obtained gains are clear. It is also worth emphasizing that, unlike in the case of standard database tuning techniques, the whole idea does not introduce any additional administrative complexity.

7. Grondin, R., Fadeitchev, E., Zarouba, V.: Searchable archive. US Patent 7,243,110 (2007)
8. Guha, S., Rastogi, R., Shim, K.: Cure: An efficient clustering algorithm for large databases. In: Proc. of SIGMOD, pp. 73–84 (1998)
9. Hellerstein, J.M., Stonebraker, M., Hamilton, J.R.: Architecture of a database system. Foundations and Trends in Databases 1(2), 141–259 (2007)
10. Infobright: http://www.infobright.com
11. Ioannidis, Y.E.: The history of histograms (abridged). In: Proc. of VLDB, pp. 19–30 (2003)
12. Jain, A.K., Murty, M.N., Flynn, P.J.: Data clustering: A review. ACM Comput. Surv. 31(3), 264–323 (1999)
13. Kerdprasop, N., Kerdprasop, K.: Semantic knowledge integration to support inductive query optimization. In: Song, I.-Y., Eder, J., Nguyen, T.M. (eds.) DaWaK 2007. LNCS, vol. 4654, pp. 157–169. Springer, Heidelberg (2007)
14. Kersten, M.L.: The database architecture jigsaw puzzle. In: Proc. of ICDE, pp. 3–4 (2008)
15. Kloesgen, W., Żytkow, J.M. (eds.): Handbook of Data Mining and Knowledge Discovery. Oxford University Press, Oxford (2002)
16. Metzger, J.K., Zane, B.M., Hinshaw, F.D.: Limiting scans of loosely ordered and/or grouped relations using nearly ordered maps. US Patent 6,973,452 (2005)
17. MySQL manual: Storage engines, http://dev.mysql.com/doc/refman/6.0/en/storage-engines.html
18. Pawlak, Z., Skowron, A.: Rudiments of rough sets. Inf. Sci. 177(1), 3–27 (2007)
19. Pedrycz, W., Skowron, A., Kreinovich, V. (eds.): Handbook of Granular Computing. Wiley, Chichester (2008)
20. Rasin, A., Zdonik, S., Trajman, O., Lawande, S.: Automatic vertical-database design. WO Patent Application, 2008/016877 A2 (2008)
21. Ślęzak, D., Eastwood, V.: Data warehouse technology by Infobright. In: Proc. of SIGMOD, pp. 841–845 (2009)
22. Ślęzak, D., Kowalski, M., Eastwood, V., Wróblewski, J.: Methods and systems for database organization. US Patent Application, 2009/0106210 A1 (2009)
23. Ślęzak, D., Wróblewski, J., Eastwood, V., Synak, P.: Brighthouse: an analytic data warehouse for ad-hoc queries. PVLDB 1(2), 1337–1345 (2008)
24. Stonebraker, M., Abadi, D., Batkin, A., Chen, X., Cherniack, M., Ferreira, M., Lau, E., Lin, A., Madden, S., O'Neil, E., O'Neil, P., Rasin, A., Tran, N., Zdonik, S.: CStore: A column oriented DBMS. In: Proc. of VLDB, pp. 553–564 (2005)
25. Wojnarski, M., Apanowicz, C., Eastwood, V., Ślęzak, D., Synak, P., Wojna, A., Wróblewski,

```sql
GROUP BY sales_person HAVING SUM(sales_commission) > 9
ORDER BY sales_person DESC LIMIT 5;


-- Q3 --
SELECT COUNT(f.sales_person) FROM fact_sales f
INNER JOIN dim_sales_area s ON (f.sales_area_id = s.sales_area_id)
WHERE f.trans_date between '2006-05-15' AND '2006-05-31'
    AND f.sales_commission > 9.0 AND s.sales_state LIKE 'NY%';


-- Q4 --
SELECT MIN(comm), MAX(comm), AVG(comm), SUM(comm)
FROM    (SELECT f.dlr_trans_amt*(f.sales_commission/100) AS comm
        FROM fact_sales f INNER JOIN dim_dealers d ON (f.dealer_id = d.dealer_id)
        INNER JOIN dim_dates dates ON (f.trans_date = dates.trans_date)
        WHERE dates.trans_year = 2007 AND dates.trans_month = 'JANUARY'
            AND d.dealer_name LIKE 'BHUTANI%' ) AS maxcomm;


-- Q5 --
SELECT COUNT(DISTINCT trans_date) FROM fact_sales;


-- Q6 --
SELECT dlr_trans_amt*(sales_commission/100)
FROM fact_sales
WHERE trans_date IN (SELECT trans_date FROM dim_dates
                WHERE trans_year = 2007 AND trans_month = 'FEBRUARY')
    AND dealer_id IN
        (SELECT dealer_id FROM dim_dealers WHERE dealer_name LIKE 'BHUTANI%'
                    OR dealer_state = (SELECT sales_state FROM dim_sales_area
                            WHERE sales_area_id = 40))
    AND dlr_trans_amt*(sales_commission/100) IS NOT NULL
    AND dlr_trans_amt*(sales_commission/100) > 4300 LIMIT 1000,1000;


-- Q7 --
SELECT car_year, car_colour, sales_person,
    COUNT(DISTINCT dim_dealers.dealer_id) AS dealer_cnt
FROM fact_sales, dim_dealers
WHERE fact_sales.dealer_id = dim_dealers.dealer_id
    AND car_colour <> 'YELLOW' AND sales_person NOT LIKE 'RA%'
    AND car_year IN (2000, 2003, 2005)
    AND fact_sales.make_id NOT IN (SELECT make_id FROM dim_cars
                WHERE model_name LIKE 'E%X%')
GROUP BY car_year, car_colour, sales_person
ORDER BY dealer_cnt DESC, car_year, car_colour, sales_person;


-- Q8 --
SELECT dim_dealers.dealer_id, COUNT(*) AS numdeal
FROM dim_dealers, fact_sales f1, dim_sales_area WHERE f1.dealer_id =
dim_dealers.dealer_id
    AND f1.sales_area_id = dim_sales_area.sales_area_id
```

minami@kiis.ac.jp
² Kyushu University Library, 6-10-1 Hakozaki, Higashi, Fukuoka 812-8581 Japan
{minami,ejkim}@lib.kyushu-u.ac.jp

Abstract. Our society is rapidly changing to information society, where the needs and requests of the people on information access are different widely from person to person. Library's mission is to provide its users, or patrons, with the most appropriate information. Libraries have to know the profiles of their patrons, in order to achieve such a role. The aim of library marketing is to develop methods based on the library data, such as circulation records, book catalogs, book-usage data, and others. In this paper we discuss the methodology and imporatnce of library marketing at the beginning. Then we demonstrate its usefulness through some examples of analysis methods applied to the circulation records in Kyushu University and Guacheon Library, and some implication that obtained as the results of these methods. Our research is a big beginning towards the future when library marketing is an unavoidable tool.

Keywords: Library Marketing, Data Analysis, Circulation Data, Usage of Areas, Intelligent Bookshelf (IBS), Usage Data Analysis.

1 Introduction

According to the American Marketing Association (AMA) [1], the concept of marketing used to be as follows: "Marketing is an organizational function and a set of processes for creating, communicating, and delivering value to customers and for managing customer relationships in ways that benefit the organization and its stakeholders." They now define marketing as follows: "Marketing is the activity, set of institutions, and processes for creating, communicating, delivering, and exchanging offerings that have value for customers, clients, partners, and society at large."

By comparing these two definitions, we recognize that marketing was considered as the activities that benefit the organization (company); which matches with the ordinary people's intuition. It is now considered as wider activities that benefit the customers and our society. So it is natural to apply marketing to non-profit organizations like libraries including public and university libraries.

not used sufficiently so far. It is truly a big waste of potentially very useful data. We carry out our research on library marketing by dividing the process into four levels.

(1) Preliminary Investigation

In this level we invesitgate what information, tips, and knowledge could be obtained by analysing some kinds of data. We do not worry much about if we can really get such data or the extracted information is very useful or not. Our aim in this level is to create as many possible ideas as we can imagine which could be and/or may be used for library marketing.

(2) Real Data Analysis

In this level we apply the methods obtained in the preliminary investigation level. By using the real data, we can evaluate the analysis methods from the practical point of view. If we find out that an analysis method is very useful, then we apply this method to another data. It could happen that we can apply a method to other types of data by modifing it, slightly or largely.

Most of analysis methods presented in this paper can be considered to be those in this level. We will continue our research on this level and try hard to find as many practically useful methods as possible.

(3) Combination of Methods

Even though one type of data can be useful enough for library marketing, we would be able to extract even more useful information by combining the extracted information/knowledge and cobining more than one types of data. We will investigate this type of analysis methods after we investigate the level (2) sufficiently.

(4) Development of the Automated Methods

As we have found a very useful analysis method, it should be convenient to apply it by automating the analysis method. This method is a kind of macro procedure so that it is a pack of analysis methods and thus can be considered as one method. As a result, this analysis is easy to use as well as it can be used as a part of more sophisticated automated methods.

In this paper we will demonstrate the importance of library marketing through presenting some example analysis methods for such data as the circulation data, usage data of library materials, those data about areas in library, and so on.

The rest of this paper is organized as follows: In Section 2, we show some example analysis methods and results from a circulation record for 2007 of Kyushu University Library in order to demonstrate its potential usefulness. Even though we are in the

one student and analyze the student's behavior.

2.1 Data and Analysis Methods

We use the circulation data of the Central Library of KUL for the school year 2007; from April 1, 2007 to March 31, 2008. See also [8] for other statistical data in KUL. One record item consists of, roughly speaking, the book ID, book profile including classification and call number, borrower ID, the borrower's profile including affiliation, type (professor, student, staff, etc.), and the timestamps, i.e. date (yyyy:mm:dd) and time (hh:mm:ss), for borrow and return. The total number of circulated items is about 67 thousands.

2.2 Analysis Results from All Records

Figure 1 illustrates the ratios of borrowed materials according to patron type. About half of borrowed materials are borrowed by undergraduate students and about 40% are by graduate students. Thus almost 90% are borrowed by students. This result matches to the ratio of visiting patrons reported in [5], in which 53% of about 327 thousand visitors are undergraduate students and 28% are graduate students. Thus 81% of visitors are students in April 2009. This ratio does not vary a lot. In the fiscal year 2007 81% of visitors to the central library are the students, while 87% is the student ratio for the visitors to all libraries in KUL that consists of the central library and 6 branch libraries.

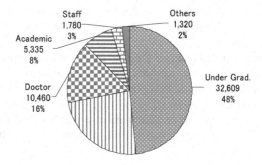

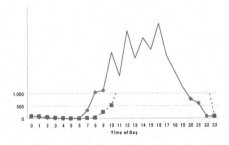
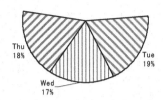

Fig. 2. Books Borrowed and Returned in Time of a Day

Fig. 3. Rates of Books Borrowed in Week

In the data for the fiscal year 2008, the ratio for the central library was 83% and that for all the KUL libraries was 88%. As a conclusion the ratio of student visitors among all the visitors is roughly from 80% to 90%. Another conclusion is this ratio is bigger for all libraries than that for the central library only. Furthermore the ratios increase by comparing the data in two years. So we have to say that the importance of library services to students is also increasing. We have to put more efforts on student services for university libraries.

If we assume this ratio is also applicable to the data in 2007, we can say that the undergraduate students who are 53% of visitors borrow 48%, while the graduate students who are 28% of visitors borrow 39% of books. From these data we have values by dividing the borrow ration by the visitor ratio, which are the index for how many books one person borrows. The values are about 0.91 for undergraduate students and about 1.39 for graduate students. The average value is exactly 1 because 100% of visitors borrow 100% of books. By comparing these ratios, we can say that the graduate students borrow 1.4 more books in average than undergraduate students. As a conclusion we can say roughly that graduate students study harder than undergraduate students if we assume that the borrowing of library books is the index for aggressiveness for study.

Figure 2 indicates how many books are borrowed and returned as time goes in a day. The horizontal axis represents the time of the day and the vertical axis represents the number of books borrowed in an hour. The peak time for returning is about 16:00 and for returning 17:00 is the peak time. More precisely the time interval the books are mostly returned are about from 12:00 to 17:00. The time interval for books are borrowed the most is about from 12:00 to 22:00.

Figure 3 indicates the ratios of borrowed books according to day of week. The result

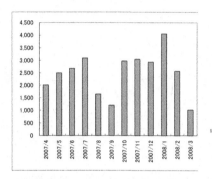

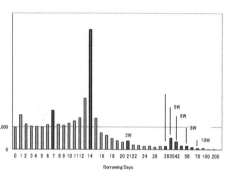

Fig. 4. Number of Books Borrowed in Month

Fig. 5. Number of Books for Renting Days

Figure 4 indicates the number of books according to month from April 2007 to March 2008. This result is natural to understand that from April to July the number of borrowed books is increasing as the students get used to study courses that start in April. The numbers become much smaller in August and September because these months are in summer holidays. The number recovers in October as the new semester starts. Then it increases suddenly in January, probably because senior students, i.e. in the 4th grade students, are very busy in writing their theses in this month because of the due dates for their graduating papers. Finally the number decreases in March because of end of the year holidays.

Figure 5 illustrates the frequencies of books according to the renting days. The peak value comes on 14 days (2 weeks), which are the due period of days for borrowing. The average is 12.2 days. Roughly speaking about 1,000 books are returned on the days that are less then 14 days; which might mean the students who borrow books from the library visit regularly. It is interesting to see that the number is also about 1,000 for 0 day, which means that the books are returned on the day they are borrowed.

To see more precisely, the number is much bigger than 1000 in the days 1, 7 and 13. Borrowing 1 day means that the books are returned on the next day. So many books are borrowed for very short time. Next peak day is 7, where the books are borrowed for one week, which is reasonable. The number increases as the day passes from 9 to 14. Many students seem to care about the return date and try to return as early as possible.

It is a surprise to see that quite a lot of books are borrowed beyond two weeks. The maximum value is 238 days. The book's title is "Introduction to German Law" and the student belongs to Engineering. The student borrowed such a long time probably because he or she did not want to return or just forgot to return.

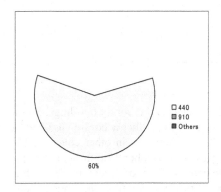

60%

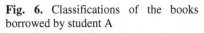
□ 440
▣ 910
■ Others

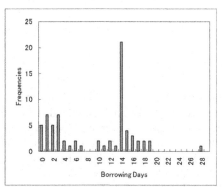

Fig. 6. Classifications of the books borrowed by student A

Fig. 7. Number of Books for Renting Days (The Book Borrowed Most Frequently)

the maximum number among all the students; which probably means that the student A is very aggressive in studying.

Figure 6 is the ratios of the classification number of books borrowed by the student. KUL takes NDC (Nippon Decimal Classification) system for books classification. In NDC 007 means information science, 410 for mathematics, 420 for physics, 430 for chemistry, 440 for astronomy space sciences, and 910 for Japanese literature. The student borrowed the books classified in 420 (physics) at the ratio 60%, followed with 410 (mathematics) with 20%.

Figure 7 illustrates the distribution of numbers of books according to the day of borrowing of student. A. As with Figure 5, student A also returned the books most of all on the 14th day. On the other hand, different from Figure 5, student A only borrowed the books only from 0 to 3 days much more than from 4 to 13 days. He or she also borrowed a number of books more than 14 days. The maximum day is 28.

3 Other Library Marketing Cases

3.1 Area Usage Data Analysis

The second author and other librarians of Gwacheon Public Library of Information & Science (hereafter Gwacheon Library, GL) [4] in Korea carried out a series of experiments by putting barcode readers at the entrance of some rooms in the library and collected the data for analyzing how their rooms are used by the visiting patrons [6]. It was an excellent research example for library marketing. In this section we show how data were collected and analyzed and what are their implications are induced from

rooms are relatively small and are distributedly located in the library buildings. So the patrons are supposed to move from one room or area to another according to what he or she wants to read or do, in comprison with other libraries in other countries like Japan. The librarians of GL had experimenting from November 15th through December 25th 2005 by putting barcode readers at the entrance door of several rooms such as DIR-I and II, FRR, CR. They also put a reader at the exit gate from the library building. With these readers they collect the data about how the patrons used the rooms of GL. In order to have the data as accurate as possible, they even arranged the librarians so that they took turns and waiting at the readers and asked the patrons to scan their ID cards when they entered and exited the rooms and the library.

From the experiment, they found a lot of results. One example is that among 6,633 patrons using the DIR-I and II, CR, FRR, 26% of patrons used DIR-I, 30% for DIR-II, 35% for CR, and 9% for FRR. Thus nearly 60% of patrons used DIR-I in the 4th fllor and DIR-II in the 3rd floor as total. So, one possible idea for them is to combine the two rooms into one so that they can provide better convinience to the patrons.

The usage data are automatically collectable for EDR. From the data, they found that about 90% used for accessing the Internet. The ratio was increasing in comparison with the usage of document editing without using the Internet. So, one possible idea for more convinience is to relocate the EDR from the 3rd floor to the 1st floor, or the entrance floor of the library.

3.2 Circulation Data Analysis in Ehime University Japan

Yamada [12] analyzed the circulation data of a university library. He compared the relationship between the years after publication of books and the ratios of borrowing and found that (1) the newly published books are well prefered to be borrowed and (2) still a number of books, or evergreen gooks, are constantly borrowed.

He concluded that it is very important for libraries to do their best so that newly published books are provided for service as soon as possible. He also concluded that by collecting and comparing the evergreen books of a lot of libraries, librarians may be able to know what books are supported by students of the libraries and thus what books are the must for them.

3.3 Usage Data Analysis with Bookshelf Equipped with RFID-Reader

society, we have to investigate more on developing methods for utilizing usage data.

4 Concluding Remarks

The aim of this paper is to demonstrate the importance of the concept of library marketing through some examples. Firstly we investigate the definition of library marketing. As case studies for library marketing, we chose the circulation records of the central library of Kyushu University. From the point of view of library marketing, the ordinary statistical results such as total number of borrowed books, average number of borrowed books per patron, the total number of the patrons who borrowed at least one book, etc. [8, 9], are not enough. In this paper we tried to find other analysis methods such as the pattern of borrowing and returning time zones, patterns of borrowing days, comparison of borrowing days of week, and others.

The results presented in this paper are just a beginning in our approach to library marketing. We need to keep investigating more in this direction. One possibility is to analyse the usage data from IBS. Another one is to combine different types of data and extracts more useful knowledge for improving patron services by libraries.

References

1. American Marketing Association (AMA): http://www.marketingpower.com/
2. Finkenzeller, K.: RFID Handbook, 2nd edn. John Wiley & Sons, Chichester (2003)
3. Gwacheon City: http://www.gccity.go.kr/foreign/english/
4. Gwacheon City Library: http://www.gclib.net/
5. Kim, E., Minami, T.: Library's Space Organization Improvement Based on Patrons' Behavioral Research-An Attempt for Library Marketing at Gwacheon Public Library in Korea and Kyushu University Library–, Research and Development Division Annual Report 2008/2009, Kyushu University Library (2009) (in Japanese)
6. Kim, E.: A Study on the Space Organization by the User's Behavior in Public Library. Gyeonggi University (2008) (in Korean)
7. Kyushu University Library: http://www.lib.kyushu-u.ac.jp
8. Kyushu University Library: Annual Report 2007/2008 (2008)
9. Kyushu University Library: Annual Report 2008/2009 (2009)

Univ. Ss. Cyril and Methodius, Skopje, Macedonia
{georgina,etfdav}@feit.ukim.edu.mk

Abstract. To understand the structure-to-function relationship, life sciences researchers and biologists need to retrieve similar structures from protein databases and classify them into the same protein fold. With the technology innovation the number of protein structures increases every day, so, retrieving structurally similar proteins using current structural alignment algorithms may take hours or even days. Therefore, improving the efficiency of protein structure retrieval and classification becomes an important research issue. In this paper we propose novel approach which provides faster classification (minutes) of protein structures. We build separate Hidden Markov Model for each class. In our approach we align tertiary structures of proteins. Additionally we have compared our approach against an existing approach named 3D HMM. The results show that our approach is more accurate than 3D HMM.

Keyword: Protein classification, Hidden Markov Model, SCOP.

1 Introduction

To understand the structure-to-function relationship, life sciences researchers and biologists need to retrieve similar structures from protein databases and classify them into the same protein fold. The structure of a protein molecule is the main factor which determines its chemical properties as well as its function. Therefore, the 3D representation of a residue sequence and the way this sequence folds in the 3D space are very important. The 3D protein structures are stored in the world-wide repository Protein Data Bank (PDB) [1]. In order to find the function of protein molecule, life sciences researchers and biologists need to classify the protein structure. There are several sophisticated methods for classifying proteins structures.

The SCOP (Structural Classification of Proteins) database, describes the structural and evolutionary relationships between proteins [2]. Classification with SCOP method is based on experts' experience. Evolutionary relationship of the proteins is

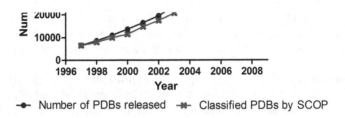

Fig. 1. Number of proteins released in PDB versus number of proteins classified by SCOP

The FSSP (Families of Structurally Similar Proteins) database [4] is created according to the DALI method [5]. It is based on secondary structure. The evaluation of a pair of proteins is a highly time consuming task, so the comparison between a macromolecule and all the macromolecules of the database requires days. Therefore, one representative protein for each class is defined, so that no two representatives have more than 25 percent amino-acid sequence identity. The unclassified protein is compared only to the representative protein of each class that requires an entire day. The DALI algorithm is based on the best alignment of protein structures.

SCOP, CATH, FSSP and many other sophisticated classifiers are very time consuming. SCOP method is the slowest due to manual classification form experts. CATH method is semi-manual, while FSSP is totally automated, but still is not able to follow the speed of determining novel protein structures.

Fig. 1 presents the gap of number of released proteins in PDB database and number of proteins classified by SCOP. As it can be seen, the number of determined protein structures which are yet not classified by SCOP increases every day. Therefore, a need for fast and accurate methods for protein classification is obvious.

There are many classification algorithms that can be used for protein classification as Naive Bayesian classifier, k nearest neighbour (K-NN), decision trees, neural networks, Support vector machines (SVM), Hidden Markov Model (HMM) and so on.

ProCC [6], first decomposes protein structures into multiple SSE (secondary structure elements) triplets. The algorithm then extracts ten features from a SSE triplet based on the spatial relationships of SSEs such as distances and angles. R*-Tree is utilized to index feature vectors of SSE triplets. For each database protein, a weighted bipartite graph is generated based on the matched SSE triplets of retrieval results. A

ary structures. In [12], it is shown that HMM approach based on tertiary structure is more accurate (10% higher precision) than the approach based on secondary structure. This is due to the fact that tertiary structure cares much more information than the secondary structure.

Several works [13], [14], [15] apply a consensus strategy to classify the protein domains or folds for newly-discovered proteins by intersecting multiple classification results from classical structural alignment algorithms such as DALI [5], MAMMOTH [16], Combinatorial Extension (CE) [17] and VAST [18]. These consensus approaches yield higher classification accuracies than each individual method. However, a combination of structural alignment algorithms is computationally expensive.

In this paper we propose novel approach for classifying protein 3D structures based on HMMs which consider the tertiary structure of protein molecules. The evaluation of our classification approach is made according to the SCOP hierarchy. Additionally we have compared our approach against an existing approach named 3D HMM [11].

The paper is organized as follows: our approach is given in section 2; section 3 gives some experimental results; while section 4 concludes the paper and gives some future work directions.

2 Our Approach

In this paper we propose novel approach for classifying protein molecules. Our approach uses the well known Hidden Markov Model for building profile for tertiary structure for corresponding class.

Hidden Markov Models (HMMs) [19] are statistical models which are generally applicable to time series or linear sequences. They have been widely used in speech recognition applications [20], and been introduced to bioinformatics in the late 80's [21]. A HMM can be visualised as a finite state machine. Finite state machines move through a series of states and produce some kind of output, either when the machine has reached a particular state or when it is moving from state to state.

Hidden Markov models, which are extensions of Markov chains, have a finite set of states $(a_1, ..., a_n)$, including a begin state and an end state. The HMM generates a protein sequence by emitting symbols as it progresses through a series of states. Each state has probabilities associated with it:

forward algorithm [24]. In this paper we have used the Viterbi algorithm. The most probable sequence is determined recursively by backtracking, see Fig. 2.

Initialize: $P_{START}(0) = 1$; $P_{s_1}(0) = 0$ for all s_1

Recursion: for $i = 1$ to $length\ (query)$

$$P_{s_2}(i) = e_{s_2}(x_i) \max_{\forall s_1} \{P_{s_1}(i-1)t_{s_1 s_2}\}$$

$$backward\_ptr_i = \underset{\forall s_1}{argmax}\{P_{s_1}(i-1)t_{s_1 s_2}\}$$

Termination: $$score(x, Path) = \max_{\forall s_1}\{P_{s_1}(length(query))t_{s_1 START}\}$$

$$Path_{length(query)} = \underset{\forall s_1}{argmax}\{P_{s_1}(length(query))t_{s_1 START}\}$$

Backtracking: for $i = length\ (query)$ to 1

$$Path_{i-1} = backward\_ptr_i Path_i$$

---

s_1, s_2 are hidden states; $START$ is start state; END is end state; $Path$ is the most probable path; $backward\_ptr$ is the backward pointer; x_i = the i-th symbol in the emission sequence; t_{ab} is the transition probability from state a to b; $e_a(b)$ is the emission probability of symbol b in state a; $P_k(i)$ = the most probable path ending in state k with observation i

Fig. 2. Viterbi algorithm

In our approach we consider the arrangement in 3D space of Cα atoms which form the protein backbone. The main idea of our approach is to model the folding of protein backbone around its centre of mass by using HMM. In this way we align tertiary structures of protein molecules.

Proteins have distinct number of Cα atoms. So, we have to find a unique way to represent all proteins with sequences with same length. In this approach, we interpolate the backbone of the protein with fixed number of points, which are equidistant along the backbone. Then, we calculate the Euclidean distances from these points to

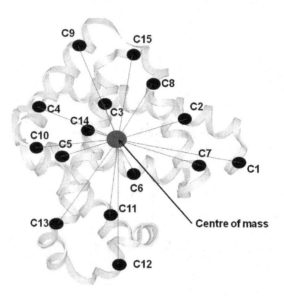

Fig. 3. Backbone interpolation

Fig. 4. Our HMM approach

Additionally, distances are quantized in order to obtain discrete values of symbols that can be emitted. Different type of quantization can be used. In order to model the

In this research we approximated the backbone with 64 approximation points which are sufficient for describing the most relevant features of proteins [25]. First, we examined the influence of number of states (Q) on classification accuracy, see Table 1. As it can be seen, by using 20 states a highest precision is achieved. By using 30 HMM states classification time increases, while classification accuracy is getting worse.

Table 1. Experimental results of our approach by using 64 approximation points

Q (number of states)	Accuracy (%)	Classification time for all test proteins (sec)
16	92.35	420
20	92.51	420
30	90.88	450

We have additionally compared our approach against an existing approach named 3D HMM [11]. We have used HMMs with $Q=20$ states. In this analysis, we have used dataset of proteins from globins and IgV (V set from immunoglobulin superfamily) families, as in [11]. We have randomly chosen one training protein from each domain, while other proteins serve as test data. Namely, test set consists of 754 proteins from globins and 1326 proteins from IgV family. Analysis showed that our approach is more accurate than existing 3D HMM approach [11], see Table 2. Namely, our approach achieves classification accuracy higher for 1.5% for globins and 1.7% for IgV family.

Table 2. Comparison of our approach against 3D HMM

Approach	Classification accuracy for globins family (%)	Classification accuracy for IgV family (%)
Our approach	99.7	98.3
3D HMM	98.2	96.6

Classifiers such as our which are based on HMM can be used for classification at

have compared our HMM approach against an existing 3D HMM approach [11]. The results show that our approach is more accurate than 3D HMM. Namely, our approach achieves classification accuracy higher for 1.5% for globins and 1.7% for IgV family.

Our future work is concentrated on investigating other protein classifiers in order to obtain higher precision. Also, we want to make a hybrid hierarchical classifier, so HMM can be used at family and lower levels of the SCOP hierarchy, while other corresponding classifiers can be used at upper levels.

References

1. Berman, H.M., Westbrook, J., Feng, Z., Gilliland, G., Bhat, T.N., Weissig, H., Shindyalov, I.N., Bourne, P.E.: The Protein Data Bank. Nucleic Acids Research 28, 235–242 (2000)
2. Murzin, A.G., Brenner, S.E., Hubbard, T., Chothia, C.: Scop: A Structural Classification of Proteins Database for the Investigation of Sequences and Structures. J. Mol. Biol. 247, 536–540 (1995)
3. Orengo, C.A., Michie, A.D., Jones, D.T., Swindells, M.B., Thornton, J.M.: CATH–A Hierarchic Classification of Protein Domain Structures. Structure 5(8), 1093–1108 (1997)
4. Holm, L., Sander, C.: The FSSP Database: Fold Classification Based on Structure- Structure Alignment of Proteins. Nucleic Acids Research 24, 206–210 (1996)
5. Holm, L., Sander, C.: Protein structure comparison by alignment of distance matrices. J. Mol. Biol. 233, 123–138 (1993)
6. Kim, Y.J., Patel, J.M.: A framework for protein structure classification and identification of novel protein structures. BMC Bioinformatics 7, 456 (2006)
7. Hastie, T., Tibshirani, R.: Discriminant adaptive nearest neighbor classification. IEEE Trans. on Pattern and Machine Intell. 18(6), 607–616 (1996)
8. Cortes, C., Vapnik, V.: Support vector networks. Machine Learning 20, 273–297 (1995)
9. Khati, P.: Comparative analysis of protein classification methods. Master Thesis. University of Nebraska, Lincoln (2004)
10. Plötz, T., Fink, G.A.: Pattern recognition methods for advanced stochastic protein sequence analysis using HMMs. Pattern Recognition 39, 2267–2280 (2006)
11. Alexandrov, V., Gerstein, M.: Using 3D Hidden Markov Models that explicitly represent spatial coordinates to model and compare protein structures. BMC Bioinformatics 5, 2 (2004)

from theory): An automated method for model comparison. Protein Science 11, 2606–2621 (2002)

17. Shindyalov, H.N., Bourne, P.E.: Protein structure alignment by incremental combinatorial extension (ce) of the optimal path. Protein Eng. 9, 739–747 (1998)

18. Gibrat, J.F., Madej, T., Bryant, S.H.: Surprising similarities in structure comparison. Curr. Opin. Struct. Biol. 6(3), 377–385 (1996)

19. Ephraim, Y., Merhav, N.: Hidden Markov processes. IEEE Transactions on Information Theory 48, 1518–1569 (2002)

20. Rabiner, L.R.: A tutorial on hidden Markov models and selected applications in speech recognition. Proc. IEEE 77(2), 257–285 (1989)

21. Churchill, G.A.: Stochastic models for heterogeneous DNA sequences. Bull. Math. Biol. 51, 79–94 (1998)

22. Karchin, R.: Hidden Markov Models and Protein Sequence Analysis. In: Seventh International Conference on Intelligent Systems for Molecular Biology – ISMB (1999)

23. Viterbi, A.J.: Error bounds for convolutional codes and an asymptotically optimum decoding algorithm. IEEE Transactions on Information Theory 13(2), 260–269 (1967)

24. Durbin, R., Edy, S., Krogh, A., Mitchison, G.: Biological sequence analysis: Probabilistic models of proteins and nucleic acids. Cambridge University Press, Cambridge (1998)

25. Mirceva, G., Kalajdziski, S., Trivodaliev, K., Davcev, D.: Comparative Analysis of three efficient approaches for retrieving protein 3D structures. In: 4-th Cairo International Biomedical Engineering Conference 2008 (CIBEC 2008), Cairo, Egypt, pp. 1–4 (2008)

26. SCOP (Structural Classification of Proteins) Database,
    http://scop.mrc-lmb.cam.ac.uk/scop/

DOME, Faculty of Engineering, The University of Melbourne, Australia
cckenneth@gmail.com, saman@unimelb.edu.au

Abstract. The average mutual information (AMI) has been claimed to be a
strong genome signature in some literatures. The range of k values is an important parameter in AMI but no standard range of k value is yet proposed. We introduce a new growth threshold (GT) equation in Growing Self-Organising
Maps (GSOM) to identify the best k range for clustering prokaryotic sequence
fragments of 10 kb. However, the results using the best k range of AMI were
still worse than our previously published results using oligonucleotide frequencies. These experiments showed that the newly proposed GT equation makes
GSOM able to efficiently and effectively analyse different data features for the
same data.

Keywords: GSOM, AMI, Species Separation, Prokaryotic Sequences.

1 Introduction

Average mutual information (AMI), which is a well-known measure of dependence of
two variables in information theory, has increasingly been used for analysing DNA
sequences. Grosse et al. [1] showed that the probability distributions of AMI are significantly different in coding and noncoding DNA; Slonim et al. [2] used AMI to
study the relationships between genes and their phenotypes; and Swati [3] applied a
mutual information function to quantify the similarities and differences between bacterial strains. The investigation of AMI on DNA sequences has been also extended to
DNA fragments. Otu and Sayood [4] revealed that fragments coming from the same
regions of the target sequence have similar AMI profiles. Bauer et al. [5] found that
the AMI profile could separate the fragments, whose sizes vary between 200 bp and
10 000 bp, of two eukaryotes and claimed that the AMI profile can be used to dis-
criminate between DNA fragments from different species. This growing evidence
supports the hypothesis that AMI may also be able to distinguish DNA fragments

successfully by spending more time and effort to experimentally determine the same map resolution for datasets with different dimensionalities, this will be difficult for the analysis of large datasets, for which a large computing time is required. This problem raised a question in the accuracy of the original GT equation. Therefore, we investigates the GT equation and then proposes a new GT equation which is generalised to a wider range of distance functions, as well as rectifying the problem of different dimensionalities so that the original purpose of introducing SF can be achieved. Then the proposed GT equation is applied to investigate the AMI for DNA sequence separation.

This paper is arranged as follows: Section 2 describes backgrounds of GSOM and the new generalised GT equation. Section 3 shows the results generated using the AMI. Finally, Section 4 provides a summary and conclusion of this paper.

2 Backgrounds

Growing Self-Organising Map (GSOM) [7] is an extension of Self-Organising Map (SOM) [8]. GSOM is a dynamic SOM which overcomes the weakness of a static map structure of SOM. Both SOM and GSOM are used for clustering high dimensional data. This is achieved by projecting the data onto a two or three dimensional feature map with lattice structure where every point of interest in the lattice represents a node in the map. The mapping preserves the data topology, so that similar samples can be found close to each other on the 2D/3D feature map.

2.1 The Problem in the Original Growth Threshold (GT) Equation in GSOM

While SOM uses a pre-specified number of nodes and map structure in training, GSOM uses a threshold to control the spread of a map in the growing phase so that the resolution of the map will be proportional to the final number of nodes generated at the end of the growing phase. This threshold can be any constant value and should be inversely proportional to the amount of detail in the hidden data structure that the user would like shown in the map. Nevertheless, in order to standardise this threshold into a parameter which is easy to use, Alahakoon et al. [7] introduced the growth threshold (GT) equation to determine the threshold:

$$dist(\mathbf{x},\mathbf{w})=\left(\sum_{d-1}|x_d - w_d|\right),$$

where $\mathbf{w}$ is the weight vector of the node, and $\mathbf{x}$ is the input vector ($\mathbf{w}$, $\mathbf{x} \in \mathfrak{R}^D$ where D is the dimensionality of data).

The growing mechanism in GSOMs depends on the comparison of the accumulated error in a node and the GT value, which is determined prior to the start of training. In order to achieve the same spread for different dimensionalities, when the GT value is increased with increased data dimensionality, the generated error should also be increased proportionally to the increment of the GT value. However, this is not the case in the original GT equation. A simple example can effectively illustrate this problem. To train a 1D dataset with SF=0.1, the original GT equation gives GT=2.3. Using the standard practice in artificial neural networks that all dimensions are normalised to values between zero and one, the maximum possible error (maxErr) is one, as shown in Fig. 1(a). However, for a 2D dataset (Fig. 1(b)) using the same spread factor (SF=0.1), the GT value is doubled to GT=4.6 but the maximum possible error is only $\sqrt{2}$ which is less than double the maximum possible error in the 1D case: GT_2D = 2*GT_1D but maxErr_2D < 2*maxErr_1D. The disproportion between GT value and generated error appears whenever the dimensionality of data is changed. Consequently, the resultant map will be smaller for dataset with a higher data dimensionality.

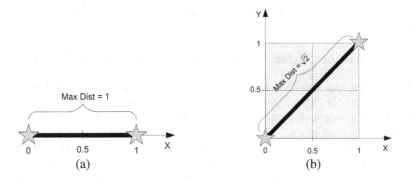

Fig. 1. Illustration of maximum Euclidean distance. (a) 1D, (b) 2D input space. Stars represent

where p is the order of the distance. If it is multiplied and divided by $D^{\frac{1}{p}}$:

$$dist(\mathbf{x}) = \frac{D^{\frac{1}{p}}}{D^{\frac{1}{p}}} \left(\sum_{d=1}^{D} |x_d|^p \right)^{\frac{1}{p}} = D^{\frac{1}{p}} \left(\frac{\sum_{d=1}^{D} |x_d|^p}{D} \right)^{\frac{1}{p}} = D^{\frac{1}{p}} AVG , \qquad (3)$$

where AVG represents a constant value over all dimensions of data and for a large D, AVG is approximately the same for different Ds.

Since GT is related to dist($\mathbf{x}$) and for the GT equation to account for dimensionality, the simplest solution is to make GT proportional to the dimensionality related part in dist(x): $GT \propto D^{\frac{1}{p}}$. Then using the same standardising control measure SF as in the original GT equation, the generalised GT equation becomes:

$$GT = -D^{\frac{1}{p}} \ln(SF) . \qquad (4)$$

It turns out that the original GT equation was defined to only suit p=1, which is the Manhattan distance, but not the intended Euclidean distance (p=2).

2.3 Average Mutual Information for DNA Sequences

Mutual information, which measures the dependence of two random variables, is originally from the field of information theory. In this paper, the average mutual information (AMI), which was used in Bauer et al. [5], is adopted. In a DNA sequence, if X is taken to be the base at location i and Y to be the base at location j, which is k downstream from i (i.e. j = i+k), the AMI function (I_k) is defined as:

$$I_k = \sum_{X \in A} \sum_{Y \in A} p_k(X,Y) \log \left(\frac{p_k(X,Y)}{p(X)p(Y)} \right) ,$$

vector for the GSOM training can be created. Each k value will correspond to a single dimension in the input vector and the dimensionality of the vector depends on the number of different k used.

2.4   Quality Measurement of the Clustering Performance in a Mixing Region

To evaluate a clustering algorithm's ability to group DNA sequence fragments into species-specific or "pure" clusters, we define two criteria that measure the clustering quality in a mixing region: intensity of mix (IoM) and level of mix (LoM), where the former measures the percentage of mixing and the later indicates the taxonomic level of ambiguity for a given pair of clusters [6].

The IoM is evaluated based on the concept of mixed pair described below. Let A and B be sets of vectors belonging to species A and B, respectively, and n(X) is the number of elements in set X. If A and B is a mixed pair, then the percentage of A in the mixing region of the two classes is n(A ∩ B | A)/n(A) and the percentage of B is n(A ∩ B | B)/n(B). For k number of species, there can be up to k(k − 1)/2 mixed pairs. Additionally, a pair of clusters is only considered to be truly mixed when both clusters are heavily overlapped. We use TH = 5% for the threshold of being truly mixed meaning that, statistically, we have a non mixing confidence of 95%. The IoM measures the amount of mixing sequences and it is nonlinearly categorised into five levels: low (L) 5%–10%, medium low (ML) 10%–20%, medium (M) 20%–40%, medium high (MH) 40%–60%, and high (H) 60%–100%.

To evaluate clustering results of species, we use LoM to describe the taxonomic level of the mixed species. Because of the evolution of organisms, nucleotide composition of genomes belonging to the same lower taxonomic levels can be very similar. Clustering organisms at higher level of taxonomy should be easier than at lower level of taxonomy. Therefore, if truly mixed pair occurs, lower LoM (e.g., Species) is more acceptable and more desirable than higher LoM (e.g., Kingdom). In summary, the proposed two measures are defined as

> IoM ∈ {L,ML,M,MH,H},

> LoM ∈ {Species, Genus, Family,Order,Class, Phylum,Kingdom}.

The two proposed measures, IoM and LoM, are only defined for truly mixed pairs to

between applications. Therefore, in our assessment, one result is better than another only when it is superior on at least two of the three measures.

3 Results

This paper investigates whether the average mutual information (AMI) can be used to separate short DNA sequence fragments, and compares the results generated by the AMI with the results created by oligonucleotide frequencies. The AMI, which was used in Bauer et al. [5], is adopted and summarised in Section 2.3. In order to compare the oligonucleotide frequency results produced in our previous publication [6], the same two sets of species genomes were used here. Similar data preprocessing was applied to produce datasets for these experiments (i.e. using a fragment length of 10 kb), except that the input vectors were created by calculating the AMI for a series of k values instead of calculating the oligonucleotide frequencies. For convenience, datasets produced using the k values ranging from X to Y will be denoted as k:X-Y. For example, k:1-100 represents the datasets which were generated using the AMI with k values ranging from 1 to 100.

Different ranges of k values have been used in literature depending on preference and no standard range of k value is yet proposed. Therefore, this investigation also tried to find out a proper range of k values for the task of species separation. To do this, the generalised GT equation can be conveniently applied here with the same SF for all different ranges of k values. The same training settings are used as in our previous publication [6] (i.e. learning length, learning rate, etc.). An SF=0.01 was found to produce a similar resolution to the maps generated for the oligonucleotide frequencies so it is used here for direct comparison. As Bauer [5] used the range of k:5-512 in his experiment to successfully separate the short DNA fragments and a longer range of dependencies between two nucleotides are improbable from the biology perspective, such range of k was used here as maximum range of k for the investigation. Four datasets were created for each of the two sets of species genomes. These datasets will be referred as long-range k values in the following discussion. They are: k:1-100, k:5-300, k:201-500 and k:5-512. The evaluation method for the mixing regions, introduced in our previous publication [6] was adopted here to evaluate results and a summary is described in Section 2.4.

The results generated by the AMI with the four long-range k values for Set1 and Set2 are tabulated in Table 1 and supp-1 respectively (all Set2 results are located in a sup-

Kingdom	--	ML:4, M, L:2	H:3, MH, ML:3, L	H:3, MH, M, ML:2, L	H:3, MH, ML:4
Phylum	--	MH, M:2, ML:3, L:5	H:3, MH:2, M:4, ML, L:3	H:3, MH, M:6, ML:2, L:2	H:3, MH:2, M:4, ML, L:3
Class	--	H, MH, M:3, ML:2, L:2	H:4, MH, M, ML:4, L:2	H:4, MH, M:4, ML:3	H:4, MH, ML:5, M, L
Order	L:2	H, MH, M, ML:2	H, MH:2, M:2	H, MH:2, M:2	H, MH:2, M, ML
Family	--	--	--	--	--
Genus	--	--	--	--	--
Species	ML, L	MH, M	H, MH, L	H, MH, ML	H, MH

Table 2. Results of using AMI with short-range k values for Set1

	Tetra	k:1-5	k:1-10	k:1-16	k: 1-25
#OfMix	4	31	29	27	30
Kingdom	--	ML:4, L:2	ML:4, L	M:2, ML:3	M:2, ML:3
Phylum	--	MH, M, ML:4, L	M:2, ML:2, L:5	MH, M, ML:3, L:3	M:3, L:7
Class	--	H, MH:2, M:3, L:3	H, MH, M:2, ML:2, L:2	H, M:5, L	H, M:4, ML, L:2
Order	L:2	H, MH:2, M, ML:2	H, MH, M, ML:2	H, M:2, ML:2	H, M:2, ML:2
Family	--	--	--	--	--
Genus	--	--	--	--	--
Species	ML, L	MH:2, L	MH:2	MH, M	H, M

and that this happened consistently in both sets. Therefore, some even shorter ranges of k values will possibly perform better.

To test the above hypothesis, another five datasets for each of Set1 and Set2 were generated using the short range of k values: k:1-5, k:1-10, k:1-16, k:1-25 and k:1-50. The results for Set1 and Set2 of each of the five datasets are shown in Table 2 and sup-2

sis. A generalised GT equation was proposed to suit a wider range of distance functions and to give GSOM the ability to analyse datasets with different numbers of dimensions through a single SF value. Then the proposed GT equation was used to effectively investigate the AMI as applied to the separation of short sequence fragments. The long-range k values performed less well than the short-range ones, perhaps because the short sequence fragments are not long enough to provide a good estimation for long-range k values [9]. The results showed that k:1-16 performed better than other short ranges of k values, such as k:1-10, and better than the longer ranges of k values, such as k:1-25. This may be because the short ranges of k values did not provide enough signals; the amount of stored signal was limited by the short length of sequences for the longer ranges of k values. Although the best range of k values (k:1-16) for the AMI could be identified after intensive tests, the results were unsatisfying comparing to the excellent results achieved by using oligonucleotide frequencies in our previous publication [6]. The bad results for the AMI may be due to the noise from the non-coding region of the fragments, as Grosse et al. [1] showed that the probability distributions of AMI are significantly different in coding and non-coding DNA. Therefore, the results should be improved if only the sequences with sufficient portions of coding DNAs are employed in the clustering.

References

1. Grosse, I., Herzel, H., Buldyrev, S.V., Stanley, H.E.: Species independence of mutual information in coding and noncoding DNA. Phys. Rev. E. J1 - PRE 61(5), 5624–5629 (2000)
2. Slonim, N., Elemento, O., Tavazoie, S.: Ab initio genotype-phenotype association reveals intrinsic modularity in genetic networks. Molecular Systems Biology 2 (2006)
3. Swati, D.: In silico comparison of bacterial strains using mutual information. J. Biosci. 32(6), 1169–1184 (2007)
4. Otu, H.H., Sayood, K.: A divide-and-conquer approach to fragment assembly. Bioinformatics 19(1), 22–29 (2003)
5. Bauer, M., Schuster, S.M., Sayood, K.: The average mutual information profile as a genomic signature. BMC Bioinformatics 9(48) (2008), doi:10.1186/1471-2105-1189-1148
6. Chan, C.-K.K., Hsu, A.L., Tang, S.-L., Halgamuge, S.K.: Using Growing Self-Organising Maps to Improve the Binning Process in Environmental Whole-Genome Shotgun Sequencing. Journal of Biomedicine and Biotechnology 2008, Article ID 513701, 10 (2008)
7. Alahakoon, L.D., Halgamuge, S.K., Srinivasan, B.: Dynamic self-organizing maps with

[1] Computer Eng. Dept., College of Computer & Information Sciences, King Saud University
yaalotaibi@ksu.edu.sa
[2] Department of Computing Science, Stirling University
ahu@cs.stir.ac.uk

Abstract. Arabic is one of the world's oldest languages and is currently the second most spoken language in terms of number of speakers. However, it has not received much attention from the traditional speech processing research community. This study is specifically concerned with the analysis of vowels in modern standard Arabic dialect. The first and second formant values in these vowels are investigated and the differences and similarities between the vowels are explored using consonant-vowels-consonant (CVC) utterances. For this purpose, an HMM based recognizer was built to classify the vowels and the performance of the recognizer analyzed to help understand the similarities and dissimilarities between the phonetic features of vowels. The vowels are also analyzed in both time and frequency domains, and the consistent findings of the analysis are expected to facilitate future Arabic speech processing tasks such as vowel and speech recognition and classification.

Keywords: MSA, Arabic, Vowels, Analysis, Speech, Recognition, Formants, HMM, ASR.

1 Background

1.1 Arabic Language and Research

Arabic is a Semitic language, and is one of the world's oldest languages. Currently it is the second most spoken language in terms of number of speakers. Modern Standard Arabic (MSA) has 36 phonemes, of which six are vowels, two diphthongs, and 28 are consonants. In addition to the two diphthongs, the six vowels are /a, i, u, a: , i:, u:/ where the first three ones are short vowels and the last three are their corresponding longer versions (that is, the three short vowels are /a, i, u /, and their three long coun-

ability of Arabic ASR training material. The lack of this information leads to many similar word forms, and consequently, decreases predictability in the language model. The three short Arabic vowels are represented using diacric symbols in the written form. The second problem is related to the morphological complexity since Arabic has a rich potential of word forms which increases the out-vocabulary rate [4], [6].

Arabic language is comparatively much less researched compared to other languages such as English and Japanese. Most of the reported studies to-date have been conducted on Arabic language and speech digital processing in general, with only a few focusing on Arabic vowels specifically. A limited number of research studies have been carried out on MSA, classical and Quraanic (Islamic Holy Scripture based) versions of Arabic. More recently, Iqbal et al. [7] reported a new preliminary study on vowels segmentation and identification using formant transitions occurring in continuous recitation of Quraanic Arabic. The paper provided an analysis of cues to identify Arabic vowels. Their algorithm extracted the formants of pre-segmented recitation audio files and recognized the vowels on the basis of these extracted formants. The study was applied in the context of recitation principles of the Holy Quraan. The vowel identification system developed showed up to 90% average accuracy on continuous speech files comprising around 1000 vowels.

In other related recent works, Razak et. al. [8] have investigated Quraanic verse recitation feature extraction using the Mel-Frequency Cepstral Coefficient (MFCC) approach. Their paper explored the viability of the MFCC technique to extract features from Quranic verse recitation. Features extraction is crucial to prepare data for the classification process. The authors were able to recognize and differentiate the Quranic Arabic utterance and pronunciation based on the extracted features vectors. Tolba et al. [9] have also reported a new method for Arabic consonant/vowel segmentation using the wavelet transform. In their paper, a new algorithm was presented for Arabic speech consonant and vowel segmentation without linguistic information. The method was based on the wavelet transform and spectral analysis and focused on searching the transient between the consonant and vowel parts in certain levels from the wavelet packet decomposition. The accuracy rate was about 88.3% for consonant/vowel segmentation and the rate remained fixed at both low and high signal to noise ratios (SNR). Previously, Newman et al. [10] worked on a frequency analysis of Arabic vowels in connected Speech. Their findings do not confirm the existence of a high classical style as an acoustically 'purer' variety of modern standard Arabic.

1.2 Hidden Markov Models

ASR systems based on the Hidden Markov Model (HMM) started to gain popularity in the mid 1980's [13]. HMM is a well-known and widely used statistical method for characterizing the spectral features of speech frame. The underlying assumption of the HMM is that the speech signal can be well characterized as a parametric random process, and the parameters of the stochastic process can be predicted in a precise, well-defined manner. The HMM method provides a natural and highly reliable way of recognizing speech for a wide range of applications [14], [15].

In the main recognition module the feature vectors are matched with reference patterns, which are called acoustic models. The reference patterns are usually Hidden HMM models trained for whole words or, more often, for phones as linguistic units. HMMs cope with temporal variation, which is important since the duration of individual phones may differ between the reference speech signal and the speech signal to be recognized. Unfortunately this is not practical in short and long Arabic vowels, where the duration is very important and dictates the word meaning. A linear normalization of the time axis is not sufficient here, since not all allophones are expanded or compressed over time in the same way. For instance, stop consonants ("d", "t", "g", "k", "b", and "p") do not change their length much, whereas the length of vowels strongly depends on the overall speaking rate [15].

The recently developed Hidden Markov Model Toolkit (HTK) [16] is a portable toolkit for building and manipulating HMM models. It is mainly used for designing, testing, and implementing ASR and its related research tasks. The HTK [16] is a general toolkit for the HMM model that is mainly geared towards speech recognition, but can also be used for other tasks. HTK includes a large number of tools for training and manipulating HMMs, working with pronunciation dictionaries, n-gram and finite-state language models, recording and transcribing speech, etc.

1.3 Formant Readings

By changing the vocal tract shape, different forms of a perfect tube are produced, which in turn, can be used to change the desired frequencies of vibration. Each of the preferred resonating frequencies of the vocal tract (corresponding to the relevant bump in the frequency response curve) is known as a formant. These are usually

The goals of this study are to investigate MSA vowels using both speech recognition and time and frequency domain information especially formants. Firstly, a recognition system will be built to classify the vowels and determine the similarities and dissimilarities among the 8 different MSA vowels under investigation. Secondly, we carry out a formant based analysis of the six Arabic vowels as used in MSA. The outcomes of these two investigative methodologies will be crosschecked to conclude the final contributions of this research regarding the MSA vowels.

The rest of this paper is organized as follows: Section II introduces the experimental framework for both methods employed in this study. The results are described and discussed in Section III. Paper conclusions and some remarks and suggestions are given in Section IV.

2 Experimental Framework

The allowed syllables in Arabic language are: consonant-vowel (CV), consonant-vowel-consonant (CVC), and consonant-vowel-consonant-consonant (CVCC), where V indicates a (long or short) vowel while C indicates a consonant. Arabic utterances can only start with a consonant [1]. Table 1 shows the eight Arabic vowels along with their names, examples, and IPA symbols. In this paper the formants of Arabic vowels will be analyzed to determine their values. These are expected to prove helpful in subsequent speech processing tasks such as vowel and speech recognition and classification. In carrying out the analysis, Arabic vowels have been viewed as if they are patterns on papers. Specifically, the vowels were plotted on paper or computer screen in the form of their time waveform, spectrograms, formants, and LPC spectrums.

2.1 Recognition System Overview

An ASR based on HMM was developed. The system was partitioned into three modules according to their functionality. First is the training module, whose function is to create the knowledge about the speech and language to be used in the system. Second is the HMM models bank, whose function is to store and organize the system knowledge gained by the first module. Finally, there is the recognition module whose function is to figure out the meaning of the speech input in the testing phase. This was

V06	Long kasrah	جِيد	i:
V07	Fatha dummah	جَوَد	aw
V08	Fatha kasrah	جَيد	ay

A second speech recognition system was also implemented using the HMM technique with the help of HTK tools. The speech ASR was designed initially as a phoneme level recognizer with 3-states: continuous, left-to-right, no skip HMM models. The system was designed by considering all 21 MSA monophones by considering a subset of the thirty-four MSA monophones as given by the KACST labeling scheme given in [17]. The silenc`e (sil) model was also included in the model set. In a later step, the short pause (sp) was created from and tied to the silence model. Since most digits consisted of more than two phonemes, context-dependent triphone models were created from the monophone models mentioned above. Prior to this, the monophones models were initialized and trained using the training data. This was done using more than one iteration and repeated again for triphones models. The pre-final training phase step was to align and tie the model by using a decision tree method. The last step in the training phase involved re-estimating the HMM parameters using the Baum-Welch algorithm [14] three times.

2.2 Database

An in-house database was built to help in investigating Arabic vowels depending on good selected and fixed phonemes. The utterances of ten male Arabic speakers, all aged between 23 to 25 years with the exception of one child, were recorded. Nine of the speakers were from different regions in Saudi Arabia and the remaining one from Egypt. Each of the ten speakers participated in five different trials for every carrier word in the data set used along with all the eight intended Arabic phonemes. Some of the speakers recorded the words in one session and others in two or three sessions.

The carrier words were chosen to represent different consonants before and after the intended vowel. These carrier words are displayed in Table 2 using the second vowel /a:/. The sampling rate used in recording these words was 16 kHz and 16-bit resolution mono. Total of the recorded audio tokens was 4000 (i.e., eight phonemes times ten speakers times ten carrier words times five trials for each speaker). These audio tokens were used for analyzing the intended phonemes in frequency, during the

(CVC)	Arabic	IPA	Info.	IPA	Info.
CW01	سار	/s/	unvoiced fricative	/r/	voiced lateral
CW02	صار	/sˤ/	unvoiced fricative emphatic	/r/	voiced lateral
CW03	بات	/b/	voiced stop	/t/	unvoiced stop
CW04	عاد	/ʕ/	voiced fricative glottal	/d/	voiced stop
CW05	طار	/tˤ/	unvoiced stop emphatic	/r/	voiced lateral
CW06	زاد	/z/	voiced fricative	/d/	voiced nasal
CW07	صام	/sˤ/	unvoiced fricative emphatic	/m/	voiced nasal
CW08	فاز	/f/	unvoiced fricative	/z/	voiced fricative
CW09	نام	/n/	voiced nasal	/m/	voiced nasal
CW10	جاع	/ʒ/	voiced affricative	/ʔ/	voiced fricatives glottal

3 Results

3.1 Speech Recognition Analysis

An HMM based speech recognition system was designed, tested, and used for recognizing Arabic vowels using the given database. The overall system performance (recognition success rate (%) with respect to Arabic vowels was 91.6% as depicted in Table 3. This table shows the confusion matrix that was generated by the recognition system. The last three columns in the table show, respectively, individual system accuracies for each vowel separately, total number of speech tokens for each individual vowel, and missed tokens per vowel. In addition to this, the table depicted the number of inserted and deleted tokens for each vowel – all of which were with zero deletion and insertion in this experiment.

It can be seen from Table 3, that the totals of missed tokens were 135 out of 1599. The best vowel accuracy was encountered with Vowel 8 which is the diphthong "Fatha Kasrah" vowel. The accuracy for this vowel is 99% and only two tokens of Vowel 8 were missed by the system. On the other hand, the worst accuracy was encountered for the case of Vowel 1 which is the "Short Fatha". The system accuracy for this vowel was 77.5% with a total of 45 missed tokens. Five of the vowels achieved over 90% accuracy but the remaining three did not.

the duration in HMM states and force the system to distinguish between short and long vowel in Arabic vowels since it is phonemic. For the fourth and fifth pairs we found that Vowel 2 (a:) was confused with Vowel 3 (u). This is considered a strange outcome due to the big difference between these vowels. The same thing can be said for the last pair. Also we can conclude from the recognition system outcomes that the vowel "Short Fatha" is the trouble source for the system where it made 3 major confusions to other vowels. Next, we will crosscheck the recognition system performance with the analysis carried out using the formant based approach.

Table 3. Confusion matrix and other statistics from the vowel recognition system

Vowel (IPA)	VWL1	VWL2	VWL3	VWL4	VWL5	VWL6	VWL7	VWL8	Del	Acc. (%)	Tokens	Missed
VWL1 (a)	155	33	5	0	6	0	1	0	0	77.5	200	45
VWL2 (a:)	4	195	0	0	0	0	1	0	0	97.5	200	5
VWL3 (u)	11	3	173	7	3	0	3	0	0	86.5	200	27
VWL4 (u:)	0	0	6	190	0	0	4	0	0	95	200	10
VWL5 (i)	8	5	5	0	166	15	0	0	0	83.4	199	33
VWL6 (i:)	0	0	0	1	0	194	0	5	0	97	200	6
VWL7 (ay)	1	0	1	5	0	0	193	0	0	96.5	200	7
VWL8 (ay)	0	0	0	0	0	2	0	198	0	99	200	2
Ins	0	0	0	0	0	0	0	0				
Total									0	91.6	1599	135

3.2 Formant Based Analysis

The aim of this part of the experiments was to evaluate values of the first and second formants, namely F1 and F2, in all considered Arabic vowels. This study considered frames in the middle of each vowel to minimize the co-articulation effects. Based on Fig. 2, we can estimate the Arabic vowel triangle's location as (400, 800), (700, 1100), and (400, 2100) where the first value corresponds to F1 and the second value to F2.

Fig. 2 shows a plot for all short vowels for one of the speakers for three different trials. It can be seen from Fig. 2 that the F1 value is relatively high for /a/, medium for /u/, and minimum for /i/. But in the case of F2, it is medium for /a/, minimum for /u/

classify /i/ and /u/. The vowel /a/ has the largest value of F1 and /i/ has the largest value of F2. The vowel /i/ has the smallest value of F1 and /u/ has the smallest value of F2. In addition, F1 can be used to classify /a:/ and /u:/ whereas F2 can be used to classify /i:/ and /u:/. The vowel /a:/ has the largest value of F1 and /i:/ has the largest value of F2, while the vowel /i:/ has the smallest value of F1 and /u:/ has the smallest value of F2.

In Arabic vowels, as mentioned earlier, F1 can vary from 300 Hz to 1000 Hz, and F2 can vary from 850 Hz to 2500 Hz. F3 is also important in determining the phonemic quality of a given speech sound, and the higher formants such as F4 and F5 can also be significant in determining voice quality [18]. In /a/ and /a:/ the whole tongue goes down so the vocal tract becomes wider than in producing other Arabic vowels. In /u/ and /u:/ the end of the tongue comes near to the palate while the other parts of the tongue are in the regular position. In /i/ and /i:/ the front of the tongue comes near to the palate whereas other parts remain in their regular position. Lips are more rounded for /u/ and /u:/ than for /i/ and /i:/. Also, the formants' usual patterns were noticed from their spectrograms as concluded in [18]. In addition, the similarities of the first (and final) consonant in all words can be clearly noticed since the same first and final consonants are used in all the plots (with just the vowel being varied) as can be inferred from Table 2.

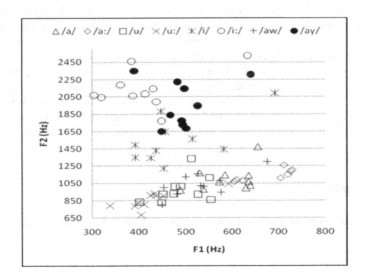

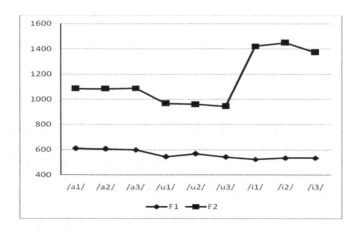

Fig. 2. Values of F1 and F2 for short vowels for Speaker 6 for three trials

3.3 Discussion

In summary, the vowel pairs (Vowel 1, Vowel 2), (Vowel 5, Vowel 6), (Vowel 3, Vowel 4), (Vowel 1, Vowel 3), and (Vowel 1, Vowel 5) that have major similarities depending on the speech recognition output, are mostly durational counterparts. This means that Vowel 1 is the short counterpart of Vowel 2 and so on. These pairs of vowels have major overlap in formant plot shown in Fig. 1. Formants can thus be seen to be very effective in classifying vowels correctly and can be used in a future speech recognition system. Formants of the vowels can be included explicitly in the feature extraction module of the recognizer. If such a system is able to recognize the different vowels then this will tremendously assist in the Arabic speech recognition process. The reason behind this is that every word and syllable in Arabic language must contain at least one vowel; hence vowel recognition will play a key role in identifying the spoken utterance. Agreement between the recognition outputs and formant analysis can be inferred from these results. In addition to this, we can say that the distinguishing acoustic features of vowels are formants, in particular formants 1 and 2. Also, for Arabic vowels we can learn that the temporal duration is very important but this is missed by both the investigative methods used in this study and we need to find a way to incorporate this feature in future speech recognition and formant-based analysis approaches.

4 Conclusions

This paper has presented automatic speech recognition and formant based analysis of

incidence between the conclusions drawn from speech recognition results and formant analysis regarding these vowels.

Acknowledgments

The authors would like to acknowledge the British Council (in Riyadh, Saudi Arabia) for funding this collaborative research between King Saud University and the University of Stirling (in Scotland).

References

1. Alkhouli, M.: Alaswaat Alaghawaiyah. Daar Alfalah, Jordan (1990) (in Arabic)
2. Deller, J., Proakis, J., Hansen, J.H.: Discrete-Time Processing of Speech Signal. Macmillan, Basingstoke (1993)
3. Alghamdi, M.: Arabic Phonetics. Al-Toubah Bookshop, Riyadh (2001) (in Arabic)
4. Omar, A.: Study of Linguistic phonetics. Aalam Alkutob, Eygpt (1991) (in Arabic)
5. Elshafei, M.: Toward an Arabic Text-to -Speech System. The Arabian Journal for Scince and Engineering 16(4B), 565–583 (1991)
6. El-Imam, Y.A.: An Unrestricted Vocabulary Arabic Speech Synthesis System. IEEE Transactions on Acoustic, Speech, and Signal Processing 37(12), 1829–1845 (1989)
7. Iqbal, H.R., Awais, M.M., Masud, S., Shamail, S.: New Challenges in Applied Intelligence Technologies. In: On Vowels Segmentation and Identification Using Formant Transitions in Continuous Recitation of Quranic Arabic, pp. 155–162. Springer, Berlin (2008)
8. Razak, Z., Ibrahim, N.J., Tamil, E.M., Idris, M.Y.I., Yakub, M. Yusoff, Z.B.M.: Quranic Verse Recitation Feature Extraction Using Mel-Frequency Cepstral Coefficient (MFCC). In: Proceedings of the 4th IEEE International Colloquium on Signal Processing and its Application (CSPA), Kuala Lumpur, Malaysia, March 7-9 (2008)
9. Tolba, M.F., Nazmy, T., Abdelhamid, A.A., Gadallah, M.E.: A Novel Method for Arabic Consonant/Vowel Segmentation using Wavelet Transform. International Journal on Intelligent Cooperative Information Systems, IJICIS 5(1), 353–364 (2005)
10. Newman, D.L., Verhoeven, J.: Frequency Analysis of Arabic Vowels in Connected Speech, pp. 77–87
11. Alghamdi, M.M.: A spectrographic analysis of Arabic vowels: A cross-dialect study. Jour-

Arabic Speech. In: IEEE International Conference on Signal Processing and Communication (ICSPC 2007), Dubai, UAE, November 24–27 (2007)

18. Alotaibi, Y.A., Hussain, A.: Formant Based Analysis of Spoken Arabic Vowels. In: BioID_MultiComm 2009: Joint COST 2101 & 2102 International Conference on Biometric ID Management and Multimodal Communication, Madrid, Spain, September 16-18 (accepted, 2009)

Faculty of Electronics Telecommunications and Information Technology,
Carol I 11, 69121 Iasi, Romania
{mdobrea,serbanm}@etti.tuiasi.ro

Abstract. The present study was done as part of a more complex project whose final aim is to design and implement an autonomic self-organizing system, mentally commanded by an user giving one of the 4 possible commands: forth, back, left, right. For this, we used the most studied method for designing non-invasive brain-computer interface (BCI), namely, the electroencephalogram (EEG) signals acquired during mental tasks. To command, in real-time, the system requires very discriminative mental tasks to be used to trigger the corresponding device commands. The novelty of our paper consists in revealing the great importance the preliminary selecting process of subject-specific set of tasks plays within the implementation of any particular BCI application. In this idea, our research focuses on an extensive analysis of twelve mental tasks; the processing and classification approaches used by us are classical ones[1].

Keywords: Brain computer interface, mental tasks, EEG autoregressive model, Bayesian classifier, artificial neural networks.

1 Introduction

The present study, as part of a more complex (on-line, EEG-based, 4-class) BCI project, aims to find, in a preliminary step, the paradigm which gives, for a given EEG processing methodology and for a specific subject, the most classifying process' advantages. Practically, in this research, we exploit the already suggested idea in the literature, namely the requirement to design a subject-specific BCI application in order to obtain high system performances. The novelty of this paper consists in quantifying the impact the subject-specific selected set of tasks has, by itself, on the classification performances, and thus, indirectly, on the global BCI performance. For this, for each of the participants to the study we find which are the 4 mental tasks (out of 12 proposed candidate tasks) that lead to the most discriminative EEG patterns.

spheres than the non-motor tasks [4]; moreover, the two silent verbal fluency tasks – namely, phonemic (letter-cued) silent word generation and semantic (category-cued) silent word generation – were found as activating two overlapping but dissociable systems in the brain [5]. Not in the last, different components of mental calculation (e.g. tasks involving number comprehension and the calculation process) [6] suggest the participation of different cortical networks reflected in significant EEG-cortical area differences. However, the aforementioned relationships are not always as predicted [2], [3], [1] due probably to neuronal substrates specificities, differences in skill, degree of laterality, degree of vigilance [7] and, not in the last, due to interpretation of the task by the subjects [8].

Nowadays, the applications involving cognitive tasks discrimination abound in the different paradigms and experimental setups they use; but, most of all, the processing and classification techniques are those that are varying the most in all the BCI papers. In this context, the question of how good the methods are is quite difficult to respond because, often, for the same set of tasks the obtained results differ significantly from subject to subject. Thus, as good as these methods can be, they can not lead to excellent results if the selected mental tasks do not give raise fundamentally to different EEG pattern activations, at least in conjunction with a given subject, a given EEG feature extracting methodology and a given electrodes montage. From this point of view, the issue of finding the subject-specific most discriminative mental tasks appears to be at least as important as the processing methods themselves.

In what follows, using a set of 12 different motor and non-motor cognitive tasks and a commonly used EEG processing and classifying methodology[1], we reveal the significant achievable gain that can be obtained in the BCI performance only by selecting the most appropriate mental tasks for each investigated subject.

2 Experimental Protocol

In this study the EEG from 4 healthy, right-handed subjects, aged between 22 and 35 years, were recorded during 12 different mental tasks (4 motor and 8 non-motor imagery tasks). The subjects were instructed not to verbalize or vocalize and not to take any overt movement. For data acquisition, we used a MindSet 24 system. The subjects were seated in a noiseless room, with dim lighting. Measurements were made

ing alternatively the right hand fingers, without any overt movement.

(4) *Left arm movement* (armL): The subjects were instructed to imagine how they are slowly rising and falling down their left arm, without any overt movement.

(5) *Right arm movement* (armR): The subjects were asked to imagine how they are slowly rising and falling down their right arm, without any overt movement.

(6) *Mental letter composing* (letter): The subjects were instructed to mentally compose a letter (with a positive emotional content) to a friend or relative.

(7) *Mathematical adding* (math): The subjects had to add the number specified before the recording to its following number; then, the result had to be added further to its corresponding following number and so on. At the end of the recording, the correctness of the subject's result was checked.

(8) *Baseline-resting* (relax): The subjects were told to relax as much as possible and try to think of nothing in particular.

(9) *Geometrical figure rotation* (rotate): The subjects had to study a mug for 30 s before the recording and after that, with the mug removed, they had to visualize mentally the object being randomly rotated about its axes.

(10) *Letter-cued silent word generation* (wordG): The subjects had to find words beginning with the alphabetical letter specified before the recording.

(11) *Letter-cued silent names generation* (wordN): The subjects had to find as many as possible names beginning with the letter specified before the recording.

(12) *Reciting poetry* (wordP): The subjects had to recite mentally a poetry, without vocalizing.

3 Data Processing and Analysis

In a first step of analysis, the subject-specific set of 4 tasks was selected using the AR model and the Bayes classifier; then, in order to quantify the gains a such particular set could provide, we employed the EEG AR model in conjunction with a MLP classifier, trained with the backpropagation (BP) algorithm.

3.1 EEG AR Model

The parameters of the six-order standard parametric AR model of the EEG signal – adopted to obtain the feature vectors – were estimated using the Yule-Walker method.

eq. 2). In eq. 2, d is the dimensionality of the feature vector and Σ_i and μ_i are the co-variance matrix and, respectively, the mean vector parameters for class i. These last parameters were estimated on the training data set (i.e. 80% of the entire data set), using the formulas in eq. 3; the rest of 20% of data formed the cross-validation set.

$$P(C_i|x) = \frac{p(x|C_i) \cdot P(C_i)}{P(x)} \tag{1}$$

$$p(x|C_i) \cong N(\mu_i, \Sigma_i) = \frac{1}{(2\pi)^{d/2}|\Sigma_i|^{1/2}} \exp\left(-\frac{1}{2}(x - \mu_i)^T \Sigma_i^{-1}(x - \mu_i)\right) \cdot \tag{2}$$

$$\mu_i = \frac{1}{N_i}\sum_{j=1}^{N_i} x_i^j \text{, and } \Sigma_i = \frac{1}{N_i}\sum_{j=1}^{N_i}(x_i^j - \mu_i)(x_i^j - \mu_i)^T \cdot \tag{3}$$

In the abovementioned formulas, N_i is the number of the training samples belonging to class i ($i \in \{1, 2\}$) and x_i^j is the sample j belonging to class i. Finally, the Bayes classifier assigns the unknown feature vector x to class C_i if and only if:

$$P(C_i|x) = \max_k\{P(C_k|x)\} \quad k = \overline{1,2} \cdot \tag{4}$$

To select the subject-specific most discriminative 4 cognitive tasks out of the 12 investigated in this paper, for each subject an exhaustive automatic analysis was done. For each subject, the all-possible four-task combinations were enumerated and the mean classification rates were computed for these based on the corresponding two-class correct classification rates compactly presented in tables 2 and 3. Of these calculated values, for each subject we selected the 4-task combination that led to the best mean classification rate. The results shown in table 4 were obtained using additionally a threshold criterion (i.e., if for at lest one pair of tasks – out of the 6 that can be derived for each 4-task combination – there were correct classification rates below a given threshold then, the corresponding 4-task combination was disregarded). Different and specific two thresholds were applied for each subject.

can be drawn from Table 2 also, from the intersections of the line *wordP* with the column *rotate* and of the line *rotate* with the column *wordP*.

The first 4-task combinations (enumerated in decreasing order of their mean classification rates), obtained for each subject, are shown in **Table 4**. The finally selected sets of tasks, for the 4 investigated subjects, are those presented in bold type in **Tabel 4**. In **Tabel 5**, the performances obtained with these selected sets are comparatively presented, together with the performances achieved for a reference set of tasks, comprising in 4 out of the 5 mental tasks proposed by Keirn and Aunon [10].

As expected, the results in **Tables 2** and **3** confirm the inter-subject variability regarding the particular way the subject EEG patterns are activated when performing the same cognitive tasks; this is primarily reflected in the various classification performances obtained by the investigated subjects for the same sets of tasks. Also, this subject-specificity is exhibited in the particular 4-task combinations we found as given the best classifying results for the 4 subjects as well as in the corresponding calculated

Table 1. The confusion matrix on CV set, for the pair of tasks (*wordP, rotate*)

Bayes results True classes	*WordP*	*Rotate*
WordP	**90.08 %**	9.92 %
Rotate	6.72 %	**93.28 %**

Table 2. Classification performances for subject S1, for all 66 pairs of tasks

S1	count	fingersL	fingersR	armL	armR	Letter	math	relax	rotate	wordG	wordN	wordP
count	•	85.71	**93.33**	81.95	87.02	76.98	69.23	72.73	74.62	87.3	**93.98**	91.34
fingersL	96.12	•	76.80	86.36	80.65	**90.70**	**94.03**	77.78	**95.65**	64.44	81.10	78.76
fingersR	93.33	67.69	•	85.94	76.98	89.92	88.72	74.81	**90.77**	63.33	82.73	72.27
armL	82.79	**91.87**	**91.34**	•	79.69	84.50	83.33	78.86	82.54	89.60	**93.62**	90.16
armR	87.10	88.55	85.27	52.76	•	75.21	85.16	66.13	77.24	**90.78**	**91.34**	90.16
letter	76.74	**92.06**	**92.86**	77.78	82.09	•	80.77	68.38	77.94	**92.25**	93.50	87.60

		count	fingersL	fingersR	armL	armR	letter	math	relax	rotate	wordG	wordN	wordP
S2	count	•	80.77	54.07	65.75	78.33	80	77.31	61.90	55.45	77.04	77.86	82.01
	fingersL	65.50	•	62.20	58.70	62.81	70.77	58.59	68.86	63.20	66.42	54.81	76.80
	fingersR	68.33	77.34	•	68.75	78.81	79.31	70.4	67.41	68.18	68.42	75.21	74.82
	armL	59.63	70.09	45.67	•	80.29	80.00	81.40	60.38	52.71	67.39	77.52	83.19
	armR	71.11	63.43	67.88	57.63	•	65.77	58.91	79.31	73.81	61.40	67.41	78.08
	letter	71.54	80.80	59.71	73.60	78.47	•	69.84	71.55	79.14	72.58	76.47	76.30
	math	73.33	70.87	61.54	75.40	78.57	67.44	•	58.02	75.91	53.68	64.81	74.81
	relax	79.84	85.00	75.83	80.51	83.45	77.70	73.39	•	83.74	77.30	65.87	76.92
	rotate	68.97	81.54	68.29	72.22	82.17	81.03	74.58	68.94	•	79.30	80.45	85.60
	wordG	75.83	69.42	59.57	61.54	81.56	76.34	68.91	70.18	67.63	•	68.75	74.40
	wordN	76.61	87.50	61.59	69.05	84.17	75.00	61.22	60.47	72.95	64.57	•	63.43
	wordP	81.9	79.23	68.97	73.94	80.73	70.00	74.17	74.40	82.30	70.00	55.37	•
S3	count	•	83.59	**92.86**	82.84	84.44	83.33	81.82	76.64	80.49	82.96	81.6	86.07
	fingersL	85.04	•	**99.22**	90.77	90.15	60.33	72.95	88.72	66.67	80.15	70.90	65.00
	fingersR	**92.31**	98.43	•	66.13	90.51	**97.60**	**97.67**	84.38	**90.70**	87.31	86.36	**94.96**
	armL	**92.56**	87.20	76.34	•	82.91	**96.12**	**94.81**	80.99	83.62	75.57	83.97	75.41
	armR	89.17	88.62	82.47	76.09	•	82.76	**90.98**	89.15	76.42	86.09	84.21	79.07
	letter	86.05	79.10	**99.23**	**94.44**	87.05	•	71.22	87.68	87.79	89.47	86.92	**93.75**
	math	75.61	79.70	**99.21**	**96.67**	**96.99**	43.97	•	80.53	62.50	87.02	81.82	86.26
	relax	80.51	90.98	89.76	73.13	84.92	85.47	84.51	•	80.69	78.26	73.02	83.06
	rotate	**90.15**	94.07	**97.62**	89.21	**93.18**	**95.16**	**96.30**	86.36	•	**95.00**	87.93	86.40
	wordG	82.50	82.35	83.47	66.13	89.29	89.34	82.26	62.39	64.44	•	78.05	65.32
	wordN	86.92	81.82	86.18	85.48	72.13	82.40	84.55	73.64	74.10	70.45	•	79.31
	wordP	**91.73**	86.96	**94.85**	86.47	**92.06**	**92.91**	**94.35**	**91.60**	73.08	89.31	89.93	•
S4	count	•	88.41	72.36	86.67	80.6	60.58	58.99	74.22	72.48	85.29	**95.20**	94.16
	fingersL	89.74	•	72.31	59.09	82.95	85.95	82.44	76.12	82.86	85.05	**90.16**	83.33
	fingersR	81.06	76.80	•	67.77	69.23	76.00	75.44	73.38	78.79	88.89	**92.31**	89.93
	armL	85.19	80.49	75.37	•	61.94	72.79	69.67	75.51	76.92	**90.98**	**95.24**	84.62
	armR	68.60	73.81	68.00	59.50	•	58.99	65.52	76.86	63.91	89.15	**93.89**	93.85
	letter	69.49	76.87	70.77	78.15	72.41	•	58.78	66.93	67.20	81.16	82.71	**93.28**
	math	77.59	**90.32**	83.69	75.94	74.10	66.13	•	73.53	74.81	89.43	87.40	**95.24**
	relax	86.61	82.64	81.90	81.20	78.36	70.31	77.31	•	87.72	72.97	82.91	**94.70**

	80	**count**	**fingersR**	**armL**	**wordN**	**88.72**
S2	60	**armR**	**relax**	**rotate**	**wordP**	**79.12**
		armR	letter	rotate	wordP	77.78
		count	armR	relax	wordP	77.33
		letter	relax	rotate	wordP	77.3
		fingersL	letter	rotate	wordP	77.23
	70	count	letter	wordG	wordP	75.66
		letter	relax	wordG	wordP	73.97
S3	70	**count**	**fingersR**	**letter**	**wordP**	**92.14**
		fingersR	letter	rotate	wordP	92
		fingersR	armR	math	wordP	91.61
		fingersR	letter	relax	wordP	91.27
		count	fingersR	letter	Rotate	91.11
	83	**count**	**fingersR**	**letter**	**wordP**	**92.14**
		fingersR	letter	relax	wordP	91.27
S4	60	**count**	**armL**	**wordN**	**wordP**	**91.99**
		count	armR	wordN	wordP	90.94
		count	rotate	wordN	wordP	90.79
		count	fingersL	wordN	wordP	90.67
		count	relax	wordN	wordP	90.67
	84	**count**	**armL**	**wordN**	**wordP**	**91.99**
		count	armL	wordG	wordP	89.69

Table 5. Confusion matrixes for the selected and for the reference sets of tasks, respectively

Selected set of tasks							
S1		**S2**		**S3**		**S4**	
count	78.48	armR	62.69	count	79.03	count	83.46
fingersR	73.92	relax	59.09	fingersR	95.65	armL	74.44
armL	73.47	rotate	82.50	letter	87.02	wordN	91.74
wordN	82.02	wordP	75.00	wordP	85.22	wordP	92.08
Reference set of tasks							
count	35.77	count	21.64	count	81.16	count	56.93
letter	60.47	letter	34.55	letter	67.20	letter	40.98
math	48.06	math	30.00	math	56.45	math	46.22
rotate	59.06	rotate	46.53	rotate	85.12	rotate	43.85

mean classification rates which vary considerably from subject to subject. Another important result of our study is that for all investigated subjects, the suitable sets of

that reflects the way in which the cognitive tasks are processed at the cortical level (i.e., hemispheric asymmetries, local and long-range synchronizations of brain activities, etc.), then, with the selected EEG features, the most subject-specific discriminative set of mental tasks (out of an extensive set of candidate tasks, including both, motor and non-motor imagery tasks) should be chosen and finally, improved versions for the already used processing methodology should be search for. The large variation in the classification performances obtained for the best-selected sets of tasks may above all suggests, for part of the subjects, either inappropriate investigated tasks (at least in conjunction with the used EEG features) or a week concentration of the subjects when performing the task, or even both of them. In order to exclude the second mentioned reason and give consistence to such preliminary analysis, in a future research we aim to reiterate the all steps we made in this study, but this time on similar data acquired in different days.

Acknowledgments. This work was supported by the Romanian National University Research Council under Grant ID 1552.

References

1. Wheeler, R.E., Davidson, R.J., Tomarken, A.J.: Frontal Brain Asymmetry and Emotional Reactivity: A Biological Substrate of Affective Style. Psychophysiol. 30(1), 82–89 (1993)
2. Bulla-Hellwig, M., Volmer, J., Götzen, A., Skreczek, W., Hartje, W.: Hemispheric Asymmetry of Arterial Blood Flow Velocity Changes During Verbal and Visuospatial Tasks. Neuropsychologia 34(10), 987–991 (1996)
3. Ray, M.K., Mackay, C.E., Harmer, C.J., Crow, T.J.: Bilateral Generic Working Memory Circuit Requires Left-Lateralized Addition for Verbal Processing. Cerebral Cortex 18(6), 1421–1428 (2008)
4. Doyle, J.C., Ornstein, R., Galin, D.: Lateral Specialization of Cognitive Mode: II EEG frequency analysis. Psychophysiol. 11, 567–578 (1974)
5. Costafreda, S.G., Fu, C.H.Y., Lee, L., Everitt, B., Brammer, M.J., David, A.S.: A Systematic Review and Quantitative Appraisal of fMRI Studies of Verbal Fluency: Role of the Left Inferior Frontal Gyrus. Hum. Brain Mapp. 27(10), 799–810 (2006)
6. Fernández, T., Harmony, T., Rodríguez, M., Bernal, J., Silva, J., Reyes, A., Marosi, E.: EEG Activation Patterns During the Performance of Tasks Involving Different Components of Mental Calculation. Electroenceph. Clin. Neuro-physiol. 94, 175–182 (1995)
7. Henning, S., Merboldt, K.D., Frahm, J.: Task- and EEG-Correlated Analyses of BOLD MRI Responses to Eyes Opening and Closing. Brain Res., 1073–1074 (2006)

Department of Media, Soongsil University
511 Sangdo-dong, Dongjak-gu, Seoul, Korea
{zooyouny,picmuse,ssudlab}@gmail.com

Abstract. According to a photography theory, lines are an important element that creates the composition and mood of a photo. In this paper, we propose a measure to compute photographic compositional dissimilarity using lines. To develop the distance measure, we investigate some attributes of line that classify composition of photos for line-used photos. And we implemented an image searching system which retrieves photo compositionally similar to given query to evaluate performance of the proposed measure. The searching system shows the precision of about 90% maximally and was capable of reliably retrieving compositionally similar to given query even if some objects were included in photos.

Keywords: Photographic Composition, Line Elements, Image Retrieval System.

1 Introduction

According to a photography theory, lines are an important element that creates composition and mood of a photo [1]. The photo composition can be identified by analyzing the pattern of lines in a photo. In this paper, we develop a distance measure for photo composition by considering pattern of lines in a photo. To develop this measure, we investigate which attributes of a line classify photo composition photos that use lines. The photo composition determined by lines includes not only straight lines but also curved lines. In this study, we deal with straight line only.

Various visual features have been used in content-based image retrieval. To represent the color feature of images, a color histogram and color set was used [1, 2]. In some sophisticated retrievals, spatial information has been considered as a visual feature. By segmenting the image into sub-regions, the spatial relation among sub-regions was used as spatial information [4-6]. In addition, Franti proposed a matching

measure. To evaluate the performance of proposed measure, we implement an image retrieval system and prove its precision and robustness.

We organize our paper as follows: Section 2 describes extraction of the line using the Hough transform and converting the extracted line to an image that is composed of points. In section 3, we analyze the converted image of the points by investigating subjective user and develop a distance measure for photo composition. We evaluate the performance of the proposed method in section 4. Finally, we discuss the conclusion and future work in section 5.

2 Line Extraction Using Hough Transform

In this study, we use the Hough transform to extract a line in a photo. The Hough transform is a feature extraction method that transforms pixels in the input image into parameter space using scoring procedure. In the case of detecting a straight line, the Hough transform calculates the parameters of all lines that pass through a pixel in the image space, and then accumulate some value to the accumulator's bin that the parameters fall into [8]. After accumulating for all pixels in the image space, a straight line in the image space is represented as a peak that has higher intensity than its neighborhood. So, lines in a photo can be found by looking for local maxima in the accumulator space.

As a preprocessing step, before conducting the Hough transform, the proposed method reduces the size of an input image to remove unnecessary information and to normalize the size of the input image. Then, we extract the edge magnitude and edge orientation by using the Sobel mask. In the accumulating procedure of the Hough transform, a scoring proportional to the edge magnitude is used to emphasize a line that is contrasted with its neighboring pixels, and scoring that is inversely proportional to the difference between the edge orientation and the angle parameter of the Hough space is used to emphasize a straight line in the same direction [9].

We used a local maximum filter to extract peaks from the Hough transformed image. If the intensity of a pixel in the Hough space is higher than the intensities of neighboring pixels, the local maximum filter outputs the difference between the intensity of the pixel and the average intensity of the neighbors, or else the local maximum

3 Distance Measure for Photo Composition

To develop an effective distance measure for photo composition, we classify images into a compositionally similar group using query image and into a dissimilar group with subjective user experiment, and identify which attributes of line classify the groups. Then we reflect the identified attribute to the distance measure.

First, to classify images into a compositionally similar group and dissimilar group to a query image, we conduct a subjective user experiment as follows. To exclude the effect of color on photo composition, only grayscale photos are used.

1. Give query images and 300 images to subjective users.
2. For all images, make the subjective users score 2 points to the image if the image is compositionally similar to a query, 1 point to the image if the image is compositionally slightly similar to the query, 0 points to the image if the image is not similar to the query compositionally at all. The scoring process is repeated for all queries.

We conducted the above experiment for 11 queries whose photo compositions are varied to avoid having the attributes of the line that classify the two groups restricted to a specific photo composition. In addition, 10 subjective users participated in the above experiment for objectivity. The queries used in the experiment are listed in fig. 2. We discovered some attributes shown in table 1 by observation of Hough transformed images classified with the above experiment. Then, we design distance measure for photo composition based on the attributes listed in table 1.

The first attribute in table 1 means that the angle, position and intensity of lines in the photos are similar if the photos are compositionally similar. With this observation, to compute the distance of two photos' composition, we use nearest point matching and matching distance as a distance measure for photo composition. Nearest point matching means finding the nearest line for each line in a photo, and using the matching distance means that we use the distance of matched lines as a distance measure for photo composition.

As the first step for measuring the compositional dissimilarity of two photos, table 2 shows the point-matching process.

After the matching process, matched points, which have a pair point or are a pair point by other, and no matched points, which have no pair point and are not a pair point with any other, are determined. We used both the average distance of the

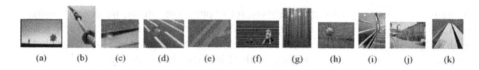

| (a) | (b) | (c) | (d) | (e) | (f) | (g) | (h) | (i) | (j) | (k) |

Fig. 2. The queries is used in the experiment

Table 1. The attributes of compositionally similar images

1.	If two photos are compositionally similar, the positions and intensities of the points in the Hough transformed images are similar to each other.
2.	If two photos are compositionally similar, the distance between the positions of the nearest two high-intensity points in the Hough transformed images should be small, and the distance between the positions of the nearest two low-intensity points may not be small.
3.	If several points in a Hough transformed image crowded around a points in another Hough transformed image are dense, the distance among the points seems to be small, or else the distance among the points seems not to be small.
4.	According to the x axis coordinate of points in the Hough space, the distance between two x axis coordinates of points seems to be smaller than the real distance in a certain range or seems not to be bigger than real distance in another range.

Table 2. Process of matching the points in two Hough transformed images

1.	Input: Two point sets, $Q = \{q_1, q_2, ..., q_M\}, T = \{t_1, t_2, ..., t_N\}$
2.	For all points q_i in Q, find the nearest pair point in T. If the distance to the nearest pair point is smaller than $penalty(q_i)$, the pair point of q_i matches the nearest point, or else, the pair point of q_i is null. $$PAIR(q_i) = \begin{cases} t_j \text{ s.t. } \min_j PD(q_i, t_j) < penalty(q_i) \\ \phi, \text{ if } \min_j PD(q_i, t_j) > penalty(q_i) \end{cases}, \forall i = 1..M$$
3.	For all points t_j in T, find the nearest pair point in Q. If the distance to the nearest pair

$$AvgMD(Q,T) = \frac{\sum_p MD(p) * (f_p + f_{\mu(Mto(p))})}{\sum_p (f_p + f_{\mu(Mto(p))})}$$

, where $p \in Q \cup T$ s.t. $Mto(p) \neq \phi$ (2)

$\mu(Mto(p))$: the mean point of the points that matches to the point p

$Mto(p) = \{p' | \ PAIR(p') = p\}$: it means a point set that matches to the point p

When several pairs point to a point, we use the distance between the point and a mean point of the pair points to the point as the distance of the matched points. As we mentioned in the third attribute in table 1, people think that the several lines densely surrounding a line similar to a line represent the lines. If only the lines are dense, the lines could be considered as a representative line, or else the distance of the matched lines should be increased. With this observation, we defined the matching distance between a point and pair points to the point as equation (3). If the pair points to a point p are spread sparsely, $\sigma(Mto(p))$ in equation (3) is computed highly so that MD is increased.

$$MD(p) = PD(\ p, \mu(Mto(p))\ ) + \sigma(Mto(p))$$

, where $p \in Q \cup T$ s.t. $Mto(p) \neq \phi$

$\mu(Mto(p))$: a mean point of the points that match to the point p (3)

$\sigma(Mto(p))$: a standard deviation of the points that match to the point p

PD : distance between two points

The distance between two points in equation (3) can be defined as the weighted sum of the distances of the positions and intensities of the two points. However, the distance of the x axis coordinates of two points is notable. As we mentioned in the fourth attribute in table 1, people feel the distance of the x axis coordinates is different from the real distance according to the x axis coordinates. An x axis coordinate of a point in the Hough transformed image is related to the angle of a line in a photo, and people feels the distance of the angles sensitively in a vertical or horizontal range but insensitively in a diagonal range. With this observation, we defined the distance between two

On the one hand, $R1$ and $R2$, as the weight of the matching points and the weight of no matching points respectively, shown in equation (5). Finally, table 3 shows the whole process for computing the compositional distance between two photos.

$$R1 = \sum_{p}(f_p + f_{\mu(Mto(p))}), \quad R2 = \sum_{p'}f_{p'}$$
$$\text{, where } p \in Q \bigcup T \text{ s.t. } Mto(p) \neq \phi \quad\quad (5)$$
$$\text{and } p' \in Q \bigcup T \text{ s.t. } PAIR(p') = \phi \text{ and } Mto(p') = \phi$$

Table 3. The entire process for computing the compositional distance between two photos

1.	For two given images Q and T, conduct the matching process as shown in table 2
2.	For all points in Q and T, compute the matching distance as equation (3)
3.	Compute the average matching distance $AvgMD$ as equation (2)
4.	Compute the photo compositional distance PCD between two given photos using weights $R1$ and $R2$ in equation (5)

4 Performance Evaluation

In this section, we conduct experiments to evaluate the performance of the proposed measure. As the first experiment, we implemented a simple retrieval system that retrieves photos that are compositionally similar to a query and evaluated the precision of the retrieval system. A database for the experiment is composed of 110 photos that are classified into 11 photo compositions. For objectivity of the database, we selected 10 high-voted photos for a query from the image set used in section 3; namely, 110 photos. The retrieval system retrieved 10 photos in the increasing order of distance computed by the proposed measure. The thresholds and constants used in the experiment are listed as follows:

$Th1(\text{Image}) = \min(300, f_{max} * 0.4)$, where f_{max} is the highest intensity in the Image

$penalty(\text{point}) = f_{point}$, where f_{point} is the intensity of the point

$\lceil 0.004, \text{if } (30 \leq i < 60 \text{ or } 120 \leq i < 150)$

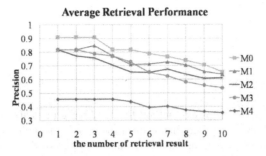

Fig. 3. The average precision of the proposed retrieval system

Fig. 3 shows the average precision of the retrieval results of our retrieval system. In fig. 3, M0 is the proposed method. M1 is identical to M0 except that M1 does not consider the intensity of matched points in equation (2) and divides the sum of *MD* by the number of matched points. M2 is identical to M0 except that M2 does not consider the standard deviation of the pair points in equation (3). M3 is identical to M0 except that M3 consider the sensitivity in equation (4) as a constant of 0.015 regardless of the angle of line. M4 is a method that does not consider the intensity of matched points in equation (2) and the standard deviation of the pair points in equation (3), and considers the sensitivity in equation (4) as a constant of 0.015. The proposed method M0 demonstrate about 90% precision for the first 3 results and about 65% for all 10 results. Moreover, M0 showed better performance than the M1-M4, relatively. The fact that M0 is better than the M1-M4 means that the attributes discovered in this study are meaningful because the M1-M4 methods are methods that do not consider the attributes.

In the second experiment, we compared the proposed distance measure to the people's subjective distance. Three queries and 190 photos were used in this experiment,

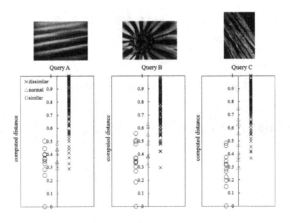

photos computed by the proposed method for the three groups are presented in fig. 4. As shown in fig. 4, the computed distances of the photos that belong to similar groups are distributed in the low region, and the distances of photos that belong to dissimilar groups are in the high region. This result means that the distance computed by the proposed method and the subjective distance are correlated.

In the third experiment, we evaluated the robustness of proposed retrieval system. We took some pictures within identical photo composition, but the number, angle and position of the lines were different, and some objects were included in the photo. In addition, we took more pictures in other places to vary the composition. We composed a database of the photos, and selected one photo as a query image to retrieve some photos by the proposed retrieval system. Fig. 5 shows the ranking of the retrieval results. Although some objects such as leaves are included in a photo or the lines in a photo are slightly different, the photos retrieved high rankings. In addition, some photos whose line patterns were similar to the query received high rankings.

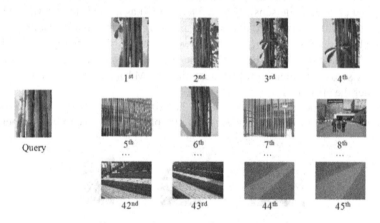

Fig. 5. The ranking of the retrieval results

5 Conclusion and Future Work

hash. The speed problem will be improved in future work.

Acknowledgement. This work was supported by Seoul R&BD Program (10581C093114).

References

1. Prakel, D.: Basics Photography: Composition. AVA Publishing, Lausanne (2006)
2. Swain, M., Ballard, D.: Color indexing. International Journal of Computer Vision 7(1), 11–32 (1991)
3. Smith, J.R., Chang, S.F.: Tools and techniques for color image retrieval. In: Proceeding of the Conference on Storage and Retrieval for Image and Video Databases IV, vol. 2670, pp. 426–437. SPIE, California (1996)
4. Faloutsos, C., Flickner, M., Niblack, W., Petkovic, D., Equitz, W., Barber, R.: Efficient and Effective Querying by Image Content. Journal of Intelligent Information Systems 4(3-4), 231–262 (1994)
5. Lu, H., Ooi, B., Tan, K.: Efficient image retrieval by color contents. In: Risch, T., Litwin, W. (eds.) ADB 1994. LNCS, vol. 819, pp. 95–108. Springer, Heidelberg (1994)
6. Smith, J.R., Chang, S.F.: Querying by color regions using the VisualSEEk content-based visual query system. In: Intelligent Multimedia Information Retrieval, pp. 23–41. MIT Press, MA (1997)
7. Franti, P., Mednonogov, A., Kyrki, V., Kalviainen, H.: Content-based matching of line-drawing images using the Hough transform. International Journal on Document Analysis and Recognition 3(2), 117–124 (2000)
8. Shapiro, L.G., Stockman, G.C.: Computer Vision. Prentice Hall, Englewood cliffs (2001)
9. Morse, B.S.: Lecture 15: Segmentation (Edge based, Hough transform). Lecture Notes, pp. 1–5. Brigham Young University (2000)

Institute for Electronics, Signal Processing and Communications
Otto-von-Guericke-University Magdeburg, Germany
{Joerg.Appenrodt,Ayoub.Al-Hamadi}@ovgu.de

Abstract. In this paper, we present our results to build an automatic
gesture recognition system using different types of cameras to compare
them in reference to their features for segmentation. Normally, the images of a mono color camera system are mostly used as input data in the
research area of gesture recognition. In comparison to that, the analysis
results of a stereo color camera and a thermal camera system are used
to determine the advantages and disadvantages of these camera systems.
With this basics, a real-time gesture recognition system is build to classify alphabets (A-Z) and numbers (0-9) with an average recognition rate
of 98% using Hidden Markov Models (HMM).

Keywords: Gesture Recognition, Stereo Camera System, Thermal
Camera, Computer Vision & Image Processing, Pattern Recognition.

1   Introduction

Gesture recognition is an important area for novel Human Computer Interaction
(HCI) systems and a lot of research has been focused on it. These systems differ
in basic approaches depending on the area in which it is used. Basically, the field
of gestures can be separated in dynamic gestures (e.g. writing letters or numbers) and static postures (e.g. sign language). The most important component
of gesture recognition systems is the exact segmentation and recognition of the
hands and the face which dependents on the data gathering. Therefor, different
camera types are established in the area of the research (e.g. mono color-, stereo
color-, thermal cameras).

Most researchers use mono color cameras for data acquisition. A big advantage
of these cameras is that they are fast and simple to control, so it is possible

system. They analyzed 36 isolated gestures and achieved the best results using Left-Right Banded topology.

In the last few years, thermal cameras are often used in the field of face recognition [3], [4], [5]. E.g. Socolinsky et al. [6], [7] described the combination of thermal and visual cameras for face recognition. Their analysis shows that thermal cameras give the same results as normal visual cameras but thermal cameras have their own advantages. Nevertheless, for the segmentation in the field of the gesture recognition thermal cameras are rarely used.

This paper introduces a novel system to recognize continuous hand gestures from alphabets A-Z and numbers from 0-9 in real-time under using the motion trajectory from a single hand with the aid of HMM. For segmentation three different types of cameras (mono color-, stereo color- and thermal camera) are analyzed by their advantages and disadvantages. The orientation between two following points was extracted and used as a basic feature for HMM. These HMM is trained by Baum-Welch (BW) algorithm and is tested by Viterbi path [8].

This paper is organized as follows: advantages and disadvantages of three different camera types for segmentation are analyzed in Section 2. In section 3, experimental results are presented. Finally, conclusion is described in Section 4.

2   Data Gathering and Evaluation

In the field of the segmentation, different types of cameras are used for data gathering (Fig.1) to build up a gesture recognition system. The mono color camera is the most used type of data acquisition because of its easy and quick possibility of data evaluation also with high resolution images. The stereo color image evaluation forms another approach with depth information in addition to the color information which is determined through a disparity calculation. Nevertheless, the disadvantage of stereo calculation is the increased computational cost. For the thermal camera forms, the temperature of an object is captured with the help of infrared radiations and afterwards shown in the image.

skin by using a Gaussian model. A large database of skin pixels is used to train the Gaussian model, which is characterized by the mean vector and covariance matrix. All skin-colored areas can be segmented using the skin color model in the image. This already shows the first deficit with mono cameras. With an inhomogeneous background, like in Fig.2(a), it is not possible to segment the hands and the face perfectly. Further, it is not possible to separate ambiguous overlapping face and hands.

(a)　　　　　　　　　　(b)　　　　　　　　　　(c)

Fig. 2. (a) Original Mono/stereo color camera (b) depth information (c) 3D structure from a stereo camera

These disadvantages can be overcome with a stereo camera system by using depth information. An unequivocal separation of the user from inhomogeneous backgrounds is possible by utilizing the depth map Fig.2(b). Furthermore, the hands can be held in front of the face and all areas are assigned ambiguously to each other. However, this approach offers some problems. Big areas like a closed hand or a head etc. are well segmentable, but on the basis of problems by calculation of disparity, sometimes no depth information is assigned for smaller areas like single spread fingers.

Thermal camera. An infrared camera is an imaging less device which detects infrared energy (temperature) and converts it into an electronic signal to generate a thermal picture on monitor or to make temperature calculations on it

(a) Original and thermal image

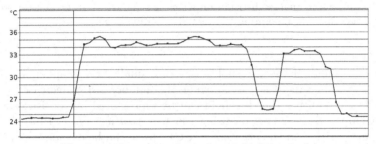

(b) Thermal gradient from the marked line in (a)

Fig. 3. Solution from thermal camera

of the head and the articulating hands can be well separated from the background. Besides, the objects have very sharp contours and it allows a good and clean segmentation even of very small areas. Fig.3(b) describes the temperature course of the straight line in Fig.3(a). Clearly, the sharp edges and exact area of the hand are recognizable. Nevertheless, overlapping of hands or the face is also not possible due to the missing depth information like in mono cameras.

2.2 Evaluation of Segmentation

For the proposed gesture recognition system, three different types of cameras are reviewed. Therefor, our experimental data are captured synchronously from a mono color, stereo color and thermal camera system in complex situations where the system had to recognize different types of gestures. The evaluation occurs by using the *Receiver Operating Characteristic* (ROC) curves. Therefor, the required ground truth of real skin pixels were marked by hand

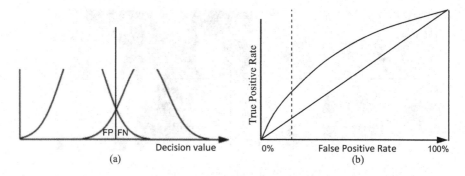

Fig. 4. (a) shows a frequency distribution which is separated into two classes and (b) shows different Receiver Operating Characteristic (ROC) curves

a normal threshold. If the threshold is getting smaller the number of false as positive (FP) values increases, mean while the number of FN decrease.

The effect of shifting the threshold can be represented by the Receiver Operating Characteristic curves by using the *true positive rate* (TPR), the *false positive rate* (FPR) and the *accuracy* (ACC), which can be calculated as follow:

$$TPR = \frac{TP}{TP + FN} \qquad FPR = \frac{FP}{FP + TN} \qquad (1)$$

$$ACC = \frac{TP + TN}{TP + FN + FP + TN} \qquad (2)$$

In Fig.4(b) an example for different types of classifiers is presented, whereas the curves differ significantly in the curvature. Furthermore, different working points A_1, EER (Error Equal Rate) and A_2 are marked. A_1 is a working point where a high TPR with a low FPR exist. In contrast to A_1 the point EER describes the area where no value (TPR or FPR) is preferred, i.e. a theoretical optimum lies. This optimum is nearby the 45° line. In general, the more the working point gets to 100% TPR and 0% FPR the better is the recognition. Figure 5(a) illustrates an image of our database captured by a mono color camera system. Thereby, parts of the background are also segmented by the skin color model Fig.5(b).

Hence, in comparison to the other camera types under consideration, a relatively low mean TPR of 79.86% and ACC of 92.56% originates with a high mean FPR of 7.07%. Without using a priori or further information this is not

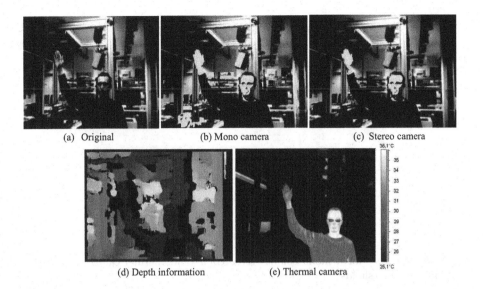

Fig. 5. A comparison of segmentation from different camera systems. (a) Original captured image, (b) The analyzed image without depth information (d), (c) The analyzed image using depth information and (e) Image from thermal camera.

real-time. In comparison to the other camera types we achieved here the best results with a mean ACC of 99.14% with a mean TPR of 78.24% and FRP of 0.267%. The improvement of stereo cameras are the depth information Fig.5(d). Thereby the high recognition rate of skin colored pixels results from fading out the background information Fig.5(c), which is only one of the advantages from stereo camera systems, described in section 2.1.

The third kind of camera was an uncooled mobile thermal camera system (FLIR SC600) with a pixel resolution of 640×480 and 30 fps. The camera specification are: spectral sensibility of 7.5-13.5μm and thermal sensibility of <45 mK. In Fig.6 the ROC curve is graphically presented for different thresholds from 33.6°C to 31.4°C by steps of 0.2°C. For segmentation the max. temperature was chosen as threshold. In our experiments we achieved an average ACC rate of ≈96%. These are not optimal results, because clothes can receive the body temperature and are partially warmer than extremities which are less intensively supplied with blood (e.g. hands) as shown in Fig.5(e). However, normally the background can also be ignored by thermal cameras. If only the face should be

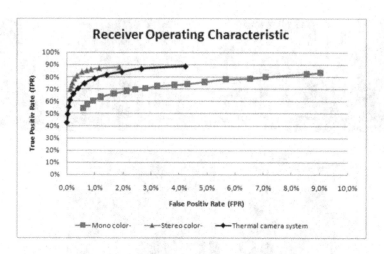

Fig. 6. ROC curves for a mono color-, stereo color- and thermal camera system by using different thresholds

3 Experimental Results

In the first part of our proposed system, we describe the classification of 36 isolated gestures (A-Z and 0-9) from stereo color image sequences or online experiments. After detecting the hands and face, the motion trajectory is generated and then analyzed by HMM. In our previous work, we designed different types of HMM topologies for comparing and getting the best results by using LRB topology [2]. Each isolated gesture is based on at least 30 video sequences, 20 video samples for training by Baum-Welch algorithm and at least 10 video samples and in addition a lot of online experiments for testing using Viterbi algorithm. We achieved an average recognition rate of 98% for isolated gestures by using the LRB topology with 9 states. Figure 7 shows the results of the isolated gesture 'W' at different times. At t=20 the highest probability for the gesture 'V' and at t=34 for the gesture 'h'. Finally at t=42 the gesture 'W' was recognized.

The second part is the classification of continuous gestures. For the separation into isolated gestures a Zero-codeword detection is realized using constant velocity as threshold [10]. The system was tested on 70 video samples for continuous gesture with more than one isolated gesture and achieved a recognition rate of 95.7%.

The system output for the continuous gesture '90' is shown in Fig 8. At t=51

Fig. 7. Result of isolated gesture 'W' at different times

Fig. 8. Result of continuous gesture '90' at different times

4 Conclusion

In this paper, we propose an automatic system to recognize continuous gestures (0-9 & A-Z). Thereby three different types of cameras (mono color-, stereo color- and thermal camera) are compared in the area of segmentation. After analyzing the advantages and disadvantages and calculating receiver operating characteristic (ROC) curves, in average stereo cameras give the best results for segmentation. Our database includes more than 30 video sequences for each gesture. We have achieved an average recognition rate of 98% for isolated gestures and a recognition rate of 95.7% for continuous gestures using a stereo camera system and in addition, we have accomplished a lot of online tests

3. Chen, X., Flynn, P., Bowyer, K.: Ir and visible light face recognition. Comput. Vis. Image Underst. 99(3), 332–358 (2005)
4. Kong, S., Heo, J., Abidi, B., Paik, J., Abidi, M.A.: Recent advances in visual and infrared face recognition - a review. Journal of CVIU 97, 103–135 (2005)
5. Selinger, A., Socolinsky, D.: Appearance-based facial recognition using visible and thermal imagery: A comparative study. Technical report, Equinox Corp (2006)
6. Socolinsky, D., Selinger, A.: Thermal face recognition in an operational scenario. In: IEEE Conference on CVPR, pp. 1012–1019 (2004)
7. Socolinsky, D., Selinger, A.: Thermal face recognition over time. In: International Conference on Pattern Recognition (ICPR), vol. 4, pp. 187–190 (2004)
8. Lawrence, R.R.: A tutorial on hidden markov models and selected applications in speech recognition. Proceeding of the IEEE 77(2), 257–286 (1989)
9. Point Grey Research, Triclops Stereo Vision System Manual Version 3.1 (2009), http://www.ptgrey.com
10. Elmezain, M., Al-Hamadi, A., Appenrodt, J., Michaelis, B.: A hidden markov model-based continuous gesture recognition system for hand motion trajectory. In: International Conference on Pattern Recognition (ICPR), pp. 1–4 (2008)

61266 Brno, Czech Republic
{idvorak,drahansky,orsag}@fit.vutbr.cz

Abstract. In this paper, there is introduced an approach to surface reconstruction of an object captured by one grayscale camera with a small resolution. The proposed solution expects a rectangular grid being projected onto the object and the camera capturing the situation from position different to the grid projector position. The crucial part of the method is exact detection of the grid. The structure of the grid is identified by the centers of the inner space between its lines. The reconstruction process itself is based on a simple math of perspective projection of the captured image. Due to the small resolution of the image some errors arise during object surface reconstruction. We proposed a correction of the calculated coordinates, which is a simple one-dimensional function depending on the distance from the camera. The method performs very well as the results in conjunction with the precision evaluation indicate at the end of the paper.

Keywords: surface reconstruction, projected grid, structured light, image processing, camera calibration.

1 Introduction

There are many solutions of a 3D surface reconstruction of an object. They differ from each other and they are typical for specific application. The first solution is based on a method, which constructs the object surface from multiple camera views. Such an example can be an early work from R. Mohr et al. [1], where the points are reconstructed from multiple uncalibrated images. In the work of P. Lavoie et al. [2] the reconstruction is done from a pair of images. On the other hand in the work of F. Pedersiny [3] the multiple camera system was calibrated in order to improve accuracy.

The next solution deals with reconstruction of the surface from one single image. Method presented by A. Saxena et al. [4, 5] is an example of such solution. Distance of the points in the image is calculated using supervised learning. Some other ap-

the projected grid. It can be characterized as a low cost and minimum dimension solution. The system consists of one grayscale camera with a low resolution (currently 640x480) and a square-structured light source such as a laser module. The known parameters are position of the camera and spacing of the projected grid in a given distance.

The reconstruction itself requires exact grid detection. Because of the low resolution of the camera the centers of grid squares (segments) are detected instead of the lines themselves. Next stage is to define the neighboring segments and the last step is reconstruction of the surface itself.

The paper is organized as follows. All phases of the algorithm are described in section 2. Due to the low resolution of the image, some errors arise during the calculation, especially while the segments are being extracted. Therefore, the calculated positions of the points are corrected by defined correction function that is depicted in section 3. In section 4, some testing examples that indicate the capability of the method are shown. The performed experiments were submitted to the accuracy evaluation and the results are stated in section 5. Some final remarks and future development are proposed in section 6.

2 Algorithm of the Surface Reconstruction

The scene is defined by a laser grid generator with a structured grid light, camera with given resolution, position and field of view, and an object. It is also necessary to know the fan angle of the laser generator. The laser itself projects a circle in the center of the grid, which can be used as a starting point for the calculation.

2.1 Image Preprocessing

We use Gaussian filter (currently with core size of 3x3) to remove the noise and to prepare the image for an adaptive thresholding. The core of the filter is defined as follows:

$$G(x, y) = \frac{1}{2\pi\sigma^2} e^{-\frac{x^2+y^2}{2\sigma^2}},\qquad(1)$$

where σ is standard deviation, x and y are variables (coordinates of the pixel in the

which comes up from the preprocessing. Therefore, the circle, which may be deformed, is detected as the residual connected segment of white pixels after the sequence of erosions.

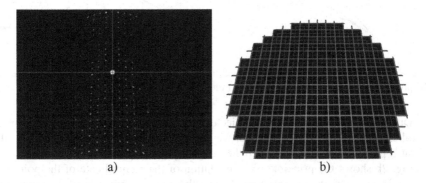

Fig. 1. a) Detected ellipse and its center in an image processed by a sequence of erosions. b) Detected segments (black) and their neighbors.

In order to determine proper count of the erosions, the average thickness of line is predicted as count of white-black crossings in vertical direction divided by count of crossed lines. Due to this process, all the lines as well as the majority of the grid corners disappear. From the remaining white areas, the largest one is the central circle. You can see an example of the detection in Fig. 1a.

The considered segment detection requires determination of corners of the segments. The projected grid holds the vertical and horizontal direction of projected lines in the camera image, which can be used to determine the corners. For the computation of the individual corners, the most extreme segment pixels are got.

It is necessary to determine the centers of all the segments for the resulting reconstruction. Computation of the center is simply given as an average position of all the pixels in the individual segment.

Using the detected corners of the segments, it is possible to determine the mutual neighbors which are detected from the mutual corners positions. Result of the segment detection of a plane is shown in Fig. 1b.

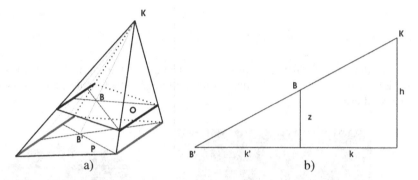

Fig. 2. a) A perspective projection of the camera image O to the plain P and one of the points B' projected as a point B. b) A principle of the calculation of the z coordinate of a point.

Due to the fact that lines are projected again as lines, and knowing the lines are parallel, in accordance with Fig. 2a, we are able to compute original position of the point B projected as the point B' to the image captured by the camera.

Fig. 2b shows the principle of computation of the z coordinate of the point in the space. If we know the camera height h and the plane coordinates of the point B then we can easily use the similarity of triangles to compute height z of the point:

$$z = h\frac{k'}{k}. \tag{3}$$

Meaning of the symbols is clear from the Fig. 2b. To begin the reconstruction process it is necessary to setup a source point which the rest of the calculation will be derived from. The segment center lying near the detected middle-grid circle is the best candidate, because the true position of the circle is known (when there is no object placed).

3 Error Correction

When the z coordinate of the point is calculated, the error arises due to the low angle between the line depicted by camera and the point and the normal vector of the grid plane. Therefore, the error is directly influenced by the distance of the point from the camera - the closer the point is the bigger the error is.

The error is in form of the polygonal function. Therefore, if we know the error, we are able to correct the calculated values to the exact ones.

which is relatively dense according to the camera distance and its low resolution.

4.1 Plane

The first experiment was done with one plane placed perpendicularly to the laser view vector. The plane was positioned 10 mm above the projection plane. The detected grid with detected center circle is shown in Fig. 3. The outer segments are ignored because they are incomplete.

The reconstructed surface of the plain is shown in Fig. 3. You can clearly see that there are some minor deformations. The plane is slightly deflected, especially at the bottom of the image.

Fig. 3. Detected grid with detected center circle of a plane on the left and reconstructed plane in 3-D space on the right

4.2 Head

The model of artificial head was chosen for the third experiment. The detected grid and the reconstructed surface in front view and in profile are shown in Fig. 4. The original model of the head is also shown in figure in order to point out the correctness of the calculations.

It is crucial for the calculation to properly detected the grid structure and set the proper mutual segments. For more complex objects, such as the head, it is harder to achieve it. Therefore we have implemented the self-repairing routines for the grid structure. These are correction of the mutual segments based on information of the

Fig. 4. The detected grid on the head (left) and the surface reconstruction (center, right)

5 Evaluation of the Results

The calculations were done for the plain experiment and the experiment with a cylindrical object. We used objects with known analytical description to be able to precisely calculate the error of our method.

At the beginning we introduce the metrics we used. The first one is an average error of all the calculated points (ERRAVG). The second one is a standard deviation of the error (ERRDEV). The maximum error is marked as ERRMAX. All of them are shown in Table 1.

Table 1. The error calculated for the given experiments

Exp.	ERRAVG (mm)	ERRDEV (mm)	ERRMAX (mm)
Plain	0,579	0,420	1,787
Cylinder	1,175	0,521	2,162

It is clear from the error evaluation that in spite of the low resolution of the camera and relatively dense grid, the errors are relatively small. The differences between the presented two cases are caused mainly by nature of the scene. The plane has a narrow surface and the grid projected on it is almost not deformed, therefore the overall error is smaller and vice versa.

Another reason causing the error is quality of the correction function, which is one-dimensional and depends only on the distance of the camera. We suppose that better correction of the errors would be achieved if a two-dimensional correction function were used.

6 Conclusion

limits.

In the future we are going to propose more sophisticated correction function in three-dimensional space. We are preparing testing of the method with real scenes as soon as a hardware prototype of the system will be available.

Acknowledgements

This research is supported by the following two grants: *"Security-Oriented Research in Information Technology"*, MSM0021630528 (CZ) and *"Information Technology in Biomedical Engineering"*, GA102/09/H083.

References

1. Mohr, R., Quan, L., Veillon, F.: Relative 3D Reconstruction Using Multiple Uncalibrated Images. The International Journal of Robotics Research 14, 619–632 (1995)
2. Luvoie, P., Ionescu, D., Petriu, E.: 3D reconstruction using an uncalibrated stereo pair of encoded images. In: Proceedings of International Conference on Image Processing, pp. 859–862 (1996)
3. Pedersini, F., Sarti, A., Tubaro, S.: Multi-Camera Acquisitions for High-Accuracy 3D Reconstruction. In: Koch, R., Van Gool, L. (eds.) SMILE 1998. LNCS, vol. 1506, pp. 124–138. Springer, Heidelberg (1998)
4. Saxena, A., Chung, S.H., Ng, A.Y.: 3-D Depth Reconstruction from a Single Still Image. International Journal of Computer Vision 76, 53–69 (2008)
5. Saxena, A., Sun, M., Ng, A.Y.: Make3D: Learning 3D Scene Structure from a Single Still Image. IEEE Transactions on Pattern Analysis and Machine Intelligence 31 (2009)
6. Park, I.K., Zhang, H., Vezhnevets, V., Choh, H.-K.: Image-based Photorealistic 3-D Face Modeling. In: Proceedings of Sixth IEEE International Conference on Automatic Face and Gesture Recognition, pp. 49–54 (2004)
7. Garcia, E., Dugelay, J.-L.: Low cost 3D face acquisition and modeling. In: Proceedings of International Conference on Information Technology: Coding and Computing, pp. 657–661 (2001)
8. Lavoie, P., Ionescu, D., Petriu, E.: A high precision 3D object reconstruction method using a colorcoded grid and NURBS. In: Proceedings of International Conference on Image

(2005)

15. Lee, K., Wong, K., Or, S., Fung, Y.: 3D Face Modeling from Perspective-Views and Con-tour-Based Generic-Model. Real-Time Imaging 7, 173–182 (2001)

Jae Weon Hong , Won Eui Hong , and Yoon sik Kwak

[1] Professor, School of Business, The Dongseo University
jwhong@benet.co.kr
[2] Lecturer, School of Business, The Jeonju University
[3] Dept. of Computer Engineering, The Chungju National University Chungbuk, Korea
yskwak@cjnu.ac.kr

Abstract. This study attempts to shed light on the factors that influence the locations of bank branches in establishing a bank's distribution network from the angle of the network analysis. Whereas the previous studies analyzed the locations of bank branches on the basis of their geographical characteristics and image, the significance of this study rests upon the fact that it endeavors to explore the location factors from a new perspective of the movement path of financial customers. For this analysis, the network between administrative districts, which form the fundamental unit of a location, was analyzed based on the financial transactional data. The important findings of this study are as follows. First, in conformity with the previous studies, the income level, the spending level, the number of businesses, and the size of workforce in the pertinent region were all found to influence the size of a bank's market. Second, the centrality index extracted from the analysis of the network was found to have a significant effect on the locations of bank branches. In particular, the degree centrality was revealed to have a greater influence on the size of a bank's market than does the closeness centrality. Such results of this study clearly suggest the needs for a new approach from the perspective of network in furtherance of other factors that have been considered important in the previous studies of the distribution network strategies.

Keywords: Distribution network strategies, bank branches.

1 Introduction

The recent introduction of Geographic Information System (GIS) can be viewed as an extension of such trend (Min Kim et al. 2004).

This study attempts to analyze the factors that influence the selection of branch location through network analysis, which is based on customer transaction data. The findings of this study are expected to contribute in the methodological expansion of previous studies. Network is the collection of nodes that are connected by lines. The nodes can be seen as persons, locations or functions, and the lines can be seen as the flow of information or physical channels between the nodes (Barabasi, 2002). Thus, the value of this study lies with the fact that it views the branch location as the networking channels of customer transactions. Furthermore, this study is also expected to contribute in establishing the future distribution network strategies.

2 Theoretical Background

2.1 The Study of Preceding Factors in Establishing Bank Distribution Network

An increase in the potential sale becomes possible with a good location, as it could attract more customers (Pastor, 1994). The location theory, which considers an ideal location of a store in order to maximize the profit, was introduced in the early 2oth century. The study of this theory became revitalized in the 1940's as the assessment of broad characteristics of a store's commercial zone and the measurement of market share within a city became the focus of the study. These studies experienced further rapid developments in the 1950's. Especially, many theories regarding the characteristics of customers' selections of retail stores were developed through the studies of the suburb shopping centers erected in the United States after World War II due to the decentralization of retail business. Based on these studies, Nelson (1960) identified the followings as the important factors in deciding the feasibility of a location: population, income, branch function, competition, land value, and future development potential, etc. In addition, Huff suggested the traffic hours and the type of traded goods as the contributing factors. Also, Kim's study (Min Kim et al. 2004) evaluated the geographical characteristics of a location as another significant factor. As a result, GIS analysis was employed to include various geographical characteristics in the consideration of a location.

As the parameters of measuring the profitability of bank divide into credits and deposits, Byung-Gil Lee (2006) assessed the branch networking efficiency by the size of credits and deposits. In a study of bank profitability, Sung-Ryong Lee (1985) concluded that a location of bank affects the size of deposits and the profit. Moreover, Lee (1985) found that as the number of branches of other financial institutions increases, the profitability of a bank branch in that region also increases. Ugg-Yeon Cho (1990) has attempted to explain whether a branch's profit and loss vary depending on its location and the density of branches in that region. In a study by Gi-In Song (2006), he has concluded that functional characteristics, such as customers' convenience, and brand image or psychological trust affect the continuous customer commitment.

In the studies pertaining to the images, the customers were found to form an image of a bank from various information sources, and such formed image had a significant influence on the profitability of the bank. Nakanish and Cooper (1974) have concluded that the branch image, level of service, value of products, and the building should be considered in the evaluation of a bank's profitability. Young Jun Kim and Yong Sik Nam (1997) expounded that, when choosing a bank, personal banking customers tend to place more emphasis on their attitude toward a bank's services and images than business banking customers do. In other words, personal bank customers tend to value the personal images they formed toward a bank and use these images as the grounds on which to continue their relationship with the bank. Myung Sik Lee (1993) agreed with the notion that a bank's image could have a positive influence on a continuous customer commitment to the bank. Furthermore, Kyung Kook Lee (2007) asserted that the greater positive image a bank establishes based on trust, the more likely it is to increase the customer satisfaction. Ki In Song (2006) confirmed such assertions by adjoining with the previous notions. He specifically suggested that customers are influenced by the functional characteristics such as convenience as well as the brand image and the psychological trust. Therefore, customers' image of a bank can be concluded as an important factor affecting the profitability of a bank.

Hence, a bank's profitability, measured by their sales or their customers' royalty, could vary depending on the factors such as its location or its image constructed by the customers. This study, however, attempts to focus on the location factor while eliminating the image factors from its analysis to put emphasis on the regional characteristics.

produced by gathering and processing the financial transaction information between the administrative districts. This data indicates the frequency of financial transactional relationship between districts. The more detailed form of data takes the binary format, which indicates the existence of relationships between administrative districts. This data was gathered by analyzing the customer transaction logs for Bank A to understand the inter-district transaction patterns and to used it in building a branch strategy.

The third type of data includes information regarding the quantity and the size of banks within each administrative district. This data was conjectured by incorporating the data from the Bank's association and the consumer surveys.

3.2 The Studying Process

This study looks at the influence of location characteristics of a bank on the profitability from the network analysis perspective. In order to achieve this, the pre-existing studies regarding the effects of the statistical population characteristics and the economical characteristics on the banks' profitability within a district were carefully studied. Through this process, the factors that carried significant values in the previous studies were employed to parallel the implications of the network analysis. Thereafter, the factors that were extracted in the network analysis were analyzed in relations to the effects on the profitability.

As in Jae Won Hong's study (2008), because the lowest level of statistics gathered by the National Statistics Office is done at the administrative district level, this study also selects the administrative district as the analytical unit to maximize the practicality.

4 The Results of the Study

4.1 The Influence of an Administrative District's Characteristics on the Market Size

A close look at the major characteristics of administrative districts – the dependent variable used in this study – reveals the following statistical data: the average population per administrative district is approximately 19, 489, the average monthly income per household is approximately 3.38 million Korean won, the average spending is

All coefficients are standardized, ** denotes significance at .01 level, and * significance at .05 level.

credits than does the level of income. The size of workforce seems to indicate the degree of work-centeredness. Furthermore, the level of spending and the number of businesses were found to affect the wealth. Here, the number of businesses indicates the degree of consumption-centeredness of the pertinent region as it includes even the simplified businesses such as restaurants.

4.2 The Effects of an Administrative District's Network Characteristics on the Market Size

This section explores, in addition to the existing studies, the influence of an administrative district's network characteristics on the market size. For the purpose of the network analysis, a dichotomous relation matrix, which depicts the presence of relationship between administrative districts, were constructed. This matrix was then analyzed using Pajek, a network analysis program. Figure 1 is a visualized result of such analysis. In this figure, the nodes represent administrative districts and the links represent the presence of financial transactional relationship between administrative districts. The administrative districts located at the center of the picture will have different levels of relative influence when compared to the ones in the outer range.

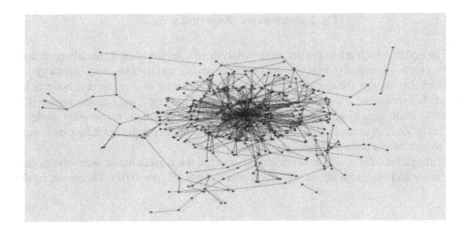

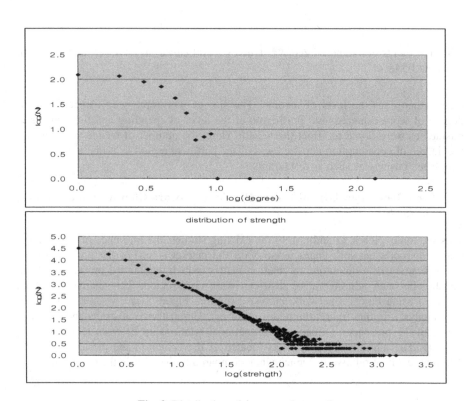

Fig. 2. Distribution of degree and strength

The nodes, which are important in the analysis of a network, are generally measured by two types of centrality indexes: the degree centrality and the closeness centrality.

Centrality means the degree of how close to the center of a network a node is located. In other words, the greater influence a node has, the closer to the center it is located. More specifically, the degree centrality indicates how many other nodes a particular node is connected to, and the closeness centrality indicates how many steps are required for a node to reach another node.

Through the analysis of network characteristics, the correlation between the degree centrality and the close centrality was found to be 0.89 ($p < 0.01$). Therefore, in the

Table 3. The effects of administrative district's closeness centrality on market size

Dependent variables	Income	Expenditure	# of company	# of employee	Closeness centrality	Adjusted R^2
Deposits	0.133**	-0.245**	-0.356**	0.835**	0.202**	0.41
Credits	0.020	-0.043	-0.148**	0.749**	0.326**	0.78
Sum	0.114**	-0.216**	-0.326**	0.846**	0.234**	0.50

All coefficients are standardized, ** denotes significance at .01 level, and * significance at .05 level.

network is necessary, in furtherance to the factors that have already been considered important in the previous location studies, such as the population, income and the number of workers.

4.3 The Achievement of Banks and the Network Characteristics of Administrative Districts

Figure 3 represents the achievements and the location characteristics viewed from the perspective of network of four banks located in Seoul. (a) illustrates the average degree centralities and closeness centralities of the administrative districts in which the four banks' branches are located. As shown in the figure, Bank A and B have relatively advantageous locations than Bank C and D. (b) illustrates the average size of credits and debits of the four banks' branches. This figure, in turns, shows that the banks having more advantageous locations (Bank A and B) have maintained relatively higher profitability in comparison to Bank C and D. Therefore, these results insinuate that the network characteristics of the administrative districts in which the bank branches are located are closely related to the individual bank's profitability.

5 Conclusion and Suggestions

This study explored the factors affecting the locations of bank branches through the network analysis with the purpose of aiding in the selection of their locations. This selection of locations is a central issue that arises in the process of executing competitive branch strategies by either establishing new branches or relocating existing

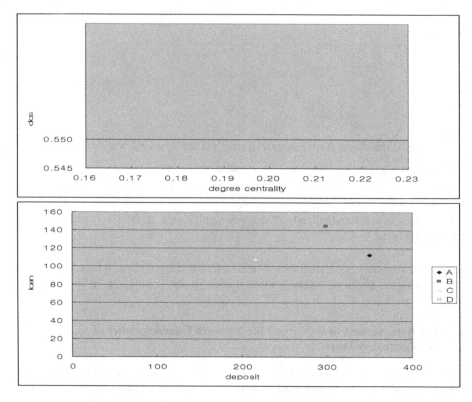

Fig. 3. Network location characteristic and achievements

utilized to make an important suggestion regarding the establishment of a location strategy.

As a result of the study, the factors such as the level of income, the level of spending, the quantity of businesses, and the number of workers were found to have a significant influence on the branch location selecting process as they did in the previous studies. Among these, the level of income and the number of workers had a positive influence, whereas the level of spending and the quantity of businesses had a negative influence. The most significant factor was found to be the number of workers.

In the study of the network approach between administrative districts, the degree centrality and the closeness centrality were found to have relatively bigger influence than the other factors, although less than the number of workers. Furthermore, the result of the network analysis of the four banks' branches revealed that the branches

References

[1] Barabasi, A.: Linked: The New Science of Networks. Perseus, Cambridge (2002)
[2] Lee, B.G.: Evaluation method of bank branch network through GIS spatial analysis. The Korean Association of Professional Geographers, Geographic research 40 (2006)
[3] Park, C.S., Lee, Y.Y.: Change of bank branch location through GIS Technics - The case of Dae Gu city -. The Korean Society for GeoSpatial Information System Publication 1(2) (1993)
[4] Cornuejols, G., Fisher, M.L., Nemhauser, G.L.: On Location of Bank Accounts to Optimize Float: An Analytic Study of Exact and Approximate Algorithms. Management Science 25(8), 808–809 (1979)
[5] Song, G.I.: Study of consumer preference in domestic banking system: Means-End Chain Theory and The Online Laddering. Korea Regional Media Communication Association, Media Science Study 6(1) (2006)
[6] Lee, H.Y., Kim, E.M.: The study of bank branch location through GIS techniques: the case of Kang Nam gu, Seoul. Geographic Information System Association of Korea Publication 5(1) (Serial Number 8), 11–26 (1997)
[7] Pastor, J.T.: Bicriterion Programs and Managerial Location Decisions: Application to the Banking Sector. The Journal of the Operational Research Society 45(12), 1351–1362 (1994)
[8] Lee, K.K.: The affects of bank's adoption of intelligent management on customer trust and satisfaction. Myung-Ji University Institute for Finance and Knowledge 5(1) (2007)
[9] Kim, M.: The GIS analysis of the selling rights of distributing organization of petroleum products. The Korean Geographical Society Publication 39(3) (Serial Number 102), 360–373 (2004)
[10] Lee, M.S.: Advertising strategy through image management in bank's marketing. Advertisement study 20(93, 9), 189–216 (1993)
[11] Nakanishi, M., Cooper, L.G.: Parameter estimate for multiplicative interactive choice model: least squares approach. Journal of Marketing Research 11, 303–311 (1974)
[12] Newman, M.E., Girvan, M.: Finding and evaluating community structure in networks. Physica, Review E 69 (2004)
[13] Nelson, R.L.: The Selection of Retail Locations. Land Economics 36(3), 307–307 (1960); The Korea Economic Daily (2007.7.31)
[14] Cho, U.Y.: The case study of the relationship between bank branch's location and profit-and-loss. Korea University Master's degree thesis (1990)
[15] Seo, W.J., Yun, S.J.: Study of bank branch's productivity by DEA modeling. POSRI

IMERL-IIE-Facultad de Ingeniería, Udelar, Montevideo, Uruguay
{canale,monzon,frobledo}@fing.edu.uy
http://www.fing.edu.uy/imerl
http://iie.fing.edu.uy/

Abstract. This article deals with the general ideas of almost global synchronization of Kuramoto coupled oscillators and synchronizing graphs. We review the main existing results and introduce new results for some classes of graphs that are important in network optimization: complete k-partite graphs and what we have called Monma graphs.

Keywords: Nonlinear systems, Network synchronization, coupled oscillators, synchronizing graphs.

1   Introduction

With the purpose of develope a formal mathematical theory for the analysis of synchronization problems, Y. Kuramoto derived a mathematical model, where each individual agent is represented by a dynamical oscillator [1]. It has several applications and has been widely studied from different points of view [2, 3]. Control community has applied classical, and has derived new, control techniques for the analysis of many synchronization properties that explain natural phenomena, like flocking, formation, self-organization, collective behavior, swarming, etc., and helps to design artificial networks of autonomous agents (see [4] and references there in). Most of these works deal with local stability properties of the synchronization. Recently, we have focused on global properties, trying to establish conditions for *almost global synchronization*, i.e., convergence to synchronization for almost all possible initial conditions. When the oscillator are all identical, the dynamical properties rely on the interconnection graph. We look for necessary and sufficient conditions for this graph, in order to have almost global synchronization of the agents (*synchronizing* graphs). In [5, 6], we de-

2 Kuramoto Model and Synchronizing Graphs

Consider n identical oscillators, described by their phases θ_i, $i = 1, \ldots, n$. Each oscillator has a set of *neighbors* $\mathcal{N}_i$, which influences its velocity in this way [1]: $\dot{\theta}_i = \omega + \sum_{k \in \mathcal{N}_i} \sin(\theta_k - \theta_i)$. The natural state space is the n-dimensional torus T^n, since $\theta_i \in [0, 2\pi)$. We assume mutual influence: $k \in \mathcal{N}_i$ if and only if $i \in \mathcal{N}_k$. The interaction is given by a graph $G = (V, E)$, with vertex set $V = \{v_1, v_2, \ldots, v_n\}$, associated to the phases $\theta_1, \theta_2, \ldots, \theta_n$ and edge set $E = e_1, e_2, \ldots, e_m{}^1$. If we endow G with an arbitrary orientation, define the vector $\theta = (\theta_1, \ldots, \theta_n) \in T^n$, introduce the incidence matrix B and reparameterize time, we obtain the compact expression [4]

$$\dot{\theta} = -B.\sin\left(B^T \theta\right). \tag{1}$$

The dynamical properties rely only on the interconnection graph. We observe that the results obtained for identical oscillators may be extended for *quasi-identical* oscillators using standard perturbation techniques. We say the systems reaches *(full) synchronization* or *consensus* when all the agents have the same phase: $\theta_i = \bar{\theta}_0$, $i = 1, 2, \ldots, n$. *Partial synchronization* describes a state with some agents at one phase $\bar{\theta}_0$ and the rest of the agents at $\bar{\theta}_0 \pm \pi$. Since system (1) depends only of the phase differences between agents, we may always assume $\bar{\theta}_0 = 0$. States with phases distributed along $[0, 2\pi)$ will be referred as *non synchronized*. Observe that for every $c \in \mathcal{R}$, we have that $-B.\sin(B^T \theta) = -B.\sin[B^T(\theta + c.\mathbf{1}_n)]$ and $\mathbf{1}_n^T.B.\sin(B^T \theta) = 0$ where $\mathbf{1}_n$ denote the n-dimensional column of ones. This means that the system is invariant under translations on the state space parallel to vector $\mathbf{1}_n$ and that the dynamics develops over hyperplanes orthogonal to this direction. Frequently, we will forget this aspect and say that a property holds for one state, meaning that the property holds for this state and for every state obtained from this one by a $\mathbf{1}_n$ translation. Equation (1) describes is a *gradient system*, with potential function [11]

$$U(\theta) = m - \sum_{ik \in E} \cos(\theta_i - \theta_k) = U_0 - \mathbf{1}_m^T.\cos(B^T \theta), \tag{2}$$

around the synchronized state $\bar{\theta} = 0 \in T^n$. Then, U takes non negative values around $\bar{\theta}$ and attains its minimum, which is 0, at $\bar{\theta}$. Thus, U is a local Lyapunov function and we have local stability of the consensus. In order to have the almost global synchronization property, we must prove that the consensus is the only equilibrium point with a non-zero measure of his basin of attraction. We need to find all the equilibrium points of (1) and analyze its local stability. The Jacobian matrix around an equilibrium point $\bar{\theta} \in T^n$ is $J(\bar{\theta})$ with elements can be written as $J(\bar{\theta}) = -B.diag(\cos(B^T\bar{\theta})).B^T$. Observe that is a symmetric matrix, due to the mutual influence of the agents and it always has 0 as an eigenvalue, since $B^T.\mathbf{1}_n = 0$. For local stability, we will require negativity of the remaining $n-1$ eigenvalues of $J(\bar{\theta})$ (*transversal stability* [5]). As was done by Kuramoto, we introduce the phasors $V_i, \dots, V_n$ associated to every agent: $V_i = e^{j\theta_i}$. Then, we may think the system as particles running in the unit circumference. Consensus means that all the particles are together. These phasors will be very useful for the stability analysis.

We recall some previous results that will be useful in our present analysis. We do not include the proofs here. They can be found in [5, 6, 7]. For a given equilibrium point $\bar{\theta}$, we define the numbers $\alpha_i = \frac{1}{V_i}\sum_{k \in \mathcal{N}_i} V_k$. They all are real and if there is some negative, then $\bar{\theta}$ is unstable. This fact is extended in Lemma 1. Concerning stability of an equilibrium point, we may affirm it if all the phase differences belongs to $[-\frac{\pi}{2}, +\frac{\pi}{2}]$. Another important result is that *a graph synchronizes if and only if its blocks do* [6]. A block of a graph is either a single vertex, a *bridge* or a *bi-connected component* (a subgraph which has always two distinct paths between any pair of nodes). The result exploits the fact that every cycle of a graph belongs to only one block. This result can be seen either as a reduction procedure or a synchronization-preserving algorithm for networks construction. So, in order to state the synchronizability of a given graph, we only have to focus on its blocks. It reduces the characterization of synchronizing graphs to bi-connected families. Applying those previous results, we have found the first two families of synchronizing graphs: **complete** graphs and **trees** [6]. We have also proved that a cycle synchronizes if and only if it has less than five nodes [7]. In the next Section, we investigate the synchronizability

of vertices V_1, V_2 *such that every link of* V_1 *joins only an element of* V_1 *with an element of* V_2.

The idea generalizes to k-*partites graphs*, when we split V as the disjoint union of *clusters* $V_1 \cup V_2 \cup \ldots \cup V_k$. In a *complete k-partite graph* $G = (V, E)$, with $V = V_1 \cup \ldots \cup V_k$, every element of V_i is connected to all the elements of V_j, $j \neq i$. Observe that all the agents in the same cluster *share* the same neighbors. We introduce the following idea.

Definition 4. *Consider two nodes u and v of a graph G. We say they are twins if the have the same set of neighbors:* $\mathcal{N}_u = \mathcal{N}_v$.

Slightly modifying previous definition, we also say that two vertices are *adjacent twins* if they are adjacent and $\mathcal{N}_u \setminus \{v\} = \mathcal{N}_v \setminus \{u\}$. Concerning synchronization, twins vertices act as a *team* in order to get equilibrium in equation (1). Observe that for a complete k-partite graph, all the vertices of the same cluster are twins. The following Lemma extends a previous result and is very important for the main result of this Section.

Lemma 1. *Let $\bar{\theta} \in T^n$ be an equilibrium point of (1). If for some i, the number α_i is non positive, then $\bar{\theta}$ is unstable.*

Proof. The case α_i negative was already proved in [5]. If we have a null α_k, the matrix $J(\bar{\theta})$ may have a multiple null eigenvalues. Looking carefully at equation (2), we observe that we can rewrite $U = U_0 - \frac{1}{2} \sum_{i=1}^{n} \alpha_i$. We chose U_0 such that $U(\bar{\theta}) = 0$. Consider the k-th element of the canonical base e_k, a small positive number δ and a perturbation $\tilde{\theta} = \bar{\theta} + \delta.e_k$. Then $U(\tilde{\theta}) = U_0 - \frac{1}{2} \sum_{\substack{i=1 \\ i \neq k}}^{n} \sum_{h \in \mathcal{N}_i} \cos\left(\bar{\theta}_h - \bar{\theta}_i\right) - \frac{1}{2} \sum_{h \in \mathcal{N}_k} \cos\left(\bar{\theta}_h - \bar{\theta}_k - \delta\right)$. After some calculations, we may write

$$ U(\tilde{\theta}) = U_0 - \frac{1}{2} \sum_{\substack{i=1 \\ i \neq k}}^{n} \sum_{\substack{h \in \mathcal{N}_i \\ h \neq k}} \cos\left(\bar{\theta}_h - \bar{\theta}_i\right) - \sum_{h \in \mathcal{N}_k} \left[\cos\left(\bar{\theta}_k + \delta - \bar{\theta}_h\right)\right] $$

it, that is, the phasors $_h$, with $_v$ are all parallel to $_v$. Moreover, if **stable**, the agents in T are fully coordinated.

Proof. Let $u \in T$ and consider the real numbers $\alpha_v = \frac{1}{V_v} \sum_{w \in \mathcal{N}} V_w$, $\alpha_u = \frac{1}{V_u} \sum_{w \in \mathcal{N}} V_w$. Then, it follows that $\alpha_v.V_v = \alpha_u.V_u$, for all $u \in T$. If there are $u_1, u_2 \in T$ linearly independent, their respective α_{u_1} and α_{u_2} must be zero, and so are all numbers α in T. Then, if there is some $\alpha_u \neq 0$, $u \in T$, all phasors in T are parallel. So, all the nodes in T are partially or fully coordinated. Now suppose that $\bar{\theta}$ is stable and that there are $u_1, u_2 \in T$ such that $u_1 = -u_2$. Then $\alpha_{u_1} = \frac{1}{V_{u_1}} \sum_{w \in \mathcal{N}} V_w = -\frac{1}{V_{u_2}} \sum_{w \in \mathcal{N}} V_w = -\alpha_{u_2}$ and we have at least one negative number α and $\bar{\theta}$ should be unstable, by Lemma 1. $\qquad\square$

We are now ready to state and prove one of the main results of this article.

Theorem 1. *A complete k-partite graph synchronizes.*

Proof. We follow the same steps as before. Let $G = (V, E)$ and $V_1, V_2, \ldots, V_k$ be a partition of V such that all the agents in V_i are twins, $i = 1, 2, \ldots, k$. For $k = 2$, we have the particular case of bi-partite graph. Let $\bar{\theta}$ be an equilibrium point of (1). We have several cases, regarding the numbers α.

Case 1: There exists some null number α. Once again, according to Lemma 1, $\bar{\theta}$ should be unstable.

Case 2: For every $u \in V$, $\alpha_u \neq 0$. Then, by Lemma 2, in order to have a stable equilibrium, all agents in V_i are fully coordinated, $i = 1, \ldots, k$. Now, consider $u_i \in V_i$ and $u_h \in V_h$, with $\alpha_{u_i} \neq 0$ and $\alpha_{u_h} \neq 0$. Denote by R the sum of all phasors in V: $R = \sum_{w \in V} V_w$. Then, since the graph is complete k-partite, $R = \sum_{w \in V_i} V_w + \sum_{w \in V \setminus V_i} V_w = |V_i|.V_{u_i} + \alpha_{u_i}.V_{u_i}$, where $|V_i|$ is the cardinality of V_i. A similar expression is also valid for u_h. So, $[|V_i| + \alpha_{u_i}].V_{u_i} = [|V_h| + \alpha_{u_h}].V_{u_h}$. If V_{u_i} and V_{u_h} are not parallel, we obtain a negative number α and by Lemma 1, $\bar{\theta}$ is unstable. So, in order to have a stable equilibrium, all the agents in all the clusters should be parallel. Then, $\bar{\theta}$ should be a full or a partial synchronized equilibrium. Suppose we have $u_i \in V_i$ and $u_h \in V_h$ with $u_i = -u_h$. Then, $\alpha_{u_i} = -\alpha_{u_h}$ and $\bar{\theta}$ is unstable. Then, the only stable equilibrium point is the synchronization $\qquad\square$

P vio   The   l   iv   f f r the s   chronization of

survivability. A commonly planning requirement is to ensure the existence of at least two-node-disjoint-paths between pairs of distinguished nodes. In this way, when occurring a failure (link or node), the network will remain in operational state, i.e. the resulting network is connected. To find a network topology verifying this restriction is known as the Steiner Node-Survivable Network Problem (STNSNP) [9]. A very important particular case of the STNSNP is the construction of a minimum-weight two-connected network spanning all the points in a set of nodes V. For this problem, in [9] Monma-Munson-Pulleyblanck introduce a characterization of optimal solutions. They prove that there exits an optimal two-connected solution whose nodes all have degree 2 or 3, and such that the removal of any edge or pair of edges leaves a bridge in the resulting connected components. Moreover, they prove that optimal solutions that are not a cycle contains, as a node induced subgraph, a graph like the one shown in figure 1-Left, with two nodes of degree 3, joined by three paths with l, m and n degree 2 nodes, that we will denote by M_{lmn}. For these graphs we will study the synchronization property. In what follows, call this class of graphs as Monma graphs [10]. Let a and b be the nodes with degree 3. We will denote by x_i, $i = 1, \ldots, l$, the nodes of the first path between nodes a and b, y_i, $i = 1, \ldots, m$, the nodes of the second path and z_i, $i = 1, \ldots, n$, the nodes of the third path. We assume that $l \geq m \geq n \geq 1$. Firstly, we consider the particular constrains imposed to nodes with degree 2.

Lemma 3. *Let $\bar{\theta}$ be a stable equilibrium point of (1) with associated graph M_{lmn}. Let x_i, be a degree 2 node of M_{lmn}. Consider the set $\mathcal{N}_{x_i} = \{u, v\}$ of neighbors of x_i and define the angles $\varphi_u = \bar{\theta}_u - \bar{\theta}_{x_i}$, $\varphi_v = \bar{\theta}_v - \bar{\theta}_{x_i}$. Then, $\varphi_u = -\varphi_v$.*

Proof. Since $\bar{\theta}$ is an equilibrium, then $\sin(\varphi_u) + \sin(\varphi_v) = 0$ and it must be either $\varphi_u = -\varphi_v$ or $\varphi_u = \pi + \varphi_v$. But if it was the last case, we would have that

configurations with the agents θ_{x_i} on one arc and agents θ_{y_i} and θ_{z_i} on the other. Let be $\varphi = \bar{\theta}_a - \bar{\theta}_b$ (or viceversa), defined such that $\varphi \in (0, \pi)$ (we explicitly exclude partial or full synchronized equilibrium points). Observe that we must prove the existence of a suitable angle φ. The equilibrium condition at node a gives $f(\varphi) = -\sin\left(\frac{2\pi - \varphi}{l+1}\right) + \sin\left(\frac{\varphi}{m+1}\right) + \sin\left(\frac{\varphi}{n+1}\right) = 0$, where we have introduced the auxiliar function f, which is well defined and C^∞. Observe that $f(0) = -\sin\left(\frac{2\pi}{l+1}\right)$ and $f(\pi) = -\sin\left(\frac{\pi}{l+1}\right) + \sin\left(\frac{\pi}{m+1}\right) + \sin\left(\frac{\pi}{n+1}\right)$. If $l \geq 2$, $f(0) < 0$. On the other hand, since the sine is an increasing function in $(0, \pi/2)$ and $l \geq m \geq n$, it follows that $\sin\left(\frac{\pi}{l+1}\right) \leq \sin\left(\frac{\pi}{m+1}\right) \leq \sin\left(\frac{\pi}{n+1}\right)$. If $n \geq 1$, $f(\pi) > 0$. Then, in this conditions, there exists an angle $\varphi \in (0, \pi)$ such that we have a non synchronized equilibrium point. Now, we care about the stability of this equilibrium. A sufficient condition is that all involved phase differences belongs to $(-\pi/2, \pi/2)$ (see [5])). But all the phase differences are $\frac{2\pi - \varphi}{l+1}$, $\frac{\varphi}{m+1}$, $\frac{\varphi}{n+1}$. So, as $\varphi \in (0, \pi)$, it is enough to require $l \geq 3$. At this point, we must prove that the graphs M_{lmn} with $l \leq 3$ (M_{111}, M_{211}, M_{221}, M_{222}) are synchronizing. We only present the analysis of one of these cases, since the proofs are all quite similar. Let us consider the graph M_{221}. Then, at an equilibrium point $\bar{\theta}$, the phases must correspond to one of the situations showed in figure 2. In case (I), the equilibrium condition for node a gives $-\sin(\delta) + 2\sin(\beta) = 0$, with the associated constrain $2\delta + 3\beta = 2\pi$. We eliminate $\delta = \pi - \frac{3\beta}{2}$ and get the equation $2\sin(\beta) - \sin\left(\frac{3\beta}{2}\right) = 0$. Since $\delta \geq 0$, the solutions must belong to the interval $[0, \frac{2\pi}{3}]$ and we obtain the only roots $\beta = 0$ and $\delta = \pi$, which corresponds to a partial synchronized (unstable) equilibrium point. The same ideas apply to case (II). The final case has the only solution $\delta = 0$, which corresponds to a full synchronized equilibrium. Then, M_{221} is synchronizing. □

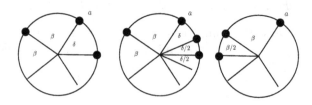

The techniques we have presented here show how ideas from graph and control theory can be combined in order to obtain more insight about the dynamics and the graph structure.

References

[1] Kuramoto, Y.: International symposium on mathematical problems in theoretical physics. Lecture notes in Physics 39, 420 (1975)
[2] Strogatz, S.: Nonlinear Dynamics and Chaos: with Applications to Physics, Biology, Chemistry and Engineering. Perseus, Cambridge (1994)
[3] Acebrón, J., Bonilla, L., Pérez, C., Ritort, F., Spigler, R.: The Kuramoto model: A simple paradigm for synchronization. Review of Modern Physics 77, 137–185 (2005)
[4] Jadbabaie, A., Motee, N., Barahona, M.: On the stability of the Kuramoto model of coupled nonlinear oscillators. In: ACC (2004)
[5] Monzón, P.: Almost global stability of dynamical systems. Ph.D. Thesis, Udelar, Uruguay (2006)
[6] Canale, E., Monzón, P.: Gluing Kuramoto coupled oscillators. In: Proceedings of the 46th IEEE CDC, New Orleans, pp. 4596–4601 (2007)
[7] Canale, E., Monzón, P.: On the Characterization of Families of Synchronizing Graphs for Kuramoto Coupled Oscillators. In: 1st IFAC NECSYS 2009, Venice (2009)
[8] Godsil, C., Royle, G.: Algebraic Graph Theory. Series Texts in Mathematics, vol. 207. Springer, New York (2001)
[9] Monma, C.L., Munson, B.S., Pulleyblank, R.: Minimum-Weight Two-Connected Spanning Networks. Mathematical Programming 46, 153–171 (1990)
[10] Robledo, F.: GRASP Heuristics for Wide Area Network Design. Ph.D. Thesis, IRISA/INRIA Université de Rennes I (2005)
[11] Khalil, H.: Nonlinear Systems. Prentice-Hall, Englewood Cliffs (1996)

Department of Informatics, School of Engineering, University of Minho
4710-057 Braga, Portugal
nmd.guerreiro@gmail.com, obelo@di.uminho.pt

Abstract. GRID environments are privileged targets for computation-intensive problem solving in areas from weather forecasting to seismic analysis. Mainly composed by commodity hardware, these environments can deliver vast computational capacity, at relatively low cost. In order to take full advantage of their power we need to have efficient task schedulers with the ability to maximize resource effectiveness, shortening execution times. GRID schedulers must not only decide taking a snapshot of the GRID's status into account, but should also consider the output involved in past decisions. In this work, we intend to show how resource usage can be analyzed, through the use of data mining techniques, to predict performance availability of a GRID environment, as a preliminary work to increase scheduling efficiency as well as adequate resource provisioning.

Keywords: GRID environments, task scheduling optimization, resource availability, data mining, performance evaluation models.

1 Introduction

Over the last decades, technological breakthroughs have changed the world so radically that we are now living in a global world, thirsty for information and unwilling to wait for that information to be discovered, captured and processed, before reaching its end consumer. Even though knowledge extraction algorithms and tools continue to evolve, processing relevant data requires usually expensive computational power. Over the last couple of decades a new trend of parallel architectures and distributed applications has emerged, presenting great advances on networking hardware and protocols, as well as in the evolution of entry-level equipments. Efforts like Beowulf [1] have turned commodity hardware into a feasible alternative for high performance

GRIDs are managed in a distributed manner, at several levels, instead of following the traditional master-slave design, whose scalability and reliability, as we know, is ultimately limited by the master node. The complexity of task scheduling on the GRID is greater than on traditional clusters, since the set of resources changes throughout time, as does their availability to perform work for application purposes. Moreover, communication between resources and applications may span from extremely fast fiber-optic based networks to conventional long distance networks with higher latency and lower bandwidth. Hence, choosing a resource to execute a previously submitted task requires balancing the cost of using powerful, but remote resources in exchange for local, but more modest resources. Despite all the sophisticated scheduling algorithms currently available, scheduling software does not learn from its past decisions. Instead, the schedulers' decision processes are usually based on a snapshot of the GRID's status and the list of tasks it needs to execute. By gathering and analyzing a GRID environment's performance data over time, it is likely that more solid scheduling strategies may arise, therefore extracting more profit from the resources in place. Along these lines, data mining techniques enable both human and automated analysis of historical data with the goal of predicting the GRID's resources status throughout time. In this paper, we aim to demonstrate how can data mining techniques be used to extract valuable knowledge about resource's load over time in a GRID environment. In particular, we intend to show how humans and automated schedulers can benefit from such knowledge in order to increase scheduling efficiency and decrease execution times.

2 Executing Tasks on a GRID

The GRID has a decentralized coordination model, where multiple schedulers coexist with multiple resource managers, to provide a scalable and fault tolerant environment. GRID applications communicate with one of the available meta-schedulers and submit the tasks whose execution is required, along with its requirements (target OS, CPU architecture, minimum RAM memory, etc). It is up to the meta-scheduler to find the appropriate resources for executing the submitted tasks, using the GRID's middleware. Ultimately, the middleware may delegate the execution of a set of tasks on a single machine or on a cluster, whose task scheduling is done by a local cluster

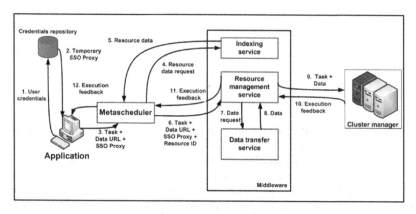

Fig. 1. Performance availability of a GRID

the middleware to provide support for the requirements that GRID applications set. Usually, the GRID's middleware does not execute the tasks itself. Instead, the middleware delegates task execution to local schedulers like Condor [8], Portable Batch System (PBS) [9] or Sun's GRID Engine [10]. The local scheduler manages local resources and a task queue and is ultimately responsible for executing tasks on the actual end nodes.

3 Evaluating the Performance of a GRID

Performance can be evaluated from multiple standpoints, depending on the type of analysis that is required. A GRID environment is no exception, since there are multiple metrics that can be thought of while evaluating the GRID's performance. Since the GRID is mostly used by applications whose execution time would be prohibitive for a single workstation, metrics that directly or indirectly relate to task execution time are among the most important. One of such metrics is performance availability, which measures the maximum amount of processing power a system is able to deliver on a given instant, considering its current load. When a system is fully loaded (i.e. cannot execute any more tasks) its performance availability is null. Conversely, if a system is idle, it is able to provide its maximum performance availability. In order to assess the GRID's performance, we chose to measure and evaluate performance availability. From our point of view, performance availability is a decisive measure that ultimately influences other ones, like execution time and success rate. It is our understanding that by scheduling tasks to resources with the best available performance, the GRID's efficiency is likely to improve.

Measuring and evaluating performance availability involves an objective meas-

deliver different performance values. So, we introduced a CPU architecture constant (kCPUARCH). The constants kCPU and kCPUARCH are then multiplied by the number of free CPUs at each moment (it is assumed that all CPUs are equal on the same node) and by its operating frequency. This portion of the formula enables us to qualify the node's CPU in considerable detail. Different memory types may have different performance levels. However, it is not possible to retrieve such details from resource indexing services we analyzed. Therefore, we only considered the amount of memory available on each node (AvailRAM). This value was multiplied by the kMEM constant to obtain the memory's influence on a node's performance availability. Although the maximum capacity of a node is important, its real ability to execute work is far more significant in terms of performance availability, since it varies with the amount of load the node experiences. Therefore, a third factor was included in our model: system load average. This coefficient's (AvailCOEF) calculation formula can be found on figure 3. If the number of processes waiting for CPU time over the last 5 minutes is greater than the unit, a node is considered to have no availability, since it already has processes it cannot give CPU time to. On the contrary, if the value is less than one, the availability value is the difference to the unit. Therefore, AvailCOEF varies between 0 and 1, that is, from null to maximum availability.

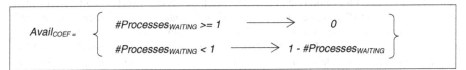

Fig. 3. Availability coefficient calculation

4 The Performance Prediction Models

To evaluate the performance of the GRID environment we decided to use two types of data mining algorithms: clustering and decision trees. In order to do that, two models were created using each algorithm: one model for analyzing the entire GRID and other model for analyzing the behavior of each individual node.

Clustering algorithms are usually used for initial data exploration, in order to find patterns that help understanding the data set in hand. These models process data and

0.005 and minimum confidence of 0.25. Tree depth was limited to a maximum of 30 levels. Our decision tree models were trained using approximately one third of the complete data set. The remaining data was left for prediction evaluation on two data sets: test and validation. RapidMiner's ClassificationPerformance operator was used to evaluate prediction accuracy.

In order to determine the effectiveness of our performance evaluation model, we simulated a typical Grid environment, using VirtualBox virtual machines on an Intel Quad Core Q9300 CPU (2.50GHz). Since VirtualBox assigns one OS process to each virtual machine, we limited the number of nodes to four, in order to allocate one of each of the four cores to a single virtual machine. Three of the nodes (gtnode-2, gtnode-3 and gtnode-4) received 1GB of RAM memory, with gtnode-1 being granted 1.5GB of memory, due to the use of an X display server and some additional services. Communication between nodes was done via a set of simulated 100Mbit Ethernet interfaces. The four virtual machines were grouped into two virtual cluster sites (gtnode-1+gtnode-3 and gtnode-2+gtnode-4). We did not create distinct VOs, since it was irrelevant for our tests. To manage each of the clusters we used Torque 2.3.0, with Ganglia Monitor being chosen for monitoring the nodes' status. Although not manda-tory, we installed the Globus Toolkit 4.0.6 on every node, to be able to gather data from each machine individually and also to have tasks being directly submitted to each machine, bypassing PBS if necessary. Ganglia's information was published on Globus' MDS Index service using the UsefulRP module. Data transfer between nodes was handled by RFT, with task management and resource allocation handled by WS-GRAM. In order to be able to submit tasks to both sites, we used Gridway 5.2.3 as the metascheduler. It was decided to install it on gtnode-1, due to its additional memory.

With the intention of simulating the load that real applications would introduce in our simulated Grid environment, we simulated three different applications, using the NAS Parallel Benchmarks [11]. We selected three benchmarks that target the processing ability for scientific applications (LU, SP and BT). Based on these benchmarks, we created three application profiles and developed a daemon that submitted tasks, for those profiles, using Gridway and its implementation of the DRMAA API. The daemon used probability values for each profile and period of the day, in order to determine if any tasks were to be launched for each profile. The three profiles were designed to simulate the activity of a fictitious organization, with different patterns of use throughout working days. On weekends, there was no

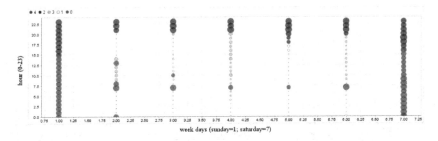

Fig. 4. Grid's available performance over the week (clustering model)

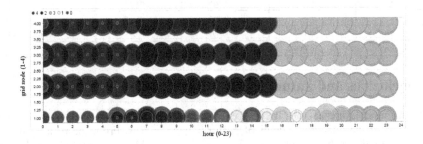

Fig. 5. Grid nodes' available performance over the day (clustering model)

In order to analyze the Grid's performance, we gathered status data during a full week, from Saturday to Friday, while the load injection daemon was executing. Since Globus Toolkit's MDS-Index module publishes node status data that can be accessed via any web services based application, we developed an additional daemon for gathering that data periodically (every 10 minutes), using Globus Toolkit's stub libraries. This daemon was installed on gtnode-1 and collected approximately 670 status snapshots in total. To perform an hour-by-hour analysis, we aggregated values on an hourly basis, by averaging values for each machine. Status data for the entire Grid was generated by summing the values for all machines on a given hour. After collecting all the data, we built and applied the data mining models that were described in the previous section (Performance Evaluation Model), using RapidMiner. All models were applied to the Grid's aggregated data and also to each of the Grid's nodes. The most relevant results are shown below, for both the clustering and decision trees models. Figure 4 shows the Grid's available performance for each test day, determined using the clustering model. The x-axis shows the weekday (from Sunday to Saturday, 1-7). The y-axis represents the time throughout a particular day (from 0.0 to 23.99). Each of the values is represented by a bubble, whose size is relates to the available

Performance class	Per node		Grid	
	Test set	Validation set	Test set	Validation set
C0	88,89%	92,50%	57,14%	70,00%
C1	0,00%	0,00%	80,00%	50,00%
C2	60,00%	90,91%	100,00%	100,00%
C3	0,00%	0,00%	0,00%	20,00%
C4	63,16%	65,00%	63,64%	100,00%
Global	75,70%	71,15%	65,52%	64,00%

5 Conclusions and Future Work

Clustering models are usually used to explore data. In this work, we neglected the constitution of the clusters in favor of performance patterns. From the results of the clustering model for the overall Grid (figure 4), it is possible to say that Grid behaved as expected. Non-working days have maximum available performance, with two of the five clusters grouping high performance availability. In the nightly period of work days, the Grid experienced extremely low available performance periods, due to the simulated Nightly application. Even though task submission ended at 2 a.m., the Grid took, in average, almost five additional hours to complete all tasks. This can be explained by the large number of tasks being submitted during the period between 12 a.m. and 2 a.m. Finally, the Grid's behavior on week days is not absolutely homogeneous, since the number and interval between tasks is not deterministic, but random. The analogous analysis for each individual machine (figure 5) revealed that gtnode-1 displayed lower values of performance availability. This can be explained by the load induced by the status data gathering daemon as well as some additional services like Gridway and an X display server.

Although clustering models favor human analysis, decision tree models provide a set of rules that can be easily used in automated analysis. Table 1 shows that our decision tree model was reasonably accurate for predicting a node's performance availability class (more than 70% accurate). The accuracy is not higher mainly due to C1 and C3 classes, in which our model scored 0%. The low accuracy can be explained by the relatively low number of instances of these classes. This fact is due to the nature of our simulated applications which resulted in many more periods of high and low performance availability than those of medium performance availability Results for

provement. Our simulated GRID was based on a low number of nodes. Besides, all nodes shared the same OS and hardware architecture. GRIDs are inherently heterogeneous so these models and techniques must be transposed to heterogeneous and real-scale GRID environments to confirm their worth in predicting the environments' available performance. Additionally, we only processed data for a period of seven days. Analyzing data of far more extended periods can also increase the support on the concepts we presented.

References

[1] Sterling, T., Becker, D., Savarese, D., Dorband, J., Ranawake, U., Packer, C.: Beowulf: A Parallel Workstation for Scientific Computation. In: Proceedings of the 24th International Conference on Parallel Processing, pp. 11–14 (1995)

[2] Kesselman, C., Foster, I.: The GRID: Blueprint for a New Computing Infrastructure. Morgan Kaufmann Publishers, San Mateo (1998)

[3] Baker, M., Apon, A., Ferner, C., Brown, J.: Emerging GRID Standards. IEEE Computer 38(4), 43–50 (2005)

[4] Huedo, E., Montero, R., Llorente, I.: The Gridway Framework for Adaptive Scheduling and Execution on Grids. Scalable Computing: Practice and Experience 6(3), 1–8 (2005)

[5] Frey, J., Tannenbaum, T., Livny, M., Foster, I., Tuecke, S.: Condor-G: A Computation Management Agent for Multi-Institutional GRIDs. Cluster Computing 5(3), 237–246 (2002)

[6] Foster, I.: Globus Toolkit Version 4: Software for Service-Oriented Systems. In: Jin, H., Reed, D., Jiang, W. (eds.) NPC 2005. LNCS, vol. 3779, pp. 2–13. Springer, Heidelberg (2005)

[7] Laure, E., Fisher, S., Frohner, A., Grandi, C., Kunszt, P., Krenek, A., Mulmo, O., Pacini, F., Prelz, F., White, J., Barroso, M., Buncic, P., Hemmer, F., Meglio, A., Edlund, A.: Programming the GRID with gLite. Computational Methods in Science and Technology 12(1), 33–45 (2006)

[8] Litzkow, M., Livny, M., Mutka, M.: Condor - a hunter for idle workstations. In: 8th International Conference on Distributed Computing Systems, pp. 104–111 (1998)

[9] Henderson, R.: Job Scheduling Under the Portable Batch System. In: Feitelson, D.G., Rudolph, L. (eds.) IPPS-WS 1995 and JSSPP 1995. LNCS, vol. 949, pp. 279–294. Springer, Heidelberg (1995)

[10] Gentzsch, W.: Sun GRID Engine: towards creating a compute power grid. In: Proceed-

[1] Department of Informatics, University of Fribourg, Switzerland
{ye.huang,amos.brocco,michele.courant,beat.hirsbrunner}@unifr.ch
[2] Department of Computing and Information Systems,
University of Bedfordshire, UK
nik.bessis@beds.ac.uk, stelios@sotiriadis.gr
[3] Department of Information and Communication Technologies,
University of Applied Sciences Western Switzerland
pierre.kuonen@hefr.ch

Abstract. Much work has been done to exploit the benefit brought by allowing job execution on distributed computational resources. Nodes are typically able to share jobs only within the same virtual organization, which is inherently bounded by various reasons such as the adopted information system or other agreed constraints. The problem raised by such limitation is thus related to finding a way to enable interoperation between nodes from different virtual organizations.

We introduce a novel technique for integrating visions from both resource users and providers, allowing to serve multiple virtual organizations as a whole. By means of snapshot data stored within each grid node, such as processing and interacting history, we propose a demand-centered heuristic scheduling approach named Critical Friend Community (CFC). To this end, a set of simplified community scheduling targeted algorithms and processing workflows are described. A prototype of our scheduling approach is being implemented within the SmartGRID project.

Keyword: Grid Scheduling, Meta-scheduling, Inter-cooperative, Critical Friend Community, SmartGRID, MaGate.

1   Motivation

During the last decade, the evolution of grid computing has resulted in different visions of the grid and technology that depend mainly on adopters point of

ferent VOs in an automatic and self-manageable way. Collaboration between VO is typically made difficult because of different non-common factors, such as agreed constraint, resource discovery approach, geographical location, security, or user preference. Those factors could be so complicated and volatile that they cannot be expected to be understandable by other VOs. Therefore, realistic implementations normally assume that two nodes from different VOs, although they might be physically connected, are not aware of the existence of each other, despite the fact that they may have complementary job execution requirement and resource configuration. In this case, a notable issue has raised, namely how to facilitate the interaction and collaboration between complementary nodes, which are normally not aware of each other due to the boundaries of different VOs.

Our idea is to use heuristic data to facilitate the scheduling decision making process. Especially, exploiting historical interoperation metadata cached on each grid node would lead to a *demand centered* grid scheduling framework across multiple VOs.

2 Principle

As mentioned above, conventional grid VOs are bounded due to various non-common reasons, so that realistic job delegations only happen between nodes within the same VO. Such approach does not take the full advantage of the fact that a node could belong to more than one VO; especially while job delegation to a node of another VO will not broke the job submission constraints, e.g., critical security issue that only allows job execution within the same VO. In this case, the integrated vision of inter-cooperative VOs is named Critical Friend Community (CFC), which inherits from the pilot work of [7]. The idea is that knowledge of neighborhood grid topology and previous interactions (either directly or indirectly) are cached on each grid node, facilitating a more effective and efficient scheduling decision. The interconnected nodes known via historical realistic collaboration records are considered as Critical Friends (CF) to each other and together they represent a Critical Friendship based Commu-

g m
both infrastructure providers, and knowledge of Critical Friends.
- A way of organizing and presenting knowledge of Critical Friends on each
  node.

3.1 Topology

Regarding the definition and classification of grid computing [8], a noteworthy point is that grids are characterized and categorized by their hardware and software properties, including operating system, machine architecture, security compromise, etc. In other words, the grids are characterized according to a provisioning perspective, and are thus *provision centered.*

One of the tendencies illustrated by emerging technologies, such as virtualization and cloud computing [9], has demonstrated that novel approaches that can remedy user's burden of deciding where to submit his jobs have a promising future. The grid services responsible for mapping jobs on proper resources are supposed to execute well-presented jobs automatically as long as appropriate resources exist and are physically interconnected, regardless of the affiliated VOs. In contrast to the traditional grid characteristics, the novel approach can thus be considered as *demand centered.* The *demand centered* topology represents a decoupled network focused on submitted job requirement, which is fundamentally different from the *provision centered* based vision.

Our idea of implementing a *demand centered* topology is the design of the Critical Friend Community (CFC). As illustrated in Figure 1, a CFC is comprised of nodes (in our case, a node refers to a grid site) affiliated to different VOs, thus the interaction between CFC nodes may cross the borders between multiple VOs. Each CFC node has a snapshot used to store historical interaction records, as well as the profile of contacted remote nodes. Each contacted remote node in the snapshot is considered as a Critical Friend of the owner node, and the Critical Friendship is weighted by the quantity and quality of previous collaboration records.

Once a node notifies a local job submission (job submitted by the user of the same site), it is considered as a job request initiator, and is able to process the fol-

only in   mp
edge and full control. The second solution broads the view by invoking nodes within the same VO, thus requiring a commonly shared Information System to guarantee that nodes of the same VO are able to find/interact with each other. The third solution behaves in a similar way with solution 2. However, solution 3 selects candidate nodes from the initiator node's Critical Friends, which are determined by means of previous interaction records independently from all constraints imposed by VO boundaries. If a selected Critical Friend is not capable of disposing the job delegation request, it could pass such request to its own friends if allowed by the terms agreed with the request initiator node. Because Critical Friends of a single node may be affiliated to different VOs, a job request can be therefore transferred within the scope of the CFC, while inconsistencies caused by VO boundaries are filled by agreed terms represented via the Critical Friend Relationship (CFR). In other words, solution 3 emphasizes on maintaining a Critical Friends Community (CFC), which is issued by *demand centered* collaboration experience, instead of factors introduced by *provision centered* grid infrastructure.

The concept of CFC mirrors the notion of relationships occurring in the real world. If a person (node in our case) is looking for a specific service but neither owns one nor knows where to get it, he will ask some of his friends (Critical Friends) who used to be helpful (decision based on past experience). If they are not able to do the favor, these friends will pass the request to their friends hoping that someone across the knowledge group (virtual organization in our case) will have the expected capability. Based on information given back via friends network, the original requester could make a decision, and invoke the service provided by friends (direct or indirect) if necessary, under agreed terms.

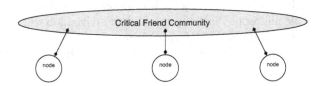

and provide a broad view by enabling the participation of remote nodes.

A coordinator is different from a meta-scheduler, although both could be physically the same component sometimes. A meta-scheduler simply assigns a job to local LRM for execution, while two coordinators have to negotiate on a job delegation from one node to the other. That is to say that a job delegation request issued by a coordinator can be refused or altered, which is not the case for a meta-scheduler.

If a job delegation request is refused or altered, the initiators coordinator has to continue by either reporting the failure to user, or releasing a re-negotiation process with modified parameters. The approach to automate the above process can be comprehended as a *workflow based* schedule, because the coordinator has already determined steps to do for handling subsequent behaviors like re-negotiation and failure. Regarding the scheduling process of each CFC node concerns many volatile factors retrieved from various environments, adaptability is a critical capability for the Community Scheduling Model, in order to exploit potential opportunities of fulfilling received job execution requests without bothering the initiator user.

Currently, the Community Scheduling Model and a set of detailed algorithms are under development. More specifically, implementation includes:

Job Orchestrating Algorithm (JOA). The philosophy of JOA is to organize a to-process job queue by merging diverse job incoming sources, with respect to local user preference.

If the preference indicates that local jobs have higher priority, the JOA will try to fill the size limited output queue with jobs from local queue firstly, and pick appropriate jobs from other sources, e.g., community queue or unprocessed queue, only if the limit of the output queue is not exceeded. If the user desires an equal treatment for all incoming job requests, the output queue will be comprised of the earliest arrived jobs, no matter where they come from. Finally, if a profitable philosophy is determined, each arrived job will be evaluated, in order to determine individual *job-profite-rate* value. In this case, the output queue will be composed by the most profitable jobs. Once the output queue

tyResourceFair is preferred, a fair selection is carried out on all known resource list. Finally, if the policy *FriendResourcePrioriy* is specified, the output list will firstly pick up a suitable resource owned either locally or by some critical friends, with other list not being considered unless the output resource list is not full.

Similarly to the aforementioned JOA, the ROA can be extended by user self-defined resource orchestration policies, but only if the expected known resource list can be found within the local node's snapshot storage.

Community Scheduling Algorithm (CSA). Once a candidate schedule (a job with its candidate resource list) arrives, an allowed maximum scheduling time duration will be given to prevent unacceptable delays and performance loss. The CSA is responsible for contacting the candidate resources simultaneously within allowed delay, in order to get a job allocation/delegation *agreement* based on the expected request (in our case, it is an *agreement offer*). An *agreement* means that the job execution request is approved by the target resource (either locally or remotely) and if such job can be delivered within a certain time, it will be accepted and executed under the agreed terms. As soon as an *agreement* has been made between the requesting node and a target resource, other *agreement offers* will be revoked.

In case no candidate resources are able to accept such *agreement offer* due to various reasons, e.g., local workload, local policy alternation, latest resource status change, the CSA needs to check whether the allocated scheduling time has expired. If not, the CSA is able to contact the locally adopted Information System, and asks for a live search from the located VO within the remaining scheduling duration. If appropriate resources can be found within such time constraints, a parallel (re-)negotiation with a newly prepared *agreement offer* can be issued again, within the shortened time duration.

As mentioned, although the job allocation is a different operation from job delegation (because the targeted resource of job allocation is an owned LRM of the local node, which cannot negotiate a job acceptance), the CSA doesn't concern such slight difference by ignoring the *agreement offer* based (re-)negotiation process if the target resource is managed by a local LRM.

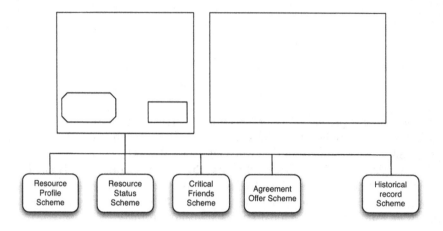

Fig. 2. Metadata Snapshot Structure

The metadata stand for information collected during each CFC node's processing history. Different kind of metadata can be collected by different adopted utilities. For instance, resource characteristics are provisioned by either a dedicated monitoring system, or an applicable grid scheduler; similarly, Critical Friend interoperation knowledge is monitored by a specific service. Finally, a weighting system provides advanced information by calculating and optimizing obtained data mentioned above.

Regarding many factors that could impact the scheduling decision, each CFC node has a metadata snapshot to preserve data provisioned for its CSM. Each metadata snapshot is comprised of sets of schemes. A scheme is a group of elements that is used for describing a particular resource or purpose. For example, a machine scheme is normally composed of elements such as machine architecture, operating system, number of CPU, etc. Other important schemes include: local resource profile, local resource status, agreement offer list, known CF (Critical Friend) profile list, known CF recent status list, historical processing records, etc. Noteworthy, data stored within each scheme is kept up-to-date over time, and is being evaluated and weighted to facilitate intelligent scheduling for the future incoming job requests.

As illustrated in Figure 2, different schemes are used together to construct a Snapshot Profile (SP) by the means of a *Snapshot Daemon*. A Snapshot Profile is a group of information encoded in a machine processable schema using a markup

on job type), prerequisite (depending on job type), time-stamp (indicating until when this information can be considered as up-to-date).

Finally, the *Snapshot Daemon* is also responsible of handling metadata exchange, either proactively or reactively, with other CFC nodes.

4 Conclusion and Future Work

This paper presents the concept of Critical Friend Community (CFC), which is inspired by the motivation of enabling interoperation between nodes from isolated grid virtual organizations. Regarding the real grid virtual organizations, which are normally bounded due to *provision centered* factors, the notion of Critical Friend Community is raised from a *demand centered* prospect. The kernel idea is that previous interaction experience, or "partner trust", overweights the physical boundaries. With this in mind, nodes of CFC are supposed to take advantage of historical data retained by each node, such as information exchange and job delegation records, to construct collaboration across multiple virtual organizations. It is noteworthy that the strength of relationship between participating nodes, i.e. the Critical Friendship, is determined by the number of previous interactions, as well as their quality.

To achieve the goals of the CFC, a Community Scheduling Model (CSM) is introduced, which respects the reality that each participating grid node has its own local scheduling polices. The CSM provides a broad view by allowing job exchange between local node and remote node by the mean of negotiation.

Regarding many volatile factors could impact the decision made by the CSM, a metadata snapshot design is proposed. This allows to assemble data collected from diverse sources to build a standard profile depending on local node's preference. Such design decouples the implementation between job scheduling and metadata collection, and matches the philosophy of CFC, i.e. a flexible approach to achieve *demand centered* prospect.

Current research focuses on a coordinator prototype, which is under implementation based on existing MaGate scheduler from the SmartGRID project that provides a platform independent communication infrastructure between nodes. Furthermore the CSF based community scheduling processing compo-

References

1. Foster, I., Kesselman, C., Tuecke, S.: The Anatomy of the Grid: Enabling Scalable Virtual Organizations. International Journal of High Performance Computing Applications 15(3), 200 (2001)
2. Krauter, K., Buyya, R., Maheswaran, M.: A taxonomy and survey of grid resource management systems for distributed computing. Software: Practice and Experience (2002)
3. Schopf, J.: Ten actions when superscheduling: A grid scheduling architecture. In: Workshop on Scheduling Architecture, Global Grid Forum, Tokyo (2003)
4. Yarmolenko, V., Sakellariou, R.: Towards increased expressiveness in service level agreements. Concurrency and Computation: Practice and Experience 19(14) (2007)
5. Waldrich, O., Wieder, P., Ziegler, W.: A meta-scheduling service for co-allocating arbitrary types of resources. In: Wyrzykowski, R., Dongarra, J., Meyer, N., Waśniewski, J. (eds.) PPAM 2005. LNCS, vol. 3911, pp. 782–791. Springer, Heidelberg (2006)
6. Huedo, E., Montero, R., Llorente, I.: The GridWay framework for adaptive scheduling and execution on grids. Scalable Computing: Practice and Experience 6(3), 1–8 (2005)
7. Huang, Y., Bessis, N., Brocco, A., Kuonen, P., Courant, M., Hirsbrunner, B.: Using Metadata Snapshots for Extending Ant-based Resource Discovery Service in Intercooperative Grid Communities. In: International Conference on Evolving Internet, INTERNET 2009, Cannes, French Riviera, France. IEEE Computer Society, Los Alamitos (2009)
8. Foster, I., Kesselman, C.: The grid: blueprint for a new computing infrastructure. Morgan Kaufmann, San Francisco (2004)
9. Buyya, R., Yeo, C., Venugopal, S., Broberg, J., Brandic, I.: Cloud computing and emerging IT platforms: Vision, hype, and reality for delivering computing as the 5th utility. Future Generation Computer Systems 25(6), 599–616 (2009)
10. Brocco, A., Frapolli, F., Hirsbrunner, B.: Bounded diameter overlay construction: A self organized approach. In: IEEE Swarm Intelligence Symposium, SIS 2009. IEEE, Los Alamitos (2009)

Kolkata-700107, India
{debnathb,chakraborty.debasri}@gmail.com
[2] Hannam University, Daejeon – 306791, Korea
taihoonn@empal.com

Abstract. In this paper two new algorithms for GIS Mobile query (point-in-area function) are proposed. This algorithm search the status of a given co-ordinate point with respect to an area (described as a set of co-ordinates without any geometric relationship). In these algorithms computational complexity are reduced. One of the algorithms is much closed to the accuracy of exhaustive search.

Keywords: GIS, image, BAS, IAS, GENerate, grid, geometric and digital.

1 Introduction

Geographic Information Systems (GISs) deal with the collection, management, and analysis of large volume of spatially referenced data [1] together with the associated logical and/or numerical attributes (semantics and thematic) [2]. The ability to manipulate these spatial data into different forms with reference to the semantics and/or thematic involved and to extract the additional information from them is the root of GIS technology.

The source of GIS data can be classified into two categories: (1) the coordinates of different features (point, line, area) along with the titles from hand drawn maps, and (2) the logical and numerical information regarding the different objects of the maps from the tables associated with the maps. GIS queries can be done in the same way either it is some logical query or query may be related with the coordinates features. A land can be defined as an area, road, rivers, rail-lines can be described by line features, a particular object in an area can be defined as a point feature (same as, an area can be defined as a point feature with respect to a vast area.). Queries can be done to find the position of a coordinate feature with respect to another coordinate feature. The coordinate objects may be still or moving.

geographic objects (features), and (2) the query processor working as an interface between the data organization and user defined queries.

The performance of any query processor is very much dependent on the respective data organization. The GEOQUEL, a special purpose language, proposed by Berman and Stonebaker [5], was one of the earlier attempts to make use of an existing DBMS for GIS data processing. This scheme decomposes every line/area feature into a sequence of line segments. It does not support geographic data types and hence, retrievals based on spatial relationships are not possible.

An attempt to extend SQL for geographical application was also made by A. Frank in the proposed MAPQUERY [6] system. This is a land information system with extra constructs to support geographical input and output facilities. It also does not support spatial operators. Pictorial SQL (PSQL) [7, 8] has been proposed as an interface language for retrieving data from pictorial database with two additional options ON and AT for selecting an area of a given picture.

B. C. Ooi in his activities [4] has adopted this approach to form a GEOgraphic Query Language (GEOQL), which is an extension of SQL. This research work is based on a special data model, named skd-tree with the additional GEOQL operators intersection, adjacent, ends at, etc.

The speed of processing of GIS queries can be enhanced by designing the algorithms to suit a parallel platform [9-11]. In fact parallelism is inherent in GIS processing though there exists no such significant effort for exploring the aspect. As the stored data does not possess any intrinsic geometrical properties, the processing of GIS queries are not at all data dependant, and, due to the large volume of data to be handled for any GIS query, application of parallel algorithms has a very significant effect [12, 13] on the processing of GIS queries.

R. Dasgupta in his research activities [16] proposed a general purpose GIS system for answering a wide spectrum of queries in a suitable parallel platform for higher efficiency. The concept of an address square has been utilized for improving the efficiency of the system. Some terminologies such as Geographic Information Unit (GIU), Address Square, Boundary Address Square (BAS), Internal Address Square (IAS) is used, where GIU is a cartographic information which is divided into some n*n grid structure and each grid was defined as address square. An area is defined as a

In the algorithm proposed by R. Dasgupta the angle between two consecutive boundary coordinates (representing the area) and the search point is determined by sine where direction of the angle is determined automatically (angle represented as d_θ). Then sum up those small angles to find the angle formed by the searched point with area (the total angle is represented as θ). The coordinate points of the area need to be stored anticlockwise fashion as per our method. If the point is inside then the ultimate angle would be 360^0 as there is no direction change but if the point is outside the area then the ultimate sum of the angles would be 0^0 as there is a direction change in time of calculating the angle.

The method proposed by us for exhaustive search is the sum angle approach says that we have to calculate the angle between each two consecutive points and the given searched point and the direction of the angle manually (angle represented as d_θ the angle is determined by cosine and direction is calculated using vector approach) [17]. Then sum up those small angles to find the angle formed by the searched point with area. The coordinate points of the area need to be stored anticlockwise fashion as per our method. If the point is inside then the ultimate angle would be 360^0 as there is no direction change but if the point is outside the area then the ultimate sum of the angles would be 0^0 as there is a direction change in time of calculating the angle.

3.2 PIA Function (Address Square Approach)

Address square approach (illustrated in fig. 1) is based on the address points. Instead of calculating angle of the test point with all the boundary point we are dividing the area into some grids and store the midpoint of those grids which are BAS. Then apply the exhaustive search or angle simulation method to find the status of a point.

3.3 Basic Terminologies

Geographic Information Unit: A geographic information unit (GIU) is defined as a piece of cartographic information containing points, lines and/or area features, each of which is expressed by a set of points with respect to GIU.

Address Square: Each GIU is divided into an n*n grid structure, where n is a positive integer. Each unit square in the grid is referred to as an address square and the

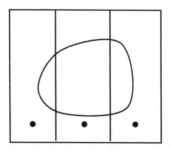

Fig. 1. Address square approach

3.4 Algorithm for Generating BAS of a Feature

Let (x_i, y_i) be the coordinate of the left top corner point of the address square (i, j), where I and j take values from 1 to n (assume a frame of n*n address squares). The right bottom point can be represented by (x_{i+1}, y_{i+1}).

INPUT: Coordinates of all the point(s) of the feature.
Coordinates of the left top and right bottom corner points of all address squares, i.e., (x_i, y_i) and (x_{i+1}, y_{i+1}), where $1 <= i <= n$ and $1 <= j <= n$.

OUTPUT: BAS of the feature.

PROCEDURE:
For i= 1 to n
Determine i for which $x_i <= x_n < x_{i+1}$
Determine i for which $y_j <= y_n < y_{j+1}$
Make bit position (i, j) of the BAS data = 1, if it is 0.
Here (x_n, y_n) represent of any point of the feature.

3.5 Algorithm for PIA Function

INPUT:
Coordinates of all the point(s) of the feature.
Coordinates of the middle points of the address squares which are BAS.
BAS and co-ordinate of the point feature.

OUTPUT: Status of the point with respect to the area feature

Functions for solving GIS queries

GENerate Function: GEN (a, b,........., p) is a function defined as a string of bits (of length 64 bits) generated with the position a,b,.......,p which are high and the remaining bits are low.

Get BAS X-Y Function: Given the (X,Y) set fo coordinates of all the peripheral points of any feature (point, line, area), the GBAXY(X,Y) function determines the BASs of the feature.

Get IAS X-Y function: Given the (X,Y) the set of coordinates of all the peripheral points of any feature and the BASs of the feature, the GIAXY(X, Y,BAS(PQ)) function determines the IAS(s) of the feature.

Point-In-Area Function (PIA): Given the coordinates of a point feature and the coordinates of an area feature, the PIA(P(x,y),A(x,y)) function determines whether the point is within the area or not.

3.7 Algorithm for Generating IAS of a Feature

INPUT:
Co-ordinates of all the points of the area feature.
BAS of the area feature.

OUTPUT: IAS of the area feature.

PROCEDURE:
Check the corner points (x_i, y_j), (x_{i+1}, y_j), (x_i, y_{j+1}), (x_{i+1}, y_{j+1}) of the address squares are inside the area or not to determine whether the address square is IAS or not.
If IAS then makes the bit position (i, j) of IAS data $=1$.

3.8 Algorithm for PIA Function

INPUT:
BAS and IAS of the area feature.
Co-ordinates of all the points of the area feature.

Go to step 3.

Step 3: do exhaustive search (sum angle approach).

4 Result

Previously we have implemented proposed algorithm of R. Dasgupta, and the result is shown in Table 1. Where, undetermined points are determined as those points those are not supporting the range. The ranges are determined with tolerance value of 355^0 to 365^0 (-5 to +5 of 360^0 for inside) and -5^0 to $+5^0$ (-5 to +5 of 0^0 for outside). It is noticed that the coordinate points those are giving abnormal results are very close to boundary points.

If the coordinate points are on the boundary then it will also give out of range exception and that is also undetermined.

Result of exhaustive search algorithm proposed by us is shown in Table 2. Here, undetermined points are determined as those points those are not supporting the range. The ranges are determined without tolerance value that of the previous (360^0 for inside and 0^0 for outside). It is noticed that the coordinate points those are giving abnormal result are only on boundary.

Though the exhaustive search is working fine but computational complexity of these algorithms is high. So, our aim is to reduce the complexity.

So, the address square approach is implemented and result is shown in Table 3. It can be noticed that number of computation in this case are drastically reduced in compare to exhaustive search. Though computational complexity is reduced but numbers of undetermined points are increased abruptly. So for the sake of accuracy this algorithm is not much more appropriate to determine the status of a point.

Finally the algorithm proposed where IASs and BASs are determined with the help of BAS and IAS algorithm. For IASs we use our proposed method of exhaustive search (intermediate angle between two consecutive points are determined by cosθ) for accuracy. The output of this algorithm is shown in Table 4. This algorithm gives pretty good result with very less computational complexity.

Table 1. Results of previously proposed exhaustive search algorithm

503	1000	762	238	0
386	1000	449	551	0

Table 3. Result of address square approach with different area and randomly generated test points

Boundary points of the area	Grid size	No of randomly generated points for test	No of points that are inside	No of points that are out-side	No of points that remain undetermined
312	8 * 8	1000	1	371	628
	16 * 16	1000	367	440	193
	32 * 32	1000	432	477	91
503	8 * 8	1000	474	112	414
	16 * 16	1000	620	148	232
	32 * 32	1000	698	187	115
386	8 * 8	1000	2	353	645
	16 * 16	1000	670	160	170
	32 * 32	1000	700	194	106

Table 4. Results of BAS-IAS approach with different area, grid values and randomly generated points

Boundary points of the area	Grid size	No of randomly generated points for test	No of points that are inside	No of points that are outside	No of points that remain undetermined
312	8 * 8	1000	681	269	50
	16 * 16	1000	925	52	23
	32 * 32	1000	966	13	21
503	8 * 8	1000	843	145	12
	16 * 16	1000	968	24	8
	32 * 32	1000	978	15	6
386	8 * 8	1000	668	274	56
	16 * 16	1000	924	68	18
	32 * 32	1000	953	37	10

ments with greater domain and optimize the cost and perfection of the algorithms remain as future work.

Acknowledgement

This work was supported by the Security Engineering Research Center, granted by the Korea Ministry of Knowledge Economy. And this work has successfully completed by the active support of Prof. Tai-hoon Kim, Hannam University, Republic of Korea.

References

1. Kasturi, R., Alemany, J.: Information extraction from images of paper-based maps. IEEE Transactions on Software Engineering 14(5), 671–675 (1988)
2. Pal, B.B., Bhattacharya, S.: Development of an efficient data structure for solving semantic queries related to cartographic database. In: International Conference on Database, Parallel Architectures and their Applications, Miami Beach, FL, USA, March 7-9, pp. 100–102 (1990)
3. Matsuyama, T., Hao, L.V., Nagao, M.: A file organization for geographic information systems based on spatial proximity. International Journal Computer Vision, Graphics and Image Processing 26(3), 303–318 (1984)
4. Ooi, B.-C.: Efficient Query Processing in Geographic Information Systems. LNCS, vol. 471, p. 208. Springer, Heidelberg (1990)
5. Berman, R., Stonebraker, M.: GEO-QUEL: A system for manipulation and display of geographic data. ACM Computer Graphics 11(2), 186–191 (1977)
6. Frank, A.: Mapquery: database query language for retrival of geometric data and their graphical representation. ACM SIGGRAPH Computer Graphics 16(3), 199–207 (1982)
7. Roussopoulos, N., Leifker, D.: An introduction to PSQL: a pictorial structured query language. In: IEEE Workshop on Visual Languages, Hirosima, Japan, December 1982, pp. 77–87 (1982)
8. Roussopoulos, N., Leifker, D.: Direct spatial search on pictorial databases using packed R-trees. In: ACM SIGMOD, International Conference on management of data, Austin, Texas, USA, May 1985, vol. 14(4), pp. 17–31 (1985)
9. Eager, D.L., Zahorjan, J., Lazowska, E.D.: Speedup versus efficiency in parallel systems.

integrated geographic information system. In: National Seminar on parallel computer systems and their applications, Calcutta, India (October 1990)

15. Dasgupta, R., Bhattacharya, S.: Design of an efficient query processor for Geographic Information. In: International Conference on Applied Informatics, Annecy, France (May 1993)

16. Dasgupta, R., Chaki, N., Bhattacharya, S.: Design of an Integrated Geographic Information System: An Algorithmic Approach. In: International Conference on Intelligent information System, Washington D.C., USA (June 1996)

17. Bhattacharyya, D., Chakraborty, D., Das, P., Bandyopadhyay, S.K., Kim, T.-h.: Mobile Queries in GIS. IJGDC - International Journal of Grid and Distributed Computing, A publication of Science and Engineering Research Support Center (August 2009)

[1] Industrial and Operations Engineering, University of Michigan,
Ann Arbor MI 48109, USA
[2] Civil and Environmental Engineering,
Seoul National University, Seoul 152-744, Republic of Korea
[3] Graduate School of Business,
Seoul National University, Seoul 151-742, Republic of Korea
hongyc@umich.edu, {kimdk95,sykho}@snu.ac.kr,
{kimsoo2,hongsuk}@snu.ac.kr

Abstract. This study proposes a new model to simulate tandem tollbooth system in order to enhance planning and management of toll plaza facilities. A discrete-event stochastic microscopic simulation model is presented and developed to evaluate the operational performance of tandem tollbooth. Traffic behavior is represented using a set of mathematical and logical algorithms. Modified versions of Max-algebra approach are integrated into this new algorithm to simulate traffic operation at toll plazas. Computational results show that the benefit of tandem tollbooth depends on the number of serial tollbooth, service time and reaction time of drivers. The capacity of tandem tollbooth increases when service time follows a normal distribution rather than negative exponential distribution. Specifically, the lower variance of service time is, the better capacity tollbooth has. In addition, the ratio of driver's reaction time to service time affects the increasing ratio of the capacity extended by tollbooth.

Keywords: simulation modeling, tandem tollbooth, toll plaza, traffic flow, capacity.

1 Introduction

The problem of traffic congestions has become one of the major critical issues throughout the globe. To this end, many researchers suggested a variety of policies,

tioned above. Furthermore, ETCS may lead inefficiency of overall toll plazas due to delays caused by manual payment lanes when ETC lanes are operating under capacity and the demand for manual payment lanes already exceeds the capacity as shown by Al-Deek et al. [2]. The difference of speed between the dedicated ETC lanes and manual payment lanes may also produce a decrease in overall safety.

A tandem tollbooth is one possible solution to traffic congestion at existing tollbooth facilities. The installment of tandem tollbooths does not require much cost while it can expand the capacity of overall toll plazas. Furthermore, Tandem tollbooths can also mitigate the risk of accidents by making traffic stream stable.

Recent literature associated with the operations of tollbooths includes general tollbooth modeling (Bai et al. [5], Hong [6], Jiang et al. [1], and Ozmen-Ertekin et al. [7]), simulation for tollbooths (Ito et al. [3], Morin et al. [8], Redding and Junga [9], and, Sadoun [10]), ETCS (Al-Deek et al. [2], Parayil et al. [4]), and tandom tollbooths (Ermakov et al. [11], Krivulin [12], [13], and [14], Grassmann et al. [15], and Foreest et al. [16]).

Bai et al. [5] formulated a minimum toll booth problem for determining a tolling strategy in a transportation network that requires the least number of toll location and causes the most efficient use of the network. They developed a methodology for using the genetic algorithm to solve the problem. The proposed method was tested based on six example networks. Hong [6] presented a service time probability distribution model and verifies that the service time depends on payment type and type of vehicle by conducting case studies. Jiang et al. [1] investigated the effect of lane expansion on the tollbooth system. Based on randomization probability, they showed that the full capacity of the single lane highway could not be restored due to the existence of the merge section in the lane expansion section. Ozmen-Ertekin et al. [7] presented an approach to estimating changes in toll plaza delays. They showed that toll plaza delays can be estimated accurately by using relatively simple macroscopic models, rather than more complicated and costly microscopic simulation tools.

Redding and Junga [9] proposed a discrete-event simulation model developed by Science Application International Corporation to simulate traffic operations at toll plazas using the General Purpose Simulation System (GPSS/H) for MS-DOS to simulate traffic at toll plazas. Al-Deek et al. [2] introduced and developed a discrete-event

This paper presents a microscopic simulation model for tandem tollbooths by using Max-Algebra approach and evaluates the operation of tandem tollbooths depending on the number of serial tollbooths under several conditions. To simulate various reaction time of driver and service time of toll collector, we generate pseudo random variables and make a variety of probability distribution by using simulation software.

The rest of this paper is divided into three sections. In section 2, we formulate simulation model for tandem tollbooth based on Max-algebra approach. Section 3 reports computational experiments for model verification and evaluation. Conclusions and suggestions for future research are discussed in the last section.

2 Formulation of Simulation Model

2.1 Model Concepts and Assumptions

Oracle Crystal Ball 11.0, which is one of the most widely used discrete event stochastic simulation model, is used to simulate tandem toll booth operation. In this paper, we generate pseudo random variables and employ a variety of probability distributions by using simulation software to simulate various reaction times of drivers and service times of toll collectors.

In this paper, Max-algebra approach is applied for simulating tandem toll booth operation. Max-algebra approach offers several benefits. First of all, the Max-algebra approach is very efficient in terms of calculation time and memory requirements. It is caused by the fact that the Max-algebra model has recursive equations that only use addition and maximization operations. The algorithms, therefore, are based on a simple computational procedure that exploits a particular order of evaluating the system state variables from the recursive equations as mentioned by Ermakov et al. [13]. Furthermore, Max-algebra model can be widely used to represent the dynamics of queuing system models because recursive equations can be easily reformulated to reflect toll plaza's unique characteristics.

It is noted that the traditional Max-algebra model for normal queuing systems should be modified to reflect unique characteristics of tollbooth operations. First, a driver in a tollbooth system can complete his or her toll payment by selecting only

nism and they are operated by FIFO (First In, First Out) as service discipline. Vehicles are served by only one of several booths and can not pass over their front vehicle. Fig. 1 illustrates the layout of a tandem tollbooth system.

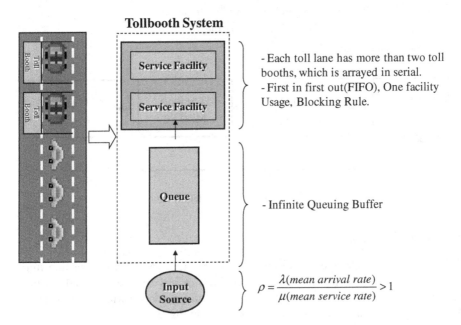

Fig. 1. Layout of Tandem Tollbooth System

The detailed descriptions of each component are summarized as follows.

- Input Source: λ (mean arrival rate) exceeds μ (mean service rate) since a tandem tollbooth is generally used at peak time. Vehicles are in queue at the beginning.

- Queue: The length of queuing buffer is infinite since demand queue is not related with the difference of service times between specific vehicles.

k : the number of vehicles in queue
N : the number of tollbooth systems
S_k : service time of the kth vehicle
R_k : reaction time of the kth vehicle
T_{ij} : waiting time of the jth vehicle in the ith vehicle set
T_{ij}^* : actual waiting time of the jth vehicle in the ith vehicle set
G_i : ending time of the ith vehicle set

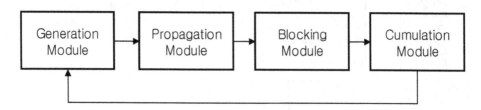

Fig. 2. Tandem Tollbooth Model Structure

1) Generation Module

The generation module is employed to generate random variables for reaction time and service time. In this module, random variables for service time, S_k, and reaction time, R_k, are generated, respectively. And then, this random variables grouped by N are assigned to each tollbooth facility as shown in Fig. 3.

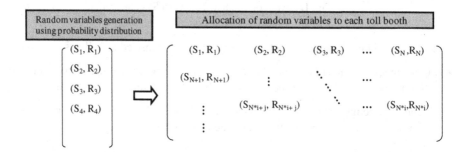

reaction effect is increased by the sum of all predecessors' reaction time included in a vehicle set i (Sum-Algebra). The procedure of the propagation module is shown in Fig. 4.

$$
\begin{pmatrix}
T_{11} & T_{12} & \cdots & T_{1N} \\
T_{21} & T_{22} & \cdots & T_{2N} \\
\vdots & \vdots & \ddots & \cdots \\
T_{i1} & T_{i2} & T_{ij} & T_{iN}
\end{pmatrix}
=
\begin{pmatrix}
R_1 + S_1 & (R_1 + R_2) + S_2 & \cdots & (R_1 + R_2 + \cdots + R_j) + S_j & \cdots \\
R_{N+1} + S_{N+1} & (R_{N+1} + R_{N+2}) + S_{N+2} & \cdots & (R_{N+1} + R_{N+2} + \cdots + R_{N+j}) + S_{N+j} & \cdots \\
\vdots & \vdots & \vdots & \vdots & \cdots \\
\vdots & \vdots & \vdots & (R_{N \cdot i+1} + R_{N \cdot i+2} + \cdots + R_{N \cdot i+j}) + S_{N \cdot i+j} & \cdots
\end{pmatrix}
$$

$$
\Rightarrow
\begin{cases}
T_{i1} = G_{i-1} + R_{i0} + S_{i0} & , j = 0 \\
T_{ij} = (R_{i1} + R_{i2} + \cdots + R_{ij}) + S_{ij} & , otherwise
\end{cases}
$$

$$T_{ij-1} - S_{ij-1} = (R_{i1} + R_{i2} + \cdots + R_{ij-1})$$

$$
\Rightarrow
\begin{cases}
T_{i1} = G_{i-1} + R_{i0} + S_{i0} & , j = 0 \\
T_{ij} = (T_{ij-1} - S_{ij-1}) + R_{ij} + S_{ij} & , otherwise
\end{cases}
$$

Fig. 4. Propagation of Reaction Time in the Same Vehicle Set

3) Blocking Module

If a preceding driver's service is not finished completely, all the following drivers are blocked independent of whether or not they have been already served completely because any following vehicles can not pass their preceding vehicle in the tollbooth facilities. This blocking "rule" may cause additional delay time. To reflect the blocking rule, waiting time of a driver j is replaced by the maximum value among the

$$
\begin{pmatrix}
T^*_{11} & T^*_{12} & \cdots & T^*_{1N} \\
T^*_{21} & T^*_{22} & \cdots & T^*_{2N} \\
\vdots & \vdots & \ddots & \cdots \\
 & & &
\end{pmatrix}
=
\begin{pmatrix}
Max(T_{11}) & Max(T_{11}, T_{12}) & \cdots & Max(T_{11}, \ldots, T_{1N}) \\
Max(T_{21}) & Max(T_{21}, T_{22}) & \cdots & Max(T_{21} +, \ldots, T_{2N}) \\
\vdots & \vdots & \vdots & \vdots \\
\vdots & \vdots & & \vdots
\end{pmatrix}
$$

lated based on the latest vehicle's waiting time in the previous vehicle set i. Therefore, the maximum waiting time of all vehicles in the previous vehicle set would become down to the first vehicle's waiting time in the next vehicle set. Fig. 6 shows the cumulation procedure of the maximum waiting time of preceding vehicle sets.

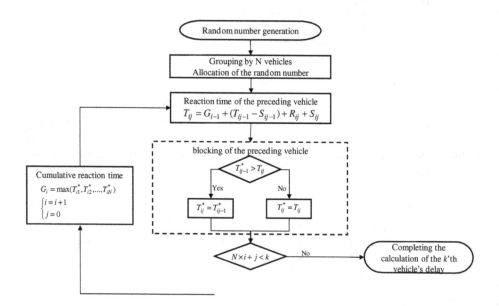

Fig. 6. Cumulation of Maximum Waiting Time of Preceding Vehicle Sets

$$\overset{k=1}{= G_{i-1} + (T_{ij-1} - S_{ij-1}) + R_{ij} + S_{ij}}$$
$$(where \quad T_{i0} = 0, S_{i0} = 0)$$
$$T_{ij}^* = \max(T_{i1}, T_{i2}, \cdots, T_{ij}) \tag{2}$$
$$= if (T_{ij-1}^* > T_{ij})\{T_{ij-1}^* : T_{ij}\}$$
$$(where \quad T_{i0}^* = 0)$$
$$G_i = \max(T_{i1}^*, T_{i2}^*, \cdots, T_{ij}^*, \cdots, T_{in}^*) \tag{3}$$
$$(where \quad G_0 = 0)$$

3 Computational Experiment

3.1 Measure of Effectiveness

To analyze the service capacity of a tandem toll booth system, the vehicle capacity per one hour ($veh/hour$) is estimated by converting waiting time of k vehicles. If k vehicles are served during T_k seconds on average, it means that $3600/T_k$ times k vehicles can be handled during one hour. The service capacity of the tollbooth system, therefore, can be calculated as equation (4). In addition to the service capacity, average waiting time of k vehicles is presented as a level of service by averaging the sum of each group of k vehicles' service time in the next section.

$$Q = \frac{3600}{T_k} \times k(veh/hour) \tag{4}$$

In this paper, distribution types and parameters are considered as independent variables. Mean and standard deviation of reaction time stand for sensitivity of a driver while those of service time are related to payment types and a toll-collector's expertness. The ratio of mean reaction time to mean service time is employed instead of the mean value since the former can represent a driver's sensitivity and toll-collector's expertness more precisely than the latter. The capacity model, therefore, is simulated

dence level.

$$n \geq (\frac{ts}{\varepsilon})^2$$

(5)

$$\left(\begin{array}{ll} where & n = required\ sample\ size \\ & t = 1.96\ (probability\ level = 95\%) \\ & s = standard\ deviation \\ & \varepsilon = allowable\ error(\pm 20) \end{array} \right.$$

3.2 Effect of Reaction Time

We assume that service time has a normal distribution with mean of a fixed value. Fig. 8 shows that the increasing ratio of the capacity of a tandem tollbooth increases as the ratio of mean reaction time to mean service time(ϕ) increases. In the case of the second tollbooth, when the ratio is 0.1 ($\phi = 0.1$), which is the case of a sensitive driver, the capacity of the second tollbooth increases by about 71% comparing with that of a single tollbooth. On the other hand, the capacity increases by only 36% in the case of an insensitive driver ($\phi = 0.9$). In the case of the third tollbooth, the increasing ratio of the capacity varies from 18% to 55% according to the driver's sensitivity.

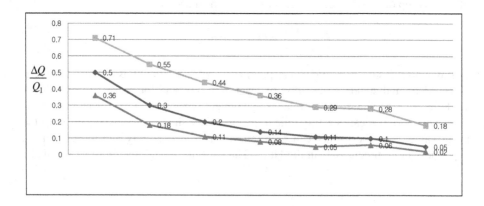

than four.

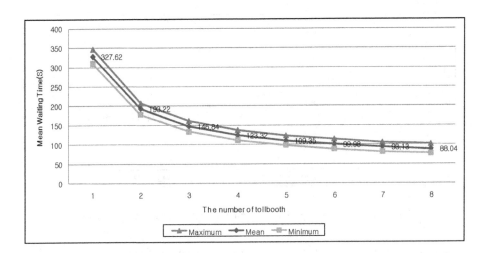

Fig. 9. Average Waiting Time according to the number of tollbooths ($\phi = 0.1$, $k = 120$ vehicle)

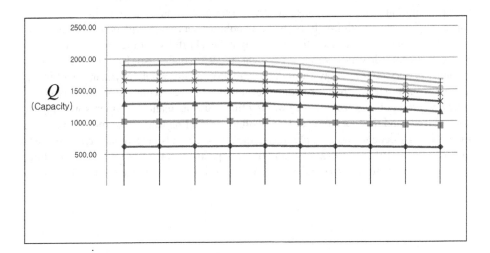

nentially distributed is more efficient.

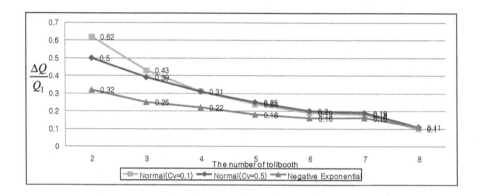

Fig. 11. Change of Capacity According to Service Distribution Types

Generally, negative exponential distribution has lager coefficient of variation than normal distribution. The increasing ratio of the capacity of a tandem tollbooth, therefore, is expected to decrease as the coefficient of variation increases. This result suggests that the standard deviation of service time of tollbooth systems should be controlled to minimize C_v since constant service time will contribute to the increase of the capacity of a tandem toll booth. In the view point of service-providers (operators), toll-collectors should be instructed to collect payments skillfully. In the view point of service-consumers (drivers), various payment types, which also lead to the various amounts of service time, may cause large variation of the whole payment distribution. These results show that providing efficient service requires various service-differentiation policies according to waiting time, such as manual payments with higher waiting time, and the touch pass or ETC with lower waiting time. The amount of service time generally depends on not only the payment types but also the vehicle types as mentioned by Hong [6]. The increasing ratio of the capacity of a tandem tollbooth, therefore, is expected to increase as ϕ and C_v decreases. These results mentioned above would

this paper presents that capacity of tandem tollbooth varies on the service time of collectors and reaction time of drivers. The capacity of tandem tollbooth goes higher when service time approximates a normal distribution rather than negative exponential distribution. This means that low variance of service time increases the capacity of tandem tollbooth. Thus, if each toll lane is separately dedicated to one payment type such that service time is uniform, it might be help to reduce delays. In addition, the ratio of reaction time to service time also has a great effect on the efficiency of tollbooth extensions. The capacity increased by second tollbooth could be reduced by half if driver reaction is not sensitive. Thus, it is recommended to consider the way to increase driver's agility to react at toll plaza.

This research focused on the new model to examine the impact of tandem tollbooth on traffic operations of existing or future toll plazas. By conducting more case studies using actual tollbooth data, we would like to suggest further practical contribution to the improvement of the tollbooth system.

Acknowledgments. The authors would like to thank to the Engineering Research Institute at Seoul National University, SNU SIR Group of the BK21 research program, and the College of Business Administration at Seoul National University for their assistance to develop this research. This research was supported by the Institute of Management Research Institute.

References

1. Jiang, R., Jia, B., Wu, Q.S.: The Lane Expansion Effect of the Tollbooth System on the Highway. International Journal of Modern Physics C 15, 619–628 (2004)
2. Al-Deek, H.M., Mohamed, A.A., Radwan, E.A.: New Model for Evaluation of Traffic Operations at Electronic Toll Collection Plazas. Transportation Research Record: Journal of the Transportation Research Board 1710, 1–10 (2000)
3. Ito, T., Hiramoto, T.: A General Simulator Approach to ETC Toll Traffic Congestion. J. Intell. Manuf. 17, 597–607 (2006)
4. Parayil, G., Yeo, T.E.D.: More Than Electronic Toll Booths: Singapore's Electronic Road Pricing Innovation. Prometheus 23, 209–226 (2005)

Toll Plaza. In: Proc. Winter Simulation Conference (1992)

10. Sadoun, B.: Optimizing the Operation of a Toll Plaza System Using Simulation: A Methodology. Simulation 81, 657–664 (2005)

11. Ermakov, S.M., Krivulin, N.K.: Efficient Algorithms for Tandem Queueing System Simulation. Applied Mathematics Letters 7, 45–49 (1994)

12. Krivulin, N.K.: A Max-Algebra Approach to Modeling and Simulation of Tandem Queuing Systems. Mathematical and Computer Modeling 22, 25–31 (1995)

13. Krivulin, N.K.: Recursive Equations Based Models of Queueing Systems. In: Proc. European Simulation Symp., Istanbul, Turkey, October 9-12, pp. 252–256 (1994)

14. Krivulin, N.K.: Using Max-Algebra Linear Models in the Representation of Queueing Systems. In: Lewis, J.G. (ed.) Proc. 5th SIAM Conf. on Applied Linear Algebra, Snowbird, UT, June 15-18, pp. 155–160 (1994)

15. Grassmann W.K., Drekic S.: An analytical solution for a tandem queue with blocking. Queuing Systems, 221–235 (2000)

16. van Foreest, N.D., Mandjes, M.R.H., van Ommeren, J.C.W., Scheinhardt, W.R.W.: A Tandem Queue with Server Slow-down and Blocking. JSAE Review 24, 403–410 (2003)

[1] Guangxi Vocational & Technical Institute of Industry, Nanning, China 530001
[2] Chinese Academy of Sciences, Beijing, China 100039
liyang@software.ict.ac.cn

Abstract. Intrusion detection is a critical component of secure information systems. Current intrusion detection systems (IDS) especially NIDS (Network Intrusion Detection System) examine all data features to detect intrusions. However, some of the features may be redundant or contribute little to the detection process and therefore they have an unnecessary negative impact on the system performance. This paper proposes a lightweight intrusion detection model that is computationally efficient and effective based on feature selection and back-propagation neural network (BPNN). Firstly, the issue of identifying important input features based on independent component analysis (ICA) is addressed, because elimination of the insignificant and/or useless inputs leads to a simplification of the problem, therefore results in faster and more accurate detection. Secondly, classic BPNN is used to learn and detect intrusions using the selected important features. Experimental results on the well-known KDD Cup 1999 dataset demonstrate the proposed model is effective and can further improve the performance by reducing the computational cost without obvious deterioration of detection performances.

Keywords: Intrusion detection, neural network, feature selection, independent component analysis.

1 Introduction

Intrusion Detection System (IDS) plays vital role of detecting various kinds of attacks. The main purpose of IDS is to find out intrusions among normal audit data and this can be considered as classification problem.

One of the main problems with IDSs is the overhead, which can become prohibitively high. As network speed becomes faster, there is an emerging need for security analysis techniques that will be able to keep up with the increased network throughput [1]. Therefore, IDS itself should be lightweight while guaranteeing high detection

tors/components from multivariate data using only the assumption that the unknown factors are mutually independent [5]. In this paper, we will propose a lightweight intrusion detection model combining back-propagation neural network (BPNN) with ICA, which has good detection performance and low computational cost by using selected important and necessary features.

The rest of this paper is organized as follows. We introduce the background of BPNN and ICA respectively in Section 2 and Section 3. Section 4 details intrusion detection model based on them. Section 5 illustrates relevant experiments and evaluations. We conclude our work in Section 6.

2 Back-Propagation Neural Network (BPNN)

An artificial neural network consists of a collection of processing elements that are highly interconnected and transform a set of inputs to a set of desired outputs. The result of the transformation is determined by the characteristics of the elements and the weights associated with the interconnections among them. By modifying the connections between the nodes the network is able to adapt to the desired outputs.

The greatest strength of BPNN is in non-linear solutions to ill-defined problems [6]. The typical back-propagation network has an input layer, an output layer, and at least one hidden layer (see Figure 1) [10]. There is no theoretical limit on the number of hidden layers but typically there are just one or two. Some work has been done

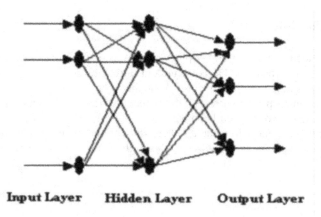

Input Layer   Hidden Layer   Output Layer

that the inputs, the output, and the desired output all have to be present at the same processing element. The complex part of this learning mechanism is for the system to determine which input contributed the most to an incorrect output and how does that element get changed to correct the error. An inactive node would not contribute to the error and would have no need to change its weights. To solve this problem, training inputs are applied to the input layer of the network, and desired outputs are compared at the output layer. During the learning process, a forward sweep is made through the network, and the output of each element is computed layer by layer. The difference between the output of the final layer and the desired output is back-propagated to the previous layer(s), usually modified by the derivative of the transfer function, and the connection weights are normally adjusted using the Delta Rule. This process proceeds for the previous layer(s) until the input layer is reached.

The most important reasons that make us to adopt BPNN to intrusion detection is that it can effective solve the problem of intrusion detection which has the following distinct characters [4]:

(1) A large amount of input (training data, including "normal" and "abnormal") /output (various attack types and normal type) data is available, but we are not sure how to relate it to the output.

(2) The problem appears to have overwhelming complexity, but there is clearly a solution.

(3) It is easy to create a number of examples of the correct behavior.

Therefore, Figure 2 illustrates the corresponding classic BP algorithm. We may use it to compute and fulfill our intrusion detection task. We will detail the relevant experimental results in Section 5.

3 Independent Component Analysis

Independent component analysis (ICA) for dimension reduction is to separate these independent components (ICs) from the monitored variables. ICA is a method for automatically identifying the underlying factors in a given data set. Dimension reduction using ICA is based on the idea that these measured variables are the mixtures of

$$Net_j = \sum_i w_{ij} 0_i$$

where

$$0_j = \frac{1}{1 + e^{-net_j}}$$

- Compute δ_j for the output layer:

$$\delta_j = (y - 0_j)0_j(1 - 0_j)$$

- Compute δ_j for each hidden layer from the back to the front:

$$\delta_j = 0_j(1 - 0_j)\sum_k W_{jk}\delta_k$$

- Compute and store each revised value:

$$\Delta W_{ij}(t) = \alpha\Delta W_{ij}(t-1)\eta\delta_j 0_i$$

- Revise the weight coefficient:

$$W_{ij}(t+1) = W_{ij}(t) + \Delta W_{ij}(t)$$

Fig. 2. BPNN algorithm

ICA techniques provide statistical signal processing tools for optimal linear transformations in multivariate data and these methods are well-suited for feature extraction, noise reduction, density estimation and regression [7], [8].

The ICA problem can be described as follows, each of h mixture signal $x_1(k), x_2(k),..., x_h(k)$ is a linear combination of q independent components $s_1(k), s_2(k),..., s_h(k)$, that is, $X = AS$ where A is a mixing matrix. Now given X, to compute A and S. Based on the following two statistical assumptions, ICA successfully gains the results: 1) the components are mutual independent; 2) each component observes nongaussian distribution. By $X = AS$, we have $S = A^{-1}X = WX$ (where $W = A^{-1}$). The task is to select an appropriate W which applied on X to maximize the

$$Y = Wx$$

Such that each component of y becomes independent of each other. If the individual marginal distributions are non-Gaussian then the derived marginal densities become a scaled permutation of the original density functions if one such W can be obtained. One general learning technique [8] for finding one W is

$$\Delta W = \eta(I - \Phi(y)y^T)W$$

Where $\Phi(y)$ is a nonlinear function of the output vector y (such as a cubic polynomial or a polynomial of odd degree, or a sum of polynomials of odd degrees, or a sigmoidal function).

4 Intrusion Detection Based on BPNN

The overall model of our approach is depicted in Figure 3:

(1) In the training phase, labled network traffic data with a lot of preset features (such as packet length, connection duration time, the ratio of SYN/ACK etc.) is passed to our ICA-based feature selection engine. Afterwards, a reduced feature subset will be acquired and the labled dataset is then used to build the BPNN classifier for intrusion detection using the selected features.

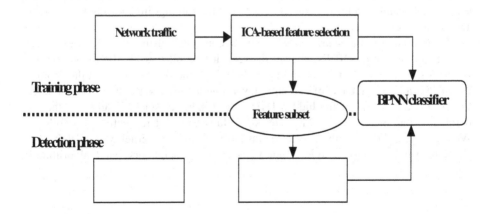

5 Experimental Results and Evaluations

All experiments were performed in a Windows machine having configurations AMD Opteron (tm) 64-bit processor 3.60GHz, 3.00GB RAM. The KDD Cup 1999 (KDD 99) dataset [9] contains 21 different types of attacks that are broadly categorized in four groups such as Probes, DoS (Denial of Service), U2R (User to Root) and R2L (Remote to Local). The original TCP dump files were preprocessed for utilization in the Intrusion Detection System benchmark of the International Knowledge Discovery and Data Mining Tools Competition. To do so, packet information in the TCP dump file is summarized into connections and each instance of data consists of 41 features.

To evaluate our method we used two major indices of performance: the detection rate (also named true positive rate, TP) and the false positive rate (FP). TP is defined as the number of intrusion instances detected by the system divided by the total number of intrusion instances present in the test set. FP is defined as the total number of normal instances that were incorrectly classified as intrusions divided by the total number of normal instances.

We have sampled 10 different datasets, each having 24701 instances, from the corpus by uniform random distribution so that the distribution of the dataset should remain unchanged. Each dataset is divided into training and testing set consisting of 18601 and 6100 instances respectively. We have carried out 10 experiments on different datasets having full features and selected features thus evaluate the intrusion detection performance in term of mean detection rate, training time, testing time, etc. to achieve low generalization.

The training of the neural networks was conducted using feed forward backpropagation algorithm-BPNN. We set the relevant parameters for BPNN as follows: we set learning rate 0.3, momentum is 0.2, training time is 50, validation threshold is 20. In addition, we take use of one input layer, one hidden layer and one output layer. We set the dimension of the hidden layer as (attribute+class)/2. Meanwhile, the experimental parameters for SVM, KNN algorithms were set respectively as follows. We use c-svc SVM algorithm, select radius basis function as kernel type in Weka. For KNN algorithm, k was set to 50, employ linear nearest neighbors search algorithm. It

effectiveness of adopting feature selection in BPNN algorithm.

Table 1. Running time results

	TP (%)	FP (%)
SVM	99.5	0.12
BPNN	99.8	0.20
KNN	99.2	0.32

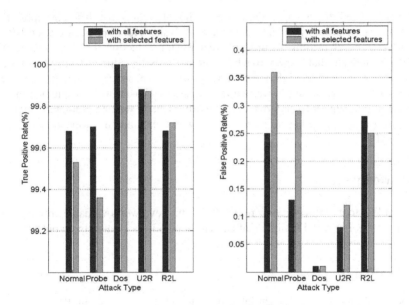

Fig. 4. TP and FP results

Table 2. Running time results using selected features

based on BPNN and ICA are amazingly good (high detection rate and low false positives), and they demonstrate two important facts: i) The selected features play the same important role in intrusion detection; ii) The computational cost can be greatly reduced without reducing any effectiveness when we make use of the selected features compared to all the 41 features. Therefore, they can be further optimized when used under realistic intrusion detection environment.

6 Conclusions and Future Work

We have presented in this paper a new idea on how to reduce the different representation spaces based on independent component analysis before applying classic BPNN machine learning algorithms to the field of intrusion detection. Experimental results on KDD 99 indicate that our approach is able not only to reduce training and testing time but also to guarantee high detection rates and low positive rates among different datasets. In our future research, we will investigate the feasibility of implementing the technique in real-time intrusion detection environment as well as characterize type of attacks such as DoS, probes, U2R and R2L, which enhance the capability and performance of IDS.

Acknowledgement

We would like to express our sincere thanks for the reviewer's valuable comments on this paper, as well as Dr. Dominik and Dr. Tai-hoon Kim's great help on our work.

References

1. Roesch, M.: Snort - Lightweight Intrusion Detection for Networks. In: Proc. of the 13th Systems Administration Conference - LISA 1999 (1999)
2. Kruege, C., Valeur, F.: Stateful Intrusion Detection for High-Speed Networks. In: Proc. of the IEEE Symposium on Research on Security and Privacy, pp. 285–293 (2002)
3. Hecht-Nielsen, R.: Theory of the backpropagation neural network. In: Proc. of the International Joint Conference on Neural Networks, pp. 593–605 (1989)

10. Introduction to Backpropagation Neural Networks,
    http://cortex.snowcron.com/neural_networks.htm
11. Li, Y., Fang, B.-X., Guo, L., Chen, Y.: A Lightweight Intrusion Detection Model Based on Feature Selection and Maximum Entropy Model. In: Proc. of 2006 International Conference on Communication Technology (ICCT 2006), pp. 1–4 (2006)
12. Chen, Y., Dai, L., Li, Y., Cheng, X.-Q.: Building Lightweight Intrusion Detection System Based on Principal Component Analysis and C4.5 Algorithm. In: Proc. of the 9th International Conference on Advanced Communication Technology (ICACT 2007), pp. 2109–2112 (2007)
13. Chen, Y., Li, Y., Cheng, X., Guo, L.: Survey and Taxonomy of Feature Selection Algorithms in Intrusion Detection System. In: Lipmaa, H., Yung, M., Lin, D. (eds.) Inscrypt 2006. LNCS, vol. 4318, pp. 153–167. Springer, Heidelberg (2006)

The Attached Institute of ETRI
P.O.Box 1, Yuseong Post Office,
Daejeon, 305-700, South Korea
{yhch,tgkim,choisj,cheolee}@ensec.re.kr

Abstract. Recently, most of malicious web pages include obfuscated codes in order to circumvent the detection of signature-based detection systems. It is difficult to decide whether the sting is obfuscated because the shape of obfuscated strings are changed continuously. In this paper, we propose a novel methodology that can detect obfuscated strings in the malicious web pages. We extracted three metrics as rules for detecting obfuscated strings by analyzing patterns of normal and malicious JavaScript codes. They are *N-gram*, *Entropy*, and *Word Size*. *N-gram* checks how many each byte code is used in strings. *Entropy* checks distributed of used byte codes. *Word size* checks whether there is used very long string. Based on the metrics, we implemented a practical tool for our methodology and evaluated it using read malicious web pages. The experiment results showed that our methodology can detect obfuscated strings in web pages effectively.

1 Introduction

JavaScript language has power that can execute dynamic work in the web browser. Therefore, malicious users attack client's system by inserting malicious JavaScript codes in a normal web page. Using JavaScript, they can steal personal information, download malware in client systems, and so on. In order to defend the attacks, security systems detect JavaScript codes in malicious web pages based on signatures. Nowadays, however, attackers circumvent the defense mechanism using obfuscation. Obfuscation is a method that changes shape of data in order to avoid pattern-matching detection. For instance, "CLIENT ATTACK" string can be changed into "CL\x73\x69NT\x20\x65T\x84ACK". Because of ob

three metrics into the strings and detect obfuscated strings. We implemented a practical tool for our methodology and experimented for real malicious web pages. The results showed that our methodology detected obfuscated strings effectively. In this paper, we focus on JavaScript codes using obfuscation among various malicious web pages.

Our contribution is like this: *After we analyzed malicious web pages including obfuscated strings, we define three metrics as rules for detecting obfuscated strings. And then, we implemented a practical tool for our methodology and evaluated it.*

Our paper is organized as follows: In section 2, we introduce researches related to malicious JavaScript codes. Next, we propose our methodology for detecting automatically obfuscated strings in malicious JavaScript codes in section 3. In section 4, we classify JavaScript strings into three cases and propose a method that extracts all doubtful strings. In section 5, we defined three metrics for detecting obfuscated strings and evaluated it using real malicious web pages. Conclusions and direction for future work are presented in section 6.

2 Related Work

There are rich researches for detecting and analyzing malicious JavaScript codes in web pages. Because attackers use JavaScript in order to execute malicious work in a client system, many researches are performed for client defense.

In [1], authors studied various JavaScript redirection in spam pages and found that obfuscation techniques are prevalent among them. Feinstein analyzed JavaScript obfuscation cases and implemented obfuscation detection tool[3]. He hooked `eval` function and the string concatenation method based on Mozilla SpiderMonkey. This method has difficulty for modifying an engine of custom web browser. He found that use of the `eval` function was relatively more common in the benign scripts than in malicious scripts. In [8], the author introduced various malicious JavaScript attacks and obfuscation methods. He found that `eval` and `document.write` functions are mostly used in malicious web pages. These researches focus on malicious JavaScript codes itself. In [2], authors proposed the tool that can deobfuscate obfuscated strings by emulating a browser

can detect malicious web pages using VM based on behavior of system, named HoneyMonkey.

In order to detect cross-site scripting, Vogt *et al.* tracked the flow of sensitive information insider the web browser using dynamic data tainting and static analysis[11]. Using static analysis, they traced every branch in the control flow by focusing on tainted value. In [6], authors proposed the method that can detect JavaScript worms based on propagation activity as worm's characters. They, however, didn't consider obfuscation of JavaScript. Wassermann *et al.* presented a static analysis for finding XSS vulnerabilities that address weak or absent input validation[13]. They traced tainted information flows in web source codes.

3 Our Methodology for Detecting Obfuscation in Malicious Web Pages

In this chapter, we propose a novel methodology for detecting obfuscated strings in malicious web pages with Javascript codes. After we extract doubtful strings in web pages, we analyze them for deciding whether they are obfuscated or not. We extract all doubtful strings in web pages using static data flow analysis and detect obfuscated strings based on three metrics that we define. We named our algorithm the the Javascript Obfuscation Detector in Web pages(JODW). In this paper, we focus on JavaScript codes using obfuscation among various malicious web pages.

JODW is a simple and strong method for detecting obfuscated string in malicious web pages. Firstly, it searches dangerous functions(`eval`, `document.write`, and so on) in web pages. The functions can execute strings of parameters. Because malicious user uses obfuscated strings in order to execute dynamic work after transmitting them as parameters of the functions, we start to parameters of the dangerous functions. Based on the parameters, we extracts all strings related to them using static data flow analysis. After analyzing the strings, JODW detects obfuscated strings. Last, JOWD deofuscates the strings. In order to detect bfuscated strin in web pages, it dema ds ma l   ts f r aut mation.

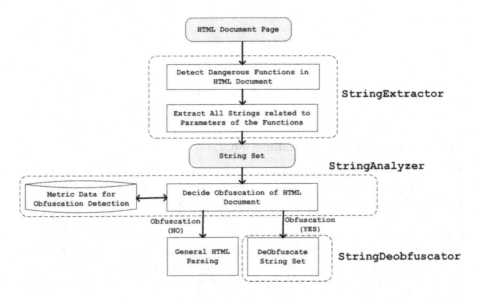

Fig. 1. Our methodology for automatic detecting of obfuscated JavaScript strings in malicious web pages

strings related to parameters of the dangerous functions have the high possibility that obfuscated strings are. We focus on the obfuscated strings. We trace all strings related to parameters of dangerous functions and extract all strings. We classify all strings of JavaScript into three cases. Based on the cases, we extract all strings using static data flow analysis. Static data flow analysis traces flow of data without executing web pages in a web browser. We will explain the mechanism of *StringExtractor* in chapter 4.

– **StringAnalyzer**. This module decides whether previous doubtful strings are obfuscated or not. We define three metrics for detecting obfuscated strings in malicious web pages: *N-gram, Entropy, Word Size*. *StringAnalyzer* detects obfuscated string based on the three metrics. We will explain the method for detecting obfuscated codes in chapter 5.

– **StringDeobfuscator**. If obfuscated strings is detected, this module deobfuscates strings, and detects malicious codes in the deobfuscated string using patterns for malicious strings. For instance, in case that `IFRAME` is included in the strin   , it i   li io   eb page because a   eb br   ing the

4.1 JavaScript String Classification

In order to extract all strings related to parameters of dangerous functions, we classify all strings in JavaScript codes into three cases. Table 1 shows the definition for all strings in JavaScript. In the table, **Y** denotes a string of JavaScript codes. In order to check whether the string is obfuscated or not, we search all **Y** in malicious web pages. f function represent changes of strings and $x_1, x_2, x_3, \ldots, x_n$ are parameters. According to f and parameters, we classify all strings into three cases. In conclusion, all cases have the possibility of obfuscation. Therefore, all strings related to parameters of dangerous functions must be checked whether they are obfuscated or not. Three cases are as follows:

- **CASE1** : $\mathbf{Y}_1 = x_1$: **NoChange**
- **CASE2** : $\mathbf{Y}_2 = \sum_{i=1}^{m} x_i$: **Concatenation**
- **CASE3** : $\mathbf{Y}_3 = \sum_{i=1}^{m} f_i(x_1, x_2, x_3, \ldots, x_n)$: **Change**

Based on three cases, we trace and extract all strings related to parameters of dangerous functions.

CASE1 : *NoChange.* The function f is constant and has one variable, and **Y** is equal to x_1. Therefore, the variable x_1 is directly transmitted to a parameter of `eval` or `document.write`. For instance, an example code is as follows: `var x1 = "3+4"; ...; eval(x1);` The `eval` function uses the string allocated in x_1 without modifying the value. However, another example shows a obfuscated string as follows: `eval("\144\157\143\165\155\145\156\164")`. This case is executed after the string is decoded. Therefore, we analyze the string whether it is decoded or not. In static data flow analysis, this case is extracted and analyzed directly.

Table 1. Definition for all strings in JavaScript

_____

In this example, x_4 is "Execute ActiveX Control". However, because the string is divided into several strings, a signature-based detect system can't detect the string. Therefore, the case must be analyzed for obfuscation detection. In static data flow analysis, we divide the string by a plus(+) character, save each strings, and analyze for obfuscaion detection.

CASE3 : *Change*. Various functions in malicious web pages decode obfuscated strings. The functions can be JavaScript functions or user-made functions. In static data flow analysis, we trace the functions and extract strings related to parameters of them. For instance, an example code is as follows:

```
Uul1ItLo["plunger"] = new Array(); var Qn2_R5kv = new
Array(32,64, 256, 32768); for (var auLRkELh = 0; auLRkELh < 6;
auLRkELh++) { for(var x8n9EKml = 0; x8n9EKml < 4; x8n9EKml++) {
    var CRrtOhOH = Uul1ItLo["plunger"].length;
    eval('Uul1ItLo["plunger"][CRrtOhOH] = GjLO8iWK.substr(0, ('
    + Qn2_R5kv[x8n9EKml] + '-6)/2);'); } }
```

In this example, $\mathbf{Y}$ is $UullItLo["plunger"][CRrtOhOH] = GjLO8iWK.substr(0, (Qn2\_R5kv[x8n9EKml]-6)/2);$. f_1 is $UullItLo["plunger"][CRrtOhOH]$, f_2 is $=$, and f_3 is $GjLO8iWK.substr(0, (Qn2\_R5kv[x8n9EKml]-6)/2)$. f_1 and f_3 are functions, and f_2 is constant. Therefore, f_1 and f_3 are changed by the decoding functions.

4.2 Extraction of Obfuscated String Using Static Data Flow Analysis

Based on three cases for strings of JavaScript, we search and extract all strings related to dangerous functions using static data flow analysis. Static data flow analysis is to trace data flow of variables in source codes without executing a program. We trace all strings dangerous functions written JavaScript in web pages. We focus on eval and document.write as dangerous functions because the function is used in most of JavaScript obfuscation.

Search dangerous functions and their function pointer reassignment
Update function list($PL\{pl_i, i = 0, 1, \ldots, n\}$)

A1 :
Trace pl_i
Analyze parameters of the functions
Classify the parameters into strings and functions($P\{p_i, i = 0, 1, \ldots, n\}$)

A2 :
Check what is p_i's case
   If p_i is string(*CASE1*), p_i is saved
   If p_i is string concatenation(*CASE2*), divide p_i, update p_i, and GOTO **A2**
   If p_i is function(*CASE3*), update PL and GOTO **A1**

Extract all strings(S) related to dangerous functions

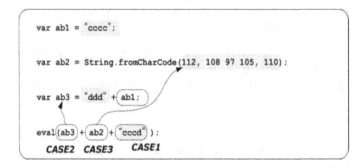

Fig. 2. An example of string extraction using static data flow analysis in JavaScript code

a malicious user uses function pointer reassignment such as `function1 = eval`.
SDFAJ traces variables related the functions, and divides them into simple
strings and functions Considering three string cases, SDFAJ traces all strings

cccc in string list. In the example, SDFAJ extracts four strings, such as "ccc", "112, 108, 97, 105, 110", "ddd", and "cccd". Using this strings, SDFAJ decides whether they are obfuscated.

5 Detection of Obfuscated Strings in JavaScript Codes

In this chapter, we propose the method to detect JavaScript obfuscated strings in a web page using all strings extracted by static data flow analysis. In order to check whether a string is obfuscated or not, we define three metrics: *N-gram*, *Entropy*, and *Word Size*. N-gram is an algorithm for text search. We search patterns for detecting obfuscated strings after analyzing normal and malicious web pages. Based on the metrics, we made experiments on detection for obfuscated strings in real malicious web pages.

5.1 Metrics for Detecting Obfuscated Strings

We define three metrics for detecting obfuscated strings. We search the usage frequency of ascii code in the strings using byte occurrence frequency as 1-gram. In order to know distribution of characters in strings, we calculate the entropy based on 1-gram. Lastly, we analyze the size of word because most of obfuscated strings are very long.

- **N – garm** check how many each byte code is used in strings
- **Entropy** check distribution of used byte codes
- **WordSize** check whether there is used very long string

In order to analyze patterns of normal web pages, we downloaded web page files including various JavaScript codes. Using OpenWebSpider[9], we collected web pages. OpenWebSpider is an open source web crawler and controls information about web pages in MySQL[7] database. Using OpenWebSpider# v0.1.3, we collected web page files in sub directories of 100 web sites and analyzed them.

N-gram. We check the usage frequency of ascii code in the strings. By doing

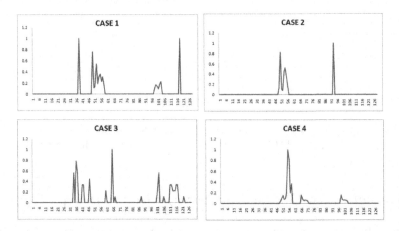

Fig. 3. Byte occurrence frequency for various JavaScript Obfuscated strings. X axis is ascii code number. Y axis is total number of each byte used in strings and we normalize values of Y axis by maximum value. The target of CASE1 is the string such as "%u9495%u4590...", and CASE2 is "\144\156". CASE3 is the case that obfuscated string uses various characters, and CASE4 uses *Alphabet* and *Number*.

Table 3. Ascii Code

Name	Ascii Code Number	Character
Alphabet	0x41-0x5A, 0x61-0x7A	A-Z, a-z
Number	0x30-0x39	0-9
Special Char	0x21-0x2F	! " # $ % & ' { } * + , - . /
	0x3A-0x40	: ; ¡ = ¿ ? @
	0x5B-0x5F, 0x7B-0x7E	[\ ] ^ _ ' { — }

We analyze various obfuscated strings in malicious web pages. Fig. 3 shows patterns of some obfuscated strings. In this chapter, we analyze four cases among various patterns of the strings. There exists various patterns except for the cases. The strings of CASE1 and CASE2 are related to the decoding mechanism that JavaScript language offers. The stings such as "%u9495%u4590..." and "\144\156" are decoded in **eval** function directly, or in **escape** and **unescape** functions. They have excessively specific characters such as "%u", "\", and so on. CASE3 and CASE4 are examples that obfuscated strings need user-made decoding functions. In cases, there are various patterns of byte occurrence fre-

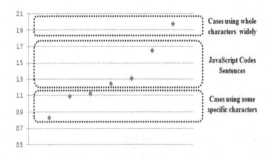

Fig. 4. Entropy for various JavaScript strings. Y axis is value of entropy. Upper region represents that the string has a whole characters widely. Middle region represents entropy for general JavaScript codes and sentences. Lower region is that the string has some specific characters excessively and has possibility of obfuscated string.

Entropy In order to analyze the distribution of bytes, we define entropy as second metric. Entropy is calculated as follows:

$$\mathbf{E(B)} = -\sum_{i=1}^{N} (\frac{b_i}{T}) \log(\frac{b_i}{T}) \begin{cases} B = \{b_i, i = 0, 1, \ldots, N\} \\ T = \sum_{i=1}^{N} b_i \end{cases}$$

In entropy($\mathbf{E}$), b_i is count of each byte values and $\mathbf{T}$ is total count of bytes in a string. If there are some bytes in a string, $\mathbf{E}$ reaches zero. Maximum value of $\mathbf{E}$ is $\log N$ and it means that byte codes are distributed widely throughout whole bytes. N is 128 because we focus on readable strings.

We calculate entropy of previous four cases. CASE1 is 1.12249, CASE2 0.82906, CASE3 1.24406, and CASE4 1.09014. The string that includes some kinds of characters has a low value of entropy, and vice verse. In search entropy ranges of ascii code, we calculate entropy of a string including all ascii code. The entropy is 1.97313. We select this as maximum value. An entropy of JavaScript codes in a general web page is roughly 1.6496. Because most strings are readable sentences, we calculate the entropy of sentences. The strings use alphabet, number and some special characters(, . " "). The entropy is about 1.3093. Collectively, range of entropy for various JavaScript strings is shown in Fig. 4. We set up two ranges: one region for some specific character, and the other region for general JavaScript codes and sentences. In Fig. 4, we exclude the case because entropy of upper region is an ideal case. *We decide that a string is obfuscated if entropy is less than 1.2.* Based   the a   ly i   1   e defi   ic2 as follow

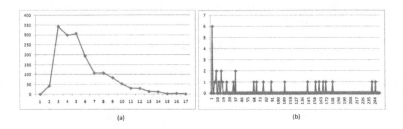

Fig. 5. Word size in sentences and JavaScript codes. (a) is the distribution of word size in general sentences. (b) is the distribution of word size in a JavaScript code.

strings use very long word size. For instance, the word size in a malicious web page that we collect is 9,212 bytes. In this metric, we target on a normal string. We divide stings into words by a space character(0x20). In order to analyze range of normal word size, we analyze various sentences and JavaScript codes as shown in Fig. 5. In the figure, (a) represents the distribution of word size in a general sentence. In the sentences, word size is under 30 on the average. (b) is the distribution of word size in a JavaScript code. The range of word size is from 0 to 300 generally. Based on the analysis result, we define metric3 as follows:

- *Metric3* : **Word Size** *Obfuscated string has excessive long size of word*

5.2 Evaluation and Experiments

In this chapter, we applied our three metrics into malicious web pages with obfuscated strings. We collected 33 real malicious pages. Among these pages, 14 pages include obfuscated strings. However, some pages are analogous to each other. We exclude similar pages and experimented 6 malicious web pages. Therefore, we applied our methodology to 6 patterns of obfuscated strings in malicious web pages. Table 4 shows patterns of each obfuscated string. We set up value of our metrics as follows:

- **Metric1** If the string includes *Special Char* excessively, it is obfuscated.
- **Metric2** If entry of the string is less than 1.2, it is obfuscated.
- **Metric3** If word size is more than 350, it is obfuscated.

Results of detection for obfuscated strings in each file based on three metrics are shown in Tabl

File3	97ACA29baca2B3A5517A99696Bae9B677d995C876a7
File4	eval(rmdiyfrT+eSS9YDtk[VFtUaNvX]);
File5	a1443oe.setTime(a1443oe.getTime()+365*24*60*60*1000);
File6	t!.Wr@i@te(#$q!.res$po#n#s$e@Bo@dy@)@'.replace(/\!|@|#|\$/ig, '')

Table 5. Results of detection for obfuscated strings. Metric1 is byte occurrence frequency, Metric2 is entropy, and Metric3 is the longest word size in the file. Values of Metric1 are byte codes used over 50% of maximum frequency number.

File Name	Metric1	Metric2	Metric3	Detection
File1	49 53 92	0.82906	750	YES
File2	40 41 49 50 101 116 124	1.71222	531	YES
File3	54 55 57	1.15289	9212	YES
File4	34 101 116	1.61563	29	NO
File5	49 51 52 59 61 97 101 111 112 114 116	1.65364	364	SUSPICIOUS
File6	33 35 36 64 101	1.4207	87	YES

- **File4 isn't Obfuscated String** Entropy is more than 1.2, and maximum word size is 29. Metrics for this pattern is false alarm.
- **File5 is suspicious of Obfuscated String** It includes bytes code evenly among all and entropy is more than 1.2. However, it has long word size more than 350 bytes.
- **File6 is Obfuscated String** It includes some special characters(33 35 36 64).

Among total 6 malicious patterns, we found obfuscated strings in 4 patterns of malicious web pages and suspected that one pattern includes an obfuscated string. However, we cannot find one malicious pattern.

6 Conclusion and Future Work

In this paper, we proposed a novel methodology that can detect obfuscated

References

1. Chellapilla, K., Maykov, A.: A Taxonomy of JavaScript Redirection Spam. In: Proceedings of the 3rd International Workshop on Adversarial Information Retrieval on Web (AIRWeb 2007) (2007)
2. Chenetee, S., Rice, A.: Spiffy: Automated JavaScript Deobfuscation. In: PacSec 2007 (2007)
3. Feinstein, B., Peck, D.: Caffeine Monkey: Automated Collection, Detection and Analysis of Malicious JavaScript. Black Hat USA (2007)
4. Hallaraker, O., Vigna, G.: Detecting Malicious JavaScript Code in Mozilla. In: Proceedings of the 10th IEEE International Conference on Engineering of Complex Computer Systems (ICECC 2005) (2005)
5. Ikinci, A., Holz, T., Freiling, F.: Monkey-Spider: Detecting Malicious Websites with Low-Interaction Honeyclients. In: Proceedings of Sicherheit 2008 (2008)
6. Livshits, B., Cui, W.: Spectator: Detection and Containment of JavaScript Worms. In: Proceedings of the USENIX 2008 Annual Technical Conference on Annual Technical Conference (2008)
7. MySQL - open source database, http://www.mysql.com
8. Nazario, J.: Reverse Engineering Malicious Javascript. In: CanSecWest 2007 (2007)
9. OpenWebSpider - open source web spider, http://www.openwebspider.org
10. Provos, N., McNamee, D., Mavrommatis, P., Wang, K., Modadugu, N.: The Ghost in the Browser Analysis of Web-based Malware. In: First Workshop on Hot Topics in Understanding Botnets (2007)
11. Vogt, P., Nentwich, F., Jovanovic, N., Kirda, E., Kruegel, C., Vigna, G.: Cross-Site Scripting Prevention with Dynamic Data Tainting and Static Analysis. In: Proceedings of the 14th Annual Network and Distributed System Security Symposium (NDSS 2007) (2007)
12. Wang, Y., Beck, D., Jiang, X., Roussev, R., Verbowski, C., Chen, S., King, S.: Automated Web Petrol with Strider HoneyMonkey. In: Proceedings of the Network and Distributed System Security Symposium (NDSS 2006) (2006)
13. Wassermann, G., Su, Z.: Static Detection of Cross-Site Scripting Vulnerabilities. In: Proceedings of the 30th International Conference Software Engineering (ICSE 2008) (2008)

Faculty of Information Technology and Multimedia,
Universiti Tun Hussein Onn Malaysia (UTHM),
86400 Parit Raja, Batu Pahat, Johor, Malaysia
{malik,mmustafa}@uthm.edu.my

Abstract. File carving is an important, practical technique for data recovery in digital forensics investigation and is particularly useful when filesystem metadata is unavailable or damaged. The research on reassembly of JPEG files with RST markers, fragmented within the scan area have been done before. However, fragmentation within Define Huffman Table (DHT) segment is yet to be resolved. This paper analyzes the fragmentation within the DHT area and list out all the fragmentation possibilities. Two main contributions are made in this paper. Firstly, three fragmentation points within DHT area are listed. Secondly, few novel validators are proposed to detect these fragmentations. The result obtained from tests done on manually fragmented JPEG files, showed that all three fragmentation points within DHT are successfully detected using validators.

Keywords: File Carving, Digital Evidence, Digital Forensics, Data Recovery.

1 Introduction

Forensics or digital investigations can be lengthy for storage with GB or TB, thus need rapid turnaround for time-sensitive cases involving potential loss of life or property. File carving tools typically produce many false positives and could miss key evidence [1]. Digital Forensics Research Workshop (DFRWS) 2007 carving challenge has boosted the pace for file carving research aimed to improve the state of the art in fully or semi-automated carving techniques [2]. [3] determined that fragmentation on a typical disk is less than 10%, however the fragmentation level of forensically important file types (like images, office files and email) is relatively high. He found that 16% of JPEGs are fragmented. As files are added, modified, and deleted, most file systems get fragmented [4]. However, in digital forensic, reassembling of

where fragments were sequential, out of order, or missing. None of the submissions to the forensic challenge of year 2007 completely solve the problems presented [2].

Baseline JPEG (simply called JPEG from this point onwards) file is used in the experiments because it is widely used in the Internet, and in many applications [9, 10]. Nevertheless, the introduced algorithms can be altered to extend the fragmentation point detection experiment to other JPEG file types (e.g. progressive, lossless and hierarchical JPEG) [11, 12]. It is important to detect fragmentation within the DHT because corrupted DHT would cause image distortion or corruption.

This paper introduces several scenarios (refer to Table 2 and Figure 3) of possible fragmentation points within DHT segment. Validators have been developed to detect these fragmentation points on JPEG files that are manually inserted with dummy data to simulate the three fragmentation scenarios.

The rest of the paper is organized as follows. Section 2 describes related work, section 3 discussed about fragmentation scenarios and validators, section 4 discussed about the experiments done, section 5 discussed about the result and discussion and finally section 6 concludes this paper.

2 Related Works

File carving processes have been defined by [3], [13] and [14]. Bifragment Gap Carving (BGC) [3] is introduced for bifragmented JPEG file recovery. The recovery is done by exhaustively searching all combinations of blocks between an identified header and footer while excluding different number of blocks until a successful decoding/validation is possible [13]. In [13], the author uses sequential hypothesis testing on data block to determine if consecutive clusters should be merged together. He uses forward fragment point detection test, and reverse sequential test only if the forward test is inconclusive. [14] focuses on solving fragmentation of JPEG image file containing RST markers that cuts through scan segment. A scan segment or area is an entropy-coded data segment which starts with start-of-scan (SOS) marker [11]. [3] and [13] are handling a general JPEG fragmentation case, while [14] is specifically focusing on fragmentation in JPEG scan area. On the other hand, this paper

baseline JPEG, but does not clearly stated on how are these DHTs are stored in the baseline JPEG file. To test this, 100 JPEG files are downloaded from the Internet (Google images) and renamed (e.g. 01.jpg). A sample of 100 JPEG files is more than enough because all baseline JPEG files have similar structure. For this reason, only a sample of five files is shown in Table 1. From the result obtained, it shows that all these files contain 4 DHTs, namely 2 DHT AC tables and 2 DHT DC tables with DHT table index 0x00, 0x10, 0x01 and 0x11. Each DHT marker is followed by one DHT table. The sequence of these DHT segments is illustrated as in Figure 1.

The offsets of 4 DHT tables and SOS in each JPEG files are tabulated as in Table 1. All the downloaded are baseline JPEG File Interchange Format (JFIF) because this type of file is the de facto standard for Internet [12]. All these files found to be using 4 different DHT tables in each file. Nevertheless, [14] found that, JPEG Exchangeable Image File Format (Exif) images taken from 76 popular digital cameras, 69 (91%) of them are using the same DHT tables.

3.1 Fragmentation Scenarios

In order to come up with DHT fragmentation detection algorithm (validator), first, we need to know all the JPEG file fragmentation possibilities or scenarios within the DHT segment. A standard structure of DHT is illustrated in Figure 2. A list of possible fragmentation scenarios is shown in Table 2. A visual representation of fragmentation scenarios is illustrated in Figure 3. Few novel validators are developed for detecting these fragmentations.

3.2 Validator for Scenario 1

After listing the possibility of fragmentation in DHT, so next, we need to know how to validate each of those scenarios. For scenario 1, the valid DHT length value for baseline JPEG must be greater than 19 because the first 2 bytes constitutes the DHT length field, followed by a byte of DC/AC table index and the next 16 bytes represent 16-bit Huffman codes (refer to Figure 2). The variable length data is not included here. If we assume that there is a minimum data of one byte in the variable length data, the size should be 20 bytes. Thus, the DHT length value of less than 20 would be detected by the validator as error (or fragmentation is detected for scenario 1 or

```
       endif
   endif
```

3.3 Validator for Scenario 2

For scenario 2, the table index value is stored in a single byte (8 bits). There are two components in a single byte of table index. The first four bits represent class component (have valid values of 0 for DC table or 1 for AC table). The next four bits represents the "Table id" (with a value 0 or 1). So, there are only four valid values for the one-byte table index i.e. 2 DC tables of values 0x00, 0x01 and another 2 AC tables of values 0x10, 0x11. If the validator found a value other than these four, error or fragmentation point (DHT-FragType-2) is detected at this location in DHT segment. The algorithm of validator for scenario 2 is illustrated below.

Example of algorithm for scenario 2.

```
get DHT structure
get DHT index (from DHT structure)
if (DHT_index<>0x0) and (DHT_index<>0x01) and
   (DHT_index<>10) and (DHT_index<>11))
          Error : Fragmentation Point Detected
                   (DHT-FragType-2)
endif
```

3.4 Validator for Scenario 3

For scenario 3, discrepancy can be detected by checking the total values stored in all sixteen bytes of Huffman codes. Nevertheless, when this occurs, it does not exactly show the exact location where the split or fragmentation point occurs. What it tells you is that, there is just a fragmentation point somewhere within the 16 byte Huffman code. To test this scenario, big values need to be used for the dummy data for creating the test file. The validator detects error or fragmentation point only when the total values stored in the 16 byte Huffman codes exceeds 255. This is because only a maximum of 255 ASCII characters can be compressed or represented as a 1-bit to 16-bit codes (or called as 16-bit Huffman codes). The algorithm of validator for scenario 3 is illustrated below.

04.jpg	177	207	270	297	347
05.jpg	177	206	268	295	334

DHT marker – DHT length (DHL)– DHT table index (DTI) DC **0x00** table – DHT 16 byte
Huffman bit code (DHT16) – Variable Length Data (VLD)
DHT marker – DHL – DTI AC **0x10** table – DHT16 - VLD
DHT marker – DHL – DTI DC **0x11** table – DHT16 – VLD
DHT marker – DHL – DTI AC **0x11** table – DHT16 - VLD

Fig. 1. Sequence of DHT segments in a single baseline JPEG image file

Table 2. Fragmentation in DHT segment scenarios

Fragmentation Scenarios	Description
Scenario 1	The JPEG file is split between the DHT marker and the "length" field (DHT structure).
Scenario 2	The JPEG file is split between the "length" and "index" field.
Scenario 3	JPEG file split in the middle of DHT structure i.e. between the index field and the "16-byte Huffman bit codes".

DHT Marker (DHT)	Length	Index	16-byte Huffman bit code (HC)	Variable Data Length (VDL)

Fig. 2. DHT without fragmentation

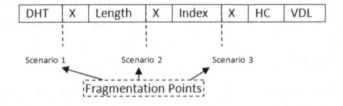

ple file structure.
- All the file headers and footers are in sequential order and not corrupted.
- Only a single pass is used. The header, footer and the fragmentation point will be indexed. This information can also be displayed to the user, but input output activities will increase the amount the processing time.
- The validator stops once the first fragmentation point is detected.
- Fragmentation codes (refer to Table 3) are introduced to represent the fragmentation points detected (refer to Table 1).

Table 3. List of fragmentation point codes used in the validators

Fragmentation Code Type	Fragmentation Scenarios
DHT-FragType-1	Scenario 1
DHT-FragType-2	Scenario 2
DHT-FragType-3	Scenario 3

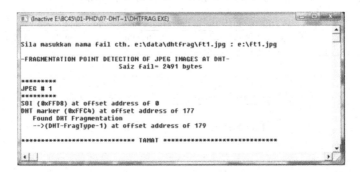

Fig. 4. The screenshot of the validator showed the fragmentation point detected for ft1.jpg

4.1 Experiment 1

Download 100 baseline JPEG images from the Internet. Baseline JPEG can be validated by checking the existence of start-of-frame (SOF) where the SOF0

The hard disk space is sanitized by creating a simple text file sanitize.txt in the 8MB partition with no content (size of 0kb). Open the file using a hex editor (e.g. HexAssistant [15]) and then use the "insert block" option to insert up to maximum size of 8MB into the file with 0x00. From the window explorer, the property for the 8MB partition shows "used space" is full. Delete the sanitize.txt file and then copy three fragmented JPEG test files (ft1.jpg to ft3.jpg) to the empty 8MB HDD partition. Image of the HDD is taken using Helix Live CD and named as hdd.dd. Similar results to experiment 1 are obtained, as shown in Table 4. The experiment can be repeated with another set of three fragmented files. Similar results are obtained but differ only in the offset address value.

Table 4. List of detected fragmentation type from the test files

Filename	Fragmentation detected	Actual fragmentation	Offset Address
ft1.jpg	DHT-FragType-1	DHT-FragType-1	DHT marker at offset address 177, DHT-FragType-1 is detected at offset address 179.
ft2.jpg	DHT-FragType-2	DHT-FragType-2	DHT marker at offset address 177, DHT-FragType-2 is detected at offset address 181.
ft3.jpg	DHT-FragType-3	DHT-FragType-3	DHT marker at offset address 177, DHT-FragType-3 is detected at offset address 182.

5 Result and Discussion

From the experiments done, all these fragmentation points (scenarios 1 to 3) are successfully detected by displaying the fragmentation codes (e.g. DHT-FragType-3) and the fragmentation point addresses.

6 Conclusion and Future Works

File carving is an important, practical technique for data recovery in digital forensics

detected using validators. For future research, experiments can be extended to carve these JPEG files fragmented within DHT.

Acknowledgement

This work was supported by Universiti Tun Hussein Onn Malaysia (UTHM).

References

1. http://www.korelogic.com/Resources/Projects/
   dfrws_challenge_2006/DFRWS_2006_File_Carving_Challenge.pdf
2. Digital Forensics Research Workshop, DFRWS (2007)
3. Garfinkel, S.: Carving contiguous and fragmented files with fast object validation. In: Proceedings of the 2007 digital forensics research workshop, DFRWS, Pittsburg (2007)
4. Pal, A., Memon, N.: Evolution of file carving. IEEE Signal Processing Magazine, 59–71 (2009)
5. Pal, A., Shanmugasundaram, K., Memon, N.: Automated Reassembly of Fragmented Images. AFOSR Grant F49620-01-1-0243 (2003)
6. Richard III, G.G., Roussev, V., Marzial, L.: In-Place File Carving. In: National Science Foundation under grant # CNS-0627226 (2007)
7. Hall, G.A., Davis, W.P.: Sliding Window Measurement for File Type Identification (2006)
8. Shannon, M.: Forensic Relative Strength Scoring: ASCII and Entropy Scoring. International Journal of Digital Evidence 2(4) (Spring 2004)
9. Li, W., Wang, K., Stolfo, S.J., Herzog, B.: Fileprints: Identifying File Types by n-gram Analysis. IEEE, Los Alamitos (2005)
10. Wallace, G.K.: The JPEG Still Picture Compression Standard. IEEE Transactions on Consumer Electronics (1991)
11. ITU T.81, CCITT: Information Technology – Digital Compression and Coding of Continuous-Tone Still Images –Requirements and Guideline (1992)
12. Hamilton, E.: JPEG file interchange format v1.02. Technical report, C-Cube Microsystems (1992)
13. Pal, A., Sencar, H.T., Memon, N.: Detecting File Fragmentation Point Using Sequential Hypothesis Testing. Journal of Digital Investigations, s2–s13 (2008)

[1] Dept. of Computer Science Engineering, Inha University
[2] School of Information & Media, Kyungin Women's College
[3] School of Management & Tourism, Kimpo College
[4] Dept. of Computer and Information Science, Sunmoon University, South Korea
kjspace@inha.ac.kr, choisymail@gmail.com, softman@kic.ac.kr,
jhchoi@kimpo.ac.kr, jhlee@inha.ac.kr, rim@sunmoon.ac.kr

Abstract. The previous key management methods are inadequate for secure data communication in cluster-based routing scheme. Because the cluster head is changed at each round, it has to take the step of authentication or shared key setting with neighbor nodes. In addition, there happens a large overhead for secure communication if the mobility of nodes is considered. Accordingly, this study proposes a secure and efficient key management mechanism suitable for cluster-based routing protocol even when the nodes are moveable and new nodes are inserted frequently.

Keywords: Cluster-based Routing, Secure Protocol, Key Management Scheme.

1 Introduction

A wireless sensor networks (WSN) consists of densely deployed sensor nodes. Because sensor nodes have very limited resources, it is not easy to apply existing public key encryption techniques such as RSA and Diffie-Hellman. In addition, as they are deployed in physical unsecure environment, a very large number of sensor nodes should allow errors and failures and are interconnected through autonomous networking, and for this reason, effective management and security functions are critical elements. Recently, intensive research is being made in WSN for developing various encryption methods through secure key distribution [1-5]. However, the previous methods for secure communication have a key distribution solution applicable limitedly to a specific structure [6]. Protocols such as LEACH [7], LEACH-C [8], and 3DE_var[13] are repre-

The Random Key Pre-Distribution (RPK) [1] guarantees secure authentication among nodes through the three-step process of random key predistribution, shared key discovery, and path key establishment. The size of key ring to be stored in each node has to be enlarged in order to increase network connection weight, and this enables a malicious attacker to get more keys through node compromise. In order to solve this problem, a method that utilizes information on sensor node deployment was proposed, but it still has the problem that a malicious attacker can use a key obtained from node compromise in other areas of the sensor network [10]. In addition, this method does not consider security analysis, through which compromised nodes can tap or hide compromise efficiently through mutual cooperation [11].

As it was considered difficult to design a secure key mechanism using a key in a sensor network where a large number of sensors are scattered, LEAP [4] was proposed, which has four keys. The four keys are private key shared with BS, broadcasted group key that base station(BS) shares with all nodes in the network, pairwise key shared with other sensor nodes, and cluster key shared with a number of neighbor nodes. Because the private key and the group key are assigned before sensor nodes are deployed, a malicious attacker may compromise a sensor node. In addition, when a sensor node is compromised before initialization as in the master key-based scheme, the malicious attacker may be able to generate all the keys used in WSN by acquiring all information stored in the sensor node within a minute [12].

HIKES[9] is a method in which BS plays the role of the Trust Authentication and assigns part of its roles to CH. It can generate a key from partial key escrow table in all nodes and can be elected as CH, and after data aggregation, information is transmitted to BS through message exchange among CHs. However, because sensor node authentication is carried out by BS and partial key escrow table has to be stored in every node, this method requires an additional storage space. When a malicious attacker obtains partial key escrow table through node compromise, it can infer from the partial key escrow table a pairwise key between CH and sensor nodes situated in other areas.

3 Proposed Approach (3DE_sec)

This step searches for a shared key with sensor nodes in the cluster. CH can know whether the sensor nodes have a shared key by broadcasting its own key ID. Using the shared key, secure links are established with nodes, and secure communication is guaranteed. The share probability(sp) that the key ring assigned to each node is shared with neighbor nodes can be calculated from $Pool$ and k as in Equation (1).

$$sp = 1 - \frac{((Pool-k)!)^2}{(Pool-2k)!Pool!} \quad , 0 \le sp \le 1 \tag{1}$$

where, since $Pool$ is very large, we use Stirling's approximation($n! \approx n^n e^{-n} \sqrt{2\pi n}$) for $n!$ to simplify the expression (1), and obtained equation (2).

$$sp = 1 - \frac{(1-\frac{k}{Pool})^{2(Pool-k+\frac{1}{2})}}{(1-\frac{2k}{Pool})^{(Pool-2k+\frac{1}{2})}} \tag{2}$$

If the number of nodes in WSN and share probability(sp) are predefined, suitable key ring size is calculated by equation (2).

3.3 Shared Key Establishment Step

Phase 1: Authentication through Shared Key Authentication
After the key predistribution step, each node has a k -sized key ring and a unique personal key for secure communication with BS. This authentication, which is called primary authentication, is made through setting a shared key among nodes using k keys assigned to each node, thus a secure communication path is established.

Phase 2: Authentication by an Authentication Center Delegated by BS
There is no shared key between newly selected CH and nodes in the cluster, if authentication is obtained from BS, it may increase the overhead of BS and network traffic. In this case, authentication can be performed quickly and overall delay time can be minimized by reusing node information obtained from previous CH. In case of

not have authentication information such as shared key or previous cluster key, it is hardly possible to be authenticated at the primary or secondary authentication step. Such a node chooses samples at random from the keys in each key ring, and sends AREQ(Authentication Request Packet) to BS, and goes through authentication by BS. In order to be authenticated by BS, it extracts some samples, and sends an encrypted message using the personal key to the selected CH. CH forwards encrypted messages from nodes without the shared key to BS, and BS decrypts the encrypted messages, and checks if they agree with the set of $< idx, BA, length, val >$ pairs, the authentication request sample code of the sender node ID. The applied idx means the index of the node in the key ring, BA is the base address, $length$ is length, and val is value. And these values are set by random functions, then val indicates the value of the key at a distance of $length$ from BA. If the samples agree with each other AREP(Authentication Reply Packet) is sent CH and requested node. Otherwise, node ID of the malicious node intending the disruption of communication is detected and sent to each CH so that malicious ID be removed from the key ring of all nodes. Because, due to the character-istic of the cluster-based scheme, CH should be changed at a regular interval of time, AREP contains the shared key's information assigned by BS.

Vulnerable nodes such as nodes do not have shared key with CH and newly in-serted nodes should be authenticated by BS. Accordingly, as in Figure 2, the nodes build $< NodeID, idx >$ pairs, information contained in large pool before key distribution and in the key ring with k keys distributed to each node, in the pool database of BS simultaneously with key predistribution. Here, $NodeID$ means the ID of each node, and idx is the index of each node ID in the key ring.

Figure 2 shows the process of checking an authentication sample code sent by a node without the shared key against the pool database owned by BS. Message (MSG_{AREQ_x}) which is the authentication sample code that node ID x encrypted using its personal key, is decrypted by BS, and $< 0,1,10, "0000000011" >$ is its part. This means that the value of 10 bits at a distance of 1 from the key at the position of 0th index in node x.

If this value coincides with the value in the BS database, tertiary authentication is performed. That is, node ID x is authenticated and AREP is sent so that CH and x can establish the shared key. The message, whose value is the same as MSG_{AREQ_x},

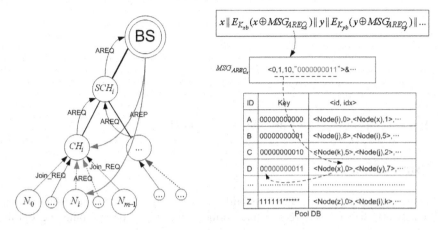

Fig. 1. The example of the authentication request and authentication reply process

Fig. 2. Example of the cryptographic message authentication validation process of BS

---

1. Advertisement Step

$CH \Rightarrow G : id_{CH}, nonce, ADV$

$A_i : choose \quad r \quad such \quad that \quad r \in (R_{CH} \cap R_{A_i})$

2. Join-Req. Step

If $r \notin \varnothing$ then

$A_i \rightarrow CH : id_{A_i}, id_{CH}, r, Join - Req., MAC_{k_{[r]}}(id_{A_i} \mid id_{CH} \mid r \mid nonce)$

Else

$A_i \rightarrow CH : id_{A_i}, id_{CH}, Join - REQ.,$

$MAC_{k_{[A_i]}}(id_{A_i} \mid id_{CH} \mid nonce \mid nonce \mid SC(..., < idx_{A_i}, BA_{A_i}, length_{A_i}, val_{A_i} >, ...))$

$CH \rightarrow BS : id_{CH}, id_{BS}, AREQ_{CH}, MAC_{k_{[CH]}}(id_{CH} \mid id_{BS} \mid nonce \mid F'(..., MAC_{A_i}, ...) \mid c_{CH})$

$\qquad$ If $\qquad\qquad val_{BS_{A_i}} = val_{A_i} \qquad\qquad\qquad\qquad$ then

$BS \rightarrow A_i : id_{BS}, id_{A_i}, AREP_{A_i}, MAC_{k_{[A_i]}}(id_{BS} \mid id_{A_i} \mid nonce \mid ASC(..., < idx_{A_i}, BA_{A_i}, length_{A_i}, val_{A_i} >, ...))$

$BS \rightarrow CH : id_{BS}, id_{CH}, AREP_{CH}, MAC_{k_{[CH]}}(id_{BS} \mid id_{CH} \mid nonce \mid ASC(..., < idx_{A_i}, BA_{A_i}, length_{A_i}, val_{A_i} >, ...))$

$\qquad$ End If

End If

3. TDMA Scheduling Step

$CH \Rightarrow G : id_{CH}, (..., < id_{A_i}, TDMA_{A_i} >, ...), TDMA \ schedule$

4. Receiving Sensing Data Step

$A_i \rightarrow CH : id_{A_i}, id_{CH}, d_{A_i}, MAC_{k_{[r]}}(id_{A_i} \mid id_{CH} \mid d_{A_i} \mid nonce + j)$

5. Sending Aggregated Information Step

($BS \rightarrow A_i$), respectively. $\Rightarrow, \rightarrow$ mean Broadcast and Unicast.

4 Simulations

The simulator used in this study was built in Visual C++. In our experiment, we limited network size ($100m \times 100m$) and formed clusters by determining the optimal number of clusters according to distance between BS and network area using Equation (3) [8].

$$k_{opt} = \frac{\sqrt{N}}{\sqrt{2\pi}} \sqrt{\frac{\varepsilon_{fs}}{\varepsilon_{mp}}} \frac{M}{d_{toBS}^2} \tag{3}$$

where, N is the number of the nodes in WSN, d_{toBS} is the distance from BS to cluster head node. For our experiments, we set $\varepsilon_{fs} = 10pJ / bit / m^2$, $\varepsilon_{mp} = 0.0013pJ / bit / m^4$, $M = 100m$, and $N = 10,000$. When the value was put in Equation (3), the optimal number of cluster k_{opt} is 62. Accordingly, the size of key ring in 3DE_sec is about 162 ($\approx 10,000 / 62$). Assuming that, transmission energy to BS for the authentication of unauthenticated nodes at each round is $n \times E_{Tx} \times Length'$ in the proposed 3DE_sec and $n \times E_{Tx} \times Length''$ in HIKES, for 3DE_sec to be more energy-efficient than HIKES, its total energy consumption should be less and this condition is satisfied in Equation (4).

$$n \times E_{Tx} \times Length' \leq n \times E_{Tx} \times Length''$$
$$Length' \leq \frac{n \times Length''}{n} \tag{4}$$

where, $Length''$ is the size of each key, and $Length'$ is the size of authentication sample code for authenticating with BS, that is, $\{< idx, BA, length, val >\}^*$.

Table 1 below shows the number of keys not shared according to the size of key ring and the size of authentication sample code for optimizing energy efficiency when is 10,000. Here, when the minimum size of key ring is 94, 3DE_sec is more energy-

100	63.58%	3,642	< 44 bit	39 bit
162	93.06%	694	< 231 bit	40 bit
200	98.31%	169	< 947 bit	40 bit
220	99.29%	71	< 2,254 bit	40 bit
250	99.84%	16	< 10,000 bit	40 bit

Table 2. Comparison of the storage requirement for cryptographic primitives(N=10,000)[9]

Cryptographic Primitive	LEAP	RKP	HIKES	3DE_sec
Initialization key	0	N/A	1	N/A
Cluster- key (Temporary Key)	1	N/A	1	1
Node-to-CH key	1	N/A	50	N/A
Node-to-Node keys	50	250	50	k
Node-to-BS key	1	N/A	1	1
Global key	1	N/A	1	1
Backup key	N/A	N/A	1	N/A
Commitment keys	50	N/A	N/A	N/A
Length of Key Chain	20	N/A	N/A	N/A
Size of Key Escrow Table	N/A	N/A	16	N/A
Total Primitives	124	250	121	k + 3

space, respectively, 21.8%, 61.2%, and 19.1% less than LEAP, RPK, and HIKES. Here, $|Key|$ indicates key size for uniqueness in the entire pool database, and in case stability within WSN is more important than energy efficiency, it can be achieved through increasing k .

Figure 4 shows the Average percentage of energy dissipation by a cluster head on key management over cluster density in both 3DE_sec and HIKES. In this case, we

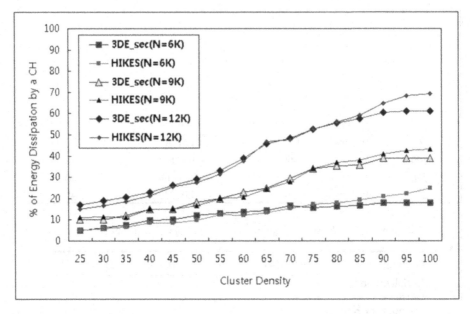

Fig. 4. Average percentage of energy dissipation by a cluster head on key management over cluster density in both 3DE_sec and HIKES

5 Conclusions and Future Works

This study proposed a cluster-based key management method that can set a shared key faster and more securely using a key ring assigned to each node before deployment in cluster formation within WSN. This key management method showed that it can work more energy-efficiently than existing key management methods even when nodes are mobile or new nodes are inserted. In future research on the application of the cluster-based routing protocol, we need to enhance the overall performance of network by minimizing the delay time in cluster formation.

Acknowledgement

"This research was supported by the MKE(The Ministry of Knowledge Economy), Korea, under the ITRC(Information Technology Research Center) Support program supervised by the NIPA(National IT industry Promotion Agency)" (NIPA-2009-C1090-0902-0020).

Network Protocols (ICNP 2003), pp. 326–335 (2003)

6. Akyildiz, I.F., Su, W., Sankarasubramaniam, Y., Cayirci, E.: A survey on sensor networks. IEEE Communications Magazine 40, 102–114 (2002)

7. Heinzelman, W.R., Chandrakasan, A.P., Balakrishnan, H.: Energy-Efficient Communication Protocol for Wireless Microsensor Networks. In: Proc. 33rd Hawaii Int'l. Conf. Sys. Sci. (2000)

8. Heinzelman, W.B., Chandrakasan, A.P., Balakrishnan, H.: An Application-Specific Protocol Architecture for Wireless Microsensor Networks. IEEE Trans. Wireless Commun. 1(4), 660–670 (2002)

9. Ibriq, J., Mahgoub, I.: A Hierarchical Key Establishment Scheme or Wireless Sensor Networks. In: Proceedings of 21st International Conference on Advanced Networking and Applications (AINA 2007), pp. 210–219 (2007)

10. Silva, R.M.S., Pereira, N.S.A., Nunes, M.S.: Applicability Drawbacks of Probabilistic Key Management Schemes for Real World Applications of Wireless Sensor Networks. In: Proceedings of the Third International Conference on Wireless and Mobile Communications, ICWMC 2007 (2007)

11. Moore, T.: A Collusion Attack on Pair-wise Key Predistribution Schemes for Distributed Sensor Networks. In: Proceedings of the Fourth Annual IEEE International Conference Pervasive Computing and Communications Workshops (PERCOMW 2006), pp. 13–17 (2006)

12. Hartung, C., Balasalle, J., Han, R.: Node Compromise in Sensor Networks: The Need for Secure Systems. Technical Report CU-CS-990-05 (2005)

13. Kim, J.S., Choi, S.Y., Han, S.J., CHoi, J.H., Lee, J.H., Rim, K.W.: Alternative Cluster Head Selection Protocol for Energy Efficiency in Wireless Sensor Networks. In: First Software Technologies for Future Dependable Distributed Systems (STFDDS 2009), pp. 159–163 (2009)

Iran University of Science and Technology
Tehran, Iran
meisam_fathi@comp.iust.ac.ir
[2] Computer Engineering Department
Iran University of Science and Technology
Tehran, Iran
parsa@iust.ac.ir

Abstract. This paper aims at automatic detection of infinite recursion at compile time in aspect-oriented programs. Infinite recursion is a known problem with aspect-oriented programming. If programmers do not take particular precautions, aspects that advise other aspects can easily and unintentionally lead to infinite recursion. The solution that is proposed in this paper informs programmers of aspects that lead to infinite recursion by showing compile time error messages and warnings. This paper, additionally, measures effectiveness of its proposed solution by applying it to several case studies. The solution that is proposed in this paper suggests that programming in aspect-oriented languages can be done more safely without restricting languages features or imposing runtime overhead.

Keywords: Infinite Recursion, Interprocedural Anlysis, Aspect-Oriented Programming, Debugging Aspect-Oriented Programs.

1 Introduction

A major problem with current mainstream aspect-oriented languages, such as AspectJ is that an aspect-oriented program can easily contain code that leads to unintentional infinite recursion. This unexpected infinite recursion is caused due to advice advising other advice or advising methods that they call. Even though recursion might be used intentionally in aspect-oriented programs by programmers for solving recursive problems, in practice, it is mostly unintended

pectJ*, which totally averts infinite recursion in aspects by layering aspects and preventing aspects from advising aspects in higher levels or aspects in the same level. This solution prevents the infinite recursion problem, but it restricts the programmers to program in AspectJ*. To remedy the restriction, Bodden et al. have offered a refactoring for transforming AspectJ programs to AspectJ* programs. However, refactoring existing programs could be burdensome for large programs.

A totally different approach is proposed in [7] and has been implemented in XFindBugs. XFindBugs examines the bytecode generated by a specific AspectJ compiler for detecting several special patterns that lead to faults in AspectJ programs. One of the patterns that is examined by XFindBugs is a pattern that leads to infinite recursion. A major difficulty with XFindBugs is its dependency on the code generated by a specific AspectJ compiler, ajc[1]. XFindBugs is incapable of finding bugs in the compiled bytcode of AspectJ programs that are not compiled with the ajc compiler.

In this paper a new approach to automatically detect infinite recursion in aspect-oriented programs is presented. The proposed approach is based upon the static analysis of source code of aspect-oriented programs. The proposed approach does not require the programmer to insert any specific instruction within the program and does not impose any runtime overhead on the program execution.

The remaining parts of this paper are organized as follows: Section 2 delves into the proposed solution. In section 3 preliminary results of applying the proposed solution to several benchmarks are presented. Finally, section 4 deals with future work and conclusion.

2 The Proposed Approach

The approach that is proposed in this paper consists of two parts. The first part, which is described in Section 2.1, is concerned with transforming an aspect-oriented program to a model that can be used for analyzing the source code. The second part, which is described in Section 2.2, is concerned with detection of infinite recursion in the transformed model.

block, inside a class constructor, inside a static initialization block, at a static field initialization, and at a non-static field initialization. When a join point does not resides in a method, several clarifications are required to keep the assumption true. These clarifications are as follows:

1. **Clarifying join points inside an advice:** The first assumption about the equivalence of methods and advice makes this clarification straightforward. Joint points that are inside an advice whose signature is $advice : param_1 \times param_2 \cdots \times param_n \longmapsto out$ are supposed to reside in a method with the same name whose signature is $advice : param_0 \times param_1 \times param_2 \cdots \times param_n \longmapsto out$. This method has an extra $param_0$ which contains the context of program at the captured join point.

2. **Clarifying join points inside an initialization block:** Joint points that are inside an initialization block are supposed to reside in a special $\langle init \rangle$ method which has no parameters.

3. **Clarifying join points inside a constructor:** Join points that are in a constructor whose signature is $new : param_1 \times param_2 \cdots \times param_n \longmapsto out$ are assumed to reside in a special method whose signature is $\langle init \rangle : param_1 \times param_2 \cdots \times param_n \longmapsto out$.

   This assumption implies that for classes with more than one constructor, there are several $\langle init \rangle$ methods with different signatures in the program model. The parameter lists of each $\langle init \rangle$ method is defined by its corresponding constructor. All constructors are supposed to call the special method $\langle init \rangle$ at their entry point before other statements inside their bodies. If there is a default constructor (i.e. constructor with no parameters), it is supposed that its body is merged with the body of $\langle init \rangle$.

4. **Clarifying join points inside a static initialization block:** Joint points that are located inside a static initialization block are supposed to reside in a special static method, $\langle static \rangle$, which takes no input parameters. If there are more than one static initialization block in a class, their corresponding join points are supposed to reside in $\langle static \rangle$ method in the order that they appear in the source code.

5. **Clarifying join points at a static field initialization:** Joint points that iated with initi lization of static fields are supp sed t ide in

```
10    // rest of the code...
11  }
```

Fig. 1. A Sample Snippet of an Aspect-Oriented Program

Table 1. Residues of join points inside the Snippet Code in Figure 1

Line#	Join Point	Residue
2	set(theNumber)	<static>()
2	new(Random)	<init>(int)
4-8	execution(maxInArray)	maxInArray(int)
5	get(array.length)	maxInArray(int)
6	call(max(double, double))	maxInArray(int)

Figure 1 is a snippet from the Null-Check benchmark that is distributed with AspectBench Compiler. Clarification for static methods and static method initializers for this snippet are shown in Table 1.

These assumptions are used to extract a program model P from the source code. This model contains, a set B_P of all methods and advice bodies defined in P, a set JP_P of join points defined in P, a relation $C_P \subset B_P \times B_P$ of all method calls in P, a relation $A_P \subset JP_P \times B_P$ which indicates join points advised by each advice, and a relation $R_P \subset JP_P \times B_P$ which indicates residues for each join point. Since this model assumes that methods and advice are equivalent, not only does the relation C_P contain method calls, but also it contains all advice bodies that are woven into join points. The B_P itself is the union of MB_P and AB_P, respectively the set of all method bodies, and the set of all advice bodies defined in P.

$$P = \langle B_P, JP_P, C_P, A_P, R_P \rangle \tag{1}$$

This model is used for constructing an extended call graph, $ECG_P = (N_P, E_P)$, in which method and advice bodies form vertices of the graphs. An edge $e = (b, b)$ belongs t   this graph provided that   f the followin   dition i

Consequently, there is an edge (b_1, b_2) in ECG if and only if b_2 is reachable from b_1 via a method call or a an advice application execution. For finding all edges it is necessary that all join points and their residues be identified.

For extracting this model *AspectBench Compiler* abc [8], which is an extensible AspectJ compiler, is used. This compiler is capable of running user defined passes and analyses, i.e. it is possible to define your desired passes and analysis and add them to abc.

2.2 Cycle Detection in the Extended Call Graph

Each edge in the extended call graph is labeled with one of the following labels:

c : An edge labeled with c is guaranteed to be executed each time its containing method is executed.

u : An edge labeled with u maybe executed each time its containing method is executed, this, however, is not guaranteed.

Let $CFG_b = (N_b, E_b, n_{entry_b}, n_{exit_b})$ be the control flow graph of method $b \in B_P$, in which N_b is the set of nodes, E_b is the set of edges, n_{entry_b} is the entry node, and n_{exit_b} is the exit node. Let's suppose that edge $e = (b, b')$ is due to node n in CFG_b, i.e. statement $n \in N_b$ is a method call statement that invokes b'. Additionally, let $\gg$ indicate the dominator relation, such that $n \gg n'$ indicates n dominates n'.

An edge $e = (b, b') \in ECG_P$ is labeled c if and only if $b \gg b_{exit_b}$, else it is labeled u.

In order to detect cycles in the extended call graph, the default cycle detection algorithm provided by abc is used. The cycle detection algorithm is applied to the call graph twice. The first application of the algorithm detects cycles whose edges are labeled with c. This application of the algorithm detects cycles which are guaranteed to lead to infinite recursion. The second application of the algorithm detects all cycles regardless of the labels of their forming edges. This second application of the algorithm detects cycles which may or may not lead to infinite recursion. In theory, not only does this application detect cycles that are detected by the previous application, and consequently are programming errors, but also

are distributed with abc [8] and are used by Dafur et al. [10]. The Non-Negative and Instrumentation benchmarks are used by Richard et al. [11]. These benchmarks have been applied to some base applications, among which the Telecom benchmark is distributed with AspectJ, and the Stack and Account applications are benchmarks that are used by Richard et al. [11].

Comparing to other benchmarks, the Profiling and Logging benchmarks have two distinct characteristics. Firstly, they have pointcuts that have the possibility to capture join points scattered in different packages and classes. As shown in line 5 of Figure 2, the Profiling benchmark defines a pointcut that captures all methods calls to the `toString()` methods.

Secondly, these benchmarks invoke several methods, which might be advised by other aspects, in the body of their advice. As shown in lines 8-11 of Figure 2 the Profiling benchmark invoke several methods over the `totalCounts` object and other objects in one of its advice bodies. Containing pointcuts that capture join points from different classes and invoking several methods in their body increases the likelihood of forming infinite recursion.

Table 2 represents the result of applying the proposed approach to the mentioned benchmarks. The first row in this table shows the name of the base application that is used. Several benchmarks have been applied to each base application. These benchmarks are marked in rows 2 to 9 of Table 2. The last four rowss show the results of applying the proposed approach to the benchmarks. The *Number of Edges in ECG* row shows the number of edges that have been constructed in the extended call graph during analysis of benchmarks.

In Table 2, the *Certain Cycles* and *Non-Certain Cycles* rows show the number of cycles that have been identified as cycles that certainly happen, and the

```
1  aspect ToStringCountingAspect {
2    private Map totalCounts = new HashMap();
3    private int myCount = 0;
4    pointcut myCall() : call(String MyClass.toString());
5    pointcut allCalls() : call(String *.toString());
6    before(): myCall() { myCount++; }
7    after() : allCalls() {
       Class c = thisJPSP.getSignature().getDeclaringType();
```

	Instrumentation			×	×	×																	
	Design by Contract				×				×														
	Number of Edges in ECG	62	43	48	9	175	69	278	98	279	841	805	275	540	550	113	755	248	256	510	95	97	230
Results	Certain-Cycles	0	0	2	0	2	2	0	2	2	0	0	2	0	0	0	0	0	2	0	0	0	0
	Non-Certain-Cycles	15	0	2	0	2	2	14	2	2	15	14	2	0	0	0	13	0	2	0	0	0	0
	False Negatives	2	0	0	0	0	0	0	0	0	2	2	0	0	0	0	0	0	0	0	0	0	0

number of cycles that might happen, respectively. As mentioned in Section 2.2 certain cycles contain edges labeled with c while non certain cycles contain edges labeled with both c and u.

All detected cycles have been examined manually to see if they really lead to infinite recursion. The last row of Table 2 shows the correctness of the solution in terms of the the number of False Negatives. As represented in Table 2, while none of the benchmarks include a fault individually, infinite recursion might occur when more than one benchmark is applied to a base application. As it was expected, when benchmarks contain pointcuts that capture join points located in different classes, in this case for Logging and Profiling benchmarks, advice advising other advice may lead to infinite recursion. Putting Logging and Profiling benchmarks away, no combination of other benchmarks has ever resulted in infinite recursion, mainly because other benchmarks have pointcuts that strictly restrict join points that they capture by explicitly identifying packages and classes that should be advised.

Additionally, the proposed approach is not capable of detecting infinite recursion when the Law-of-Demeter benchmark is woven to the base application along with Loggingg and Profiling benchmarks. The authors believe that this inabiliy to detect infinite recursion when the Law-of-Demeter benchmark is applied to the base application is due to presence of dynamic pointcuts in this benchmark which are evalueted at runtime.

4 Conclusion and Future Work

The overall experiment suggests that despite the considerable number of False

1. Laddad, R.: AspectJ in Action: Practical Aspect-Oriented Programming. Manning, Greenwich (2003)
2. Avgustinov, P., Christensen, A.S., Hendren, L., Kuzins, S., Lhoták, J., Lhoták, O., de Moor, O., Sereni, D., Sittampalam, G., Tibble, J.: Optimising AspectJ. In: PLDI 2005: Proceedings of the 2005 ACM SIGPLAN conference on Programming language design and implementation, pp. 117–128. ACM, New York (2005)
3. Bockisch, C., Kanthak, S., Haupt, M., Arnold, M., Mezini, M.: Efficient control flow quantification. In: OOPSLA 2006: Proceedings of the 21st annual ACM SIGPLAN conference on Object-oriented programming systems, languages, and applications, pp. 125–138. ACM, New York (2006)
4. Lemos, O.A.L., Vincenzi, A.M.R., Maldonado, J.C., Masiero, P.C.: Control and data flow structural testing criteria for aspect-oriented programs. J. Syst. Softw. 80(6), 862–882 (2007)
5. Zhao, J.: Data-flow-based unit testing of aspect-oriented programs. In: COMPSAC 2003: Proceedings of the 27th Annual International Conference on Computer Software and Applications, Washington, DC, USA, p. 188. IEEE Computer Society, Los Alamitos (2003)
6. Bodden, E., Forster, F., Steimann, F.: Avoiding infinite recursion with stratified aspects. In: Hirschfeld, R., Polze, A., Kowalczyk, R. (eds.) NODe/GSEM, GI. LNI, vol. 88, pp. 49–64 (2006)
7. Shen, H., Zhang, S., Zhao, J., Fang, J., Yao, S.: XFindBugs: extended FindBugs for AspectJ. In: PASTE 2008: Proceedings of the 8th ACM SIGPLAN-SIGSOFT workshop on Program analysis for software tools and engineering, pp. 70–76. ACM, New York (2008)
8. Avgustinov, P., Christensen, A.S., Hendren, L., Kuzins, S., Lhoták, J., Lhoták, O., de Moor, O., Sereni, D., Sittampalam, G., Tibble, J.: Abc: an extensible aspectj compiler. In: AOSD 2005: Proceedings of the 4th international conference on Aspect-oriented software development, pp. 87–98. ACM, New York (2005)
9. Pearce, D.J., Webster, M., Berry, R., Kelly, P.H.J.: Profiling with aspectj. Softw. Pract. Exper. 37(7), 747–777 (2007)
10. Dufour, B., Goard, C., Hendren, L., de Moor, O., Sittampalam, G., Verbrugge, C.: Measuring the dynamic behaviour of AspectJ programs. In: OOPSLA 2004: Proceedings of the 19th annual ACM SIGPLAN conference on Object-oriented programming, systems, languages, and applications, pp. 150–169. ACM, New York (2004)

[1,2] School of Information and Communication, Sung Kyun Kwan University,
Suwon 440-746 Korea
tutle7890@skku.edu, tykuc@yurim.skku.ac.kr
[3] Department of Electronic and Telecommunication Engineering,
Kangwon National University
[4] Korea Institute of Industrial Technology, Ansan 1271-18 Korea

Abstract. This paper presents a hierarchical test model and automated test
framework for robot software components of RTC(Robot Technology Component) combined with hardware module. The hierarchical test model consists of
three levels of testing based on V-model : unit test, integration test, and system
test. The automated test framework incorporates four components of test data
generation, test manager, test execution, and test monitoring. The proposed
testing model and its automation framework is proven to be efficient for testing of developed robotic software components in terms of time and cost. The
feasibility and effectiveness of proposed architecture for robot components
testing are illustrated through an application example along with embedded
robotic testbed equipped with range sensor hardware and its software component modeled as an RTC.

Keywords: Robot Software Component Testing, Robot Hardware Testing,
Hierarchical Test Model, Automated Testing System, Robotics.

1 Introduction

As robotic systems are getting more complicated and their application area broaden, the
researches on development and standardization of robotic software platform has been
reported recently. The standardization of robot software platform is aiming at more
efficient customization and manufacturing of robotic products than without. To this end,
the component based development approach has been used for generation of
RTC(Robot Technology Component) and OPRoS(Open Platform for Robotic Ser-

test object and test level defined. Together with the proposed test model, it also provides user interface, test engine, test resource repository, etc. This paper implements a test-bed for testing of the proposed system and verifies its efficacy through a series of experiments.

2 Test Model and Test Framework

2.1 Test Model Structure

Test model is based on RTC, the standard robot software component of OMG. Fig. 1 shows the structure of test model in conformity with RTC and its application example to an ultrasonic range finder sensor.

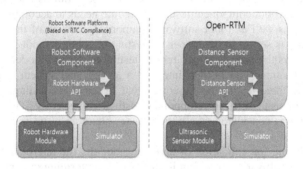

Fig. 1. Test Model Structure(left) and Its Application Example(right)

The overall robot software test system is composed of robot software platform, robot software component, robot hardware API, robot hardware module, and simulator. Robot hardware module is hardware part of robot and simulator is a virtual robot hardware platform which can accommodate robot hardware API in place of robot hardware module. Robot hardware API provides common parts of robot hardware modules in the form of prototype function. The body of robot hardware API is defined as library or DLL in accordance with robot hardware module.

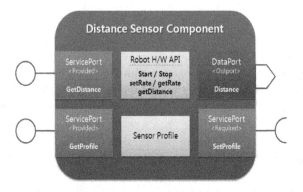

Fig. 2. Robot Software Component Test Model for Range Sensor

2.2 Outline of Hierarchical Testing Procedure

Since robot software component operates tightly coupled with its corresponding robot hardware module, robot component testing procedure needs to accommodate hardware and its interface as well as robot software component. In view of this, a hierarchical testing procedure is set up in this paper for testing of robot component conformed to RTC. Fig. 3 shows the proposed hierarchical testing procedure model which includes three levels of testing : unit testing, integration testing, and system testing for robot component. The three testing levels correspond to hardware testing, hardware API testing, and composite software component testing, respectively. That is, in Fig. 3, hardware module is considered as a basic unit for hierarchical testing of robotic software component.

After unit testing for validation of hardware module, the interoperability of hardware module and software component is checked by performing integration testing. In

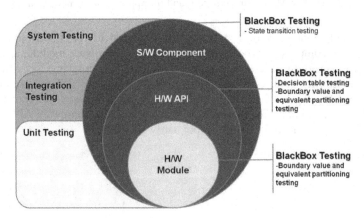

(compatibility of document, exactness of state transition, correctness of data), maintenance(comprehensibility of cause of defect), portability(functional alternativeness), etc. The testing techniques of boundary value analysis, equal partitioning testing, state transition testing, etc. are used for system testing of robot software component.

2.3 Testing Automation Framework

Although robotic software testing is crucial for development and application of standard robotic software platform and its components, lack of manpower and resources and insufficient time induces difficulty in provision of systematic testing process during robotic software development and application. In order to reduce time and cost for testing of robotic software, it is important to develop standard test model and automatic testing framework which provides systematic testing procedure.

To this end, a testing automation framework is designed for testing of robotic software component based on the hierarchical test model presented in the previous subsection. Fig. 4 shows the proposed testing framework consisting of user interface, test engine, and test resource repository. User interface implements three levels of testing hierarchy : robot hardware module test UI for document and performance test, API test UI for interface test, and robot software component UI for functional test. Test engine includes test manager, test data generation unit, test execution unit, and test monitoring unit. Test resource repository provides materials necessary for execution of test process to test engine such as test code, test plan, test case, metrics of performance measurement, etc. It is also illustrated in Fig. 4 that test engine can operate linked with robot hardware testbed or robotic simulator provided.

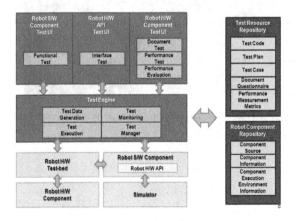

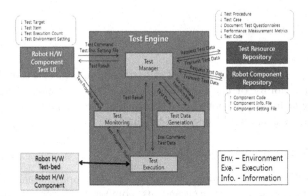

Fig. 5. Operation Flow of Test Engine

2.4 An Application Example

The proposed test model and its test framework are applied for testing of range sensor component mounted on a robot hardware testbed. Fig. 6 shows the details of test environment operating coupled with the test framework in Fig. 7.

Fig. 6. Testbed for Evaluation of Range Sensor Component

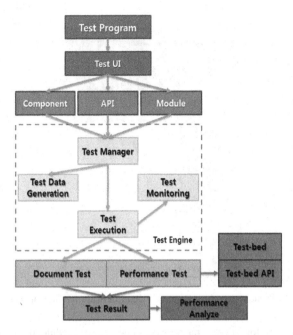

Fig. 7. Block Diagram of Overall Testing System

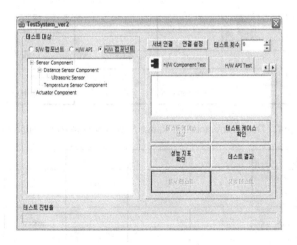

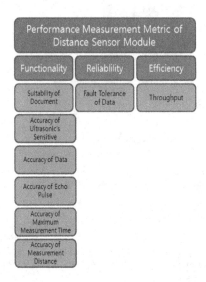

Fig. 9. Performance Indices for Evaluation of Range Sensor Module

Table 1. The Test Case for Data Correctness of Range Sensor Module by Equivalent Division Method

test case	1	2	3
distance value	2	150	400
range	distance < 3	3 <=distance<= 300	distance > 300
expected result	Timeout (unmeasurable)	distance value	Timeout (unmeasurable)

Table 2. Test Case for Data Correctness of Range Sensor Module by Boundary Value Method

test case	1	2	3	4
distance value	2	3	300	301
expected	Timeout	distance value	distance value	Timeout

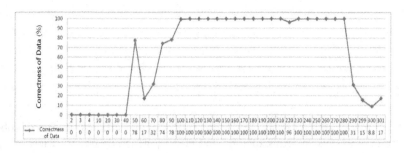

Fig. 10. Correctness of Data for Ultrasonic Sensor Module(SRF-04)

	2	3	4	10	20	30	40	50	60	70	80	90	100	110	120	130	140	150	160	170	180	190	200	210	220	230	240	250	260	270	280	290	299	300	301
Correctness of Data	0	0	0	0	0	0	0	78	17	32	74	78	100	100	100	100	100	100	100	100	100	100	100	96	100	100	100	100	100	100	100	31	15	8.8	17

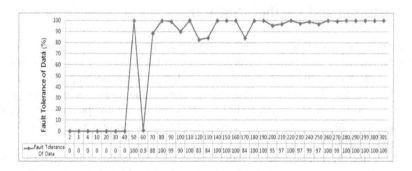

Fig. 11. Fault Tolerance of Data for Ultrasonic Sensor Module(SRF-04)

	2	3	4	10	20	30	40	50	60	70	80	90	100	110	120	130	140	150	160	170	180	190	200	210	220	230	240	250	260	270	280	290	299	300	301
Fault Tolerance Of Data	0	0	0	0	0	0	0	100	0.9	88	100	99	90	100	83	84	100	100	100	84	100	100	95	97	100	97	99	97	100	99	100	100	100	100	100

The ultrasonic sensor module used in the experiment covers a wide range of 3cm ~ 300cm. Fig. 9 plots the analyzed data correctness of ultrasonic sensor based on experiment result. In the figure, data correctness was defined as equation (1).

$$Data\ Correctness = \frac{number\ of\ test\ success}{number\ of\ trials} \times 100 \tag{1}$$

Where test success means the case that its measurement value remains within normalized error bound.

In the graph, it is found that the ultrasonic sensor SRF-04 module operates correctly in the range 100~280 cm. On the other hand, data correctness decreases notably at the distance less than 80cm or larger than 290cm. The experiment results show that performance of ultrasonic sensor module SRF-04 does not agree with the product specification for operation range of 3cm~300cm.

Fig. 10 plots fault tolerance rate of ultrasonic sensor tested. In the figure, fault tolerance is defined as the % rate of data within permissible error bound among data

chical test model and automatic test framework supports efficient testing of robotic software components in terms of time and cost by generating various test cases in systematic way.

3 Conclusion and Further Research

As personal robot system and robotic apparatus spread fast in various fields, the higher functionality and better performance are in great demand nowadays. In addition, the guaranteed reliability of interactive robot is of special importance in user's real life, since its defects might cause fatal damage to man and economic loss. In this respect, the performance and safety test of robotic software component together with robot hardware module is crucial for stable robotic interaction with human and its working environment.

Considering the importance of robotic software validation, a hierarchical testing model and its testing automation framework are developed for RTC compatible robotic software components. The effectiveness of proposed testing model is demonstrated through a series of real experiments for an embedded robotic testbed equipped with ultrasonic sensor module as range finder. Experiment results show that the proposed hierarchical testing model and testing automation framework provide an efficient way of robotic software testing in terms of time and cost. It is expected that the developed testing model and its automation framework is applicable to various standard robotic software components in real life as well as in development stage.

Acknowledgments. This work was supported by Knowledge and Economics Department of Korea Government through OPRoS project for development of standard robotic software platform.

References

1. OMG, The Robotic Technology Component Specification (2007)
2. OPRoS, Open Platform for Robotic Services Specification (2008)

13. Jervan, G., Eles, P., Peng, Z.: A Hierarchical Test Generation Technique for Embedded Systems. In: Proc. Electronic Circuits and Systems Conference, pp. 21–24 (1999)
14. Baek, C., Jang, J., Jung, G., Choi, K., Park, S.: A Case Study of Black-Box Testing for Embedded Software using Test Automation Tool. Journal of Computer Science, 144–148 (2007)
15. ISO/IEC TR 9126, Software Engineering-Product Quality-Part 1,2,3,4 (2005)

Iran University of Science and Technology, Tehran, Iran
parsa@iust.ac.ir, khalilian@comp.iust.ac.ir

Abstract. *Regression testing* is a critical activity which occurs during the maintenance stage of the software lifecycle. However, it requires large amounts of test cases to assure the attainment of a certain degree of quality. As a result, test suite sizes may grow significantly. To address this issue, *Test Suite Reduction* techniques have been proposed. However, suite size reduction may lead to significant loss of fault detection efficacy. To deal with this problem, a greedy algorithm is presented in this paper. This algorithm attempts to select a test case which satisfies the maximum number of testing requirements while having minimum overlap in requirements coverage with other test cases. In order to evaluate the proposed algorithm, experiments have been conducted on the *Siemens suite* and the *Space program*. The results demonstrate the effectiveness of the proposed algorithm by retaining the fault detection capability of the suites while achieving significant suite size reduction.

Keywords: Software regression testing, testing criteria, test suite minimization, test suite reduction, fault detection effectiveness.

1 Introduction

Software regression testing is a critical activity in the maintenance phase of evolving software. However, it requires large amounts of test cases to test any new or modified functionality within the program [1]. Re-running all existing test cases together with the new ones is often costly and even infeasible due to time and resource constraints. To address this problem, the research community proposed techniques to optimize regression testing [2], [3], [4], [5], [6], [7], [8]. Re-running test cases that do not exercise any changed or affected parts of the program makes extra cost and gives no benefit. An effective technique is to permanently discard such redundant or obsolete test cases and retain the most effective ones to reduce the excessive cost of regression

of requirements coverage. The proposed algorithm has two main features: First, it achieves significant suite size reduction and improves their fault detection effectiveness compared to other approaches. Second, the reduction process is based on the information of each program which can be obtained easily and accurately. In order to evaluate the applicability of the proposed approach, we conducted experiments on the *Siemens* suite and the *Space* program. We also implemented the well-known H algorithm [3], to compare the results of our algorithm with those of *minimizing* test suites using the H algorithm.

The rest of the paper is organized as follows: Section 2 discusses the background of the test suite reduction techniques. Section 3 contains the outline of the proposed approach. Section 4 describes the empirical studies and the obtained results. Finally, conclusions are mentioned in section 5.

2 Background and Related Work

The first formal definition of test suite reduction problem introduced in 1993 by Harrold et al. [3] as follows: Given a test suite T, $\{t_1, t_2,..., t_m\}$, from m test cases and $\{r_1, r_2,..., r_n\}$ is set of test requirements that must be satisfied in order to provide desirable coverage of the program entities and each subsets $\{T_1, T_2,..., T_n\}$ from T are related to one of r_is such that each test case t_j belonging to T_i satisfies r_i, find minimal test suite T' from T which satisfies all r_is covered by original suite T.

Generally the problem of finding the minimal subset T', $T' \subseteq T$ which satisfies all requirements of T, is NP-complete [10], because we can reduce the *minimum set-cover* problem to the problem of test suite minimization in polynomial time. Thus, researches use heuristic approaches to solve this problem. One heuristic method proposed by Harrold et al. [3], tries to find the smallest representative set that provides the same coverage as the entire test suite does.

Related work in the context of test suite reduction can be classified into two main categories: The works in which a new technique is presented [3], [4], [5], [6], [7], [9], [11] and empirical studies on the previous techniques [1], [2], [10], [12]. The works which propose a new approach commonly include heuristic algorithms [11], genetic algorithm-based techniques [13] and approaches based on integer linear programming [14]. In a recent study [10], four typical test suite reduction techniques have been

appropriate test suite reduction technique should select test cases that are both unique in exercising execution paths and effective in fault detection. The first objective attempts to remove as much redundancy from the test suite, and the second one seeks for satisfying the main purpose of software testing which is fault detection.

The proposed approach to test suite reduction uses test case-requirement matrix. This matrix shows the mappings between test cases and testing requirements. The elements consist of 1's and 0's which indicate for satisfying or dissatisfying the requirements by test cases respectively. The general idea of the proposed algorithm is as follows: At first the test case-requirement matrix is multiplied by its transposed matrix. The resultant is a square matrix of size $n * n$, such that n is the number of test cases. Each diagonal element of this matrix shows the number of unmarked requirements covered by the corresponding test case. Each non-diagonal element in the ith row and the jth column shows the number of requirements coverage in which the ith and the jth test cases overlap. Then, the algorithm *greedily* selects an optimum test case until a same coverage of testing requirements is achieved. A test case is optimum which satisfies the maximum number of unmarked requirements (the maximum diagonal element) and simultaneously having the minimum overlap in requirements coverage with other test cases (the minimum value obtained by adding the all non-diagonal elements at the corresponding row). We call our algorithm *Bi-Objective Greedy* (*BOG*). The pseudocode description of the proposed algorithm is shown in the Fig. 1. The inputs of this algorithm is a test suite with m test cases, a set of n testing requirements and also the $m*n$ test case-requirement matrix. Besides, two arrays of Boolean values namely *marked* and *selected* are considered. The first array keeps the cumulative requirements coverage of the reduced test suite. The second one keeps the selection of test cases. The proposed algorithm consists of three main steps and a helper function which is described in the following.

Step 1: In this step, the test case-requirement matrix is multiplied by its transposed matrix and is kept in a matrix called *multiplied*. Using this matrix, a vector called *sumColumns* will be computed which will indicate the number of requirements coverage overlap of a test case with others.

Step 2: In this step, the algorithm repeatedly selects an optimum test case until all testing requirements are satisfied. In each of its iteration, first the test cases with the maximum diagonal values from *multiplied* matrix are selected into the *maxList*. Also,

STEP 1:	$multiplied$:= multiplication of the $cv[m,n] * cv^{T}[n,m]$; // initialization
	foreach t_i **do** compute $sumColumns[i]$, sum of the elements in the ith row
	of the $multiplied$ matrix, except for the diagonal element;

STEP 2:   **while** there exists r_i such that $marked[i] ==$ **FALSE do**

           $maxList$:= all t_i for which the $selected[i] ==$ **FALSE** and

                $multiplied[i,i]$ is the maximum;

           $minList$:= all t_i for which the $selected[i] ==$ **FALSE** and

                $sumColumns[i]$ is the minimum;

           $interSection$:= $maxList \cap minList$;

           if Card($interSection$) $== 0$ **then**

                $nextTest$:= SelectOptimumTestCase($maxList$, $minList$,

                                $multiplied$, $sumColumns$);

           else if Card($interSection$) $== 1$ **then**

                $nextTest$:= the test case in the $interSection$;

           else

                $nextTest$:= any test case in the $interSection$;

           endif

STEP 3: RS := $RS \cup \{nextTest\}$;

           $selected[nextTest]$:= **TRUE**;

           $multiplied[nextTest,nextTest]$:= 0;

           foreach $r_j \in$ requirements where $cv[nextTest,r_j] ==$ **TRUE do**

                $marked[i]$:= **TRUE**;

           foreach t_i for which the $selected[i] ==$ **FALSE** and

                $multiplied[nextTest,t_i] > 0$ **do**

                $multiplied[t_i,t_i]$:= the number of unmarked requirements

                        covered by the t_i;

                if $multiplied[t_i,t_i] == 0$ **then**

                    $selected[t_i]$:= **TRUE**;

           endfor

        endwhile

        return RS;

end TestSuiteReduction

Fig. 1. The pseudocode description of the proposed algorithm

If during the update process, the value of an element becomes zero, it is redundant

```
minMin := the value of the sumColumns[tᵢ] for one of the tᵢ in the minList;
minListDistance := maxMax − maxMin;
maxListDistance := minMax − minMin;
if minListDistance < maxListDistance then
    testCase := the tᵢ from the minList for which multiplied[tᵢ] == maxMin;
else
    testCase := the tᵢ from the maxList for which sumColumns[tᵢ] == minMax;
endif
return testCase;
end SelectOptimumTestCase
```

Fig. 2. A helper function to select a near optimal test case from two sets of test cases

An optimum test case in the *maxList* should have the minimum respective element in the vector *sumColumns*. Oppositely, an optimum test case in the *minList* should have the maximum respective diagonal element in the *multiplied* matrix. Then, either of the two optimum test cases is selected as the near optimal test case based on which has the less distance. The distance of the optimum test case in *maxList* is the difference of its respective element in the *sumColumns* with the respective element of *sumColumns* for an arbitrary test case in *minList*. The distance of the optimum test case in *minList* is the difference of its respective diagonal element in the *multiplied* matrix with the respective diagonal element of *multiplied* for an arbitrary test case in *maxList*.

4 Empirical Studies

Our studies have been conducted on the eight C programs as subjects. *Siemens* suite includes seven programs developed by the researchers at Siemens Corporation [15]. These programs are associated with several faulty versions. Each faulty version of each program contains a single fault seeded in it. The eighth subject is the *Space* program which is a real one [5]. To investigate the effectiveness of our approach, we implemented the bi-objective greedy algorithm. Moreover, the *H* algorithm [3] has been implemented to compare the results of this approach with those of the proposed approach, since it is reported [10] as the best choice among current reduction techniques. We measured the following from the experiments:

visualize the empirical results in test suite reduction studies. Our experiments follow a setup similar to that used by Rothermel et al. [2]. For each program, we created branch coverage adequate test suites for six different suite ranges named as B, B1, B2, B3, B4 and B5. For each suite range, we first selected $X * LOC$ test cases randomly from the test pool and added to the test suite, where X is 0, 0.1, 0.2, 0.3, 0.4 and 0.5 respectively and LOC is the number of lines of code for each program. Then, randomly-selected test cases are added into the test suite as necessary so long as each test case increased the cumulative branch coverage of the suite, until the test suite becomes adequate with respect to branch coverage. In this way, the developed test suites have various types and varying levels of redundancy exist among them. For each program, we created 1000 such branch coverage adequate test suites in each suite size range. In order to gather branch coverage information of test cases, all programs were hand-instrumented.

Both the H algorithm and the BOG algorithm were applied to the generated suites with respect to branch coverage as testing criterion. The results of this experiment are shown in the box plot in the Fig. 3. It shows the distribution of the percentage of size reduction (SR) and percentage fault detection loss (FL) in the largest suite size range (B5) for each program (due to limitation of the space). In this figure, boxes are paired such that, white pair of boxes shows percentage of size reduction and gray pair of boxes shows the percentage of fault detection loss. In each pair, left side box indicates for our algorithm and the right side one indicates for the H algorithm.

Suite Size Reduction: Fig. 3 shows that the average suite size reduction is high for all programs. The results also show that both the H algorithm and the BOG algorithm could reduce the suites to the same extent. This indicates the effectiveness of the proposed algorithm in determining redundant test cases. Moreover, suite size reduction increases for larger suites. The reason is that the high number of test cases provides more opportunities for the algorithm to select among test cases.

Fault Detection Loss: The results show that the average fault detection loss has been improved except for *schedule2*. In addition, the amount of fault loss for the *tcas* and *schedule2* is relatively high among other programs. For the *tcas* program, this may be due to simplicity of this program. Many of the test cases satisfy the same branches and will be removed since they are redundant. But these test cases exercise unique execution paths with respect to some other testing criteria. Hence, using different or

Table 1. z values and the corresponding percentage of confidence

Program Name	Computed z value	Percentage of confidence for rejecting the null hypothesis
printtokens	1.56	>88%
printtokens2	-1.29	>80%
replace	2.89	>99.5%
schedule	2.56	>98.9%
schedule2	0.15	<50%
space	5.71	>99.99%
tcas	1.50	>86.6%
totinfo	8.84	>99.99%

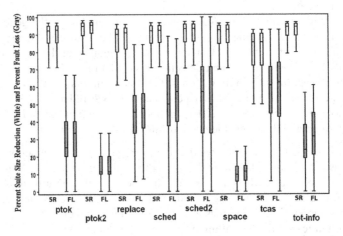

Fig. 3. The boxplot for the percentage suite size reduction and percentage fault detection loss

The fault loss for the *Siemens* programs is still high in this study as well as prior studies. The reason is that test cases in the test pools are generated to exercise various while box and black box requirements which are not considered during reduction. Thus, removing those test cases may result in significant fault loss. The major benefit of the *BOG* algorithm is to decrease the extent of fault loss as compared to the *H*

References

1. Rothermel, G., Harrold, M.J., von Ronne, J., Hong, C.: Empirical Studies of Test-Suite Reduction. Journal of Software Testing, Verification, and Reliability 12(4), 219–249 (2002)
2. Rothermel, G., Harrold, M.J., Ostrin, J., Hong, C.: An Empirical Study of the Effects of Minimization on the Fault Detection Capabilities of Test Suites. In: Proceedings of the International Conference on Software Maintenance. IEEE Computer Society, Los Alamitos (1998)
3. Harrold, M.J., Gupta, R., Soffa, M.L.: A methodology for controlling the size of a test suite. ACM Trans. Softw. Eng. Methodol. 2, 270–285 (1993)
4. Chen, T.Y., Lau, M.F.: Heuristics toward the Optimization of the Size of a Test Suite. In: Proc. 3rd Int'l. Conf. on Softw. Quality Management, Seville, Spain, April 1995, vol. 2, pp. 415–424 (1995)
5. Jones, J.A., Harrold, M.J.: Test-Suite Reduction and Prioritization for Modified Condition/Decision Coverage. IEEE Trans. Softw. Eng. 29, 195–209 (2003)
6. McMaster, S., Memon, A.: Call-Stack Coverage for GUI Test Suite Reduction. IEEE Trans. Softw. Eng. 34, 99–115 (2008)
7. Tallam, S., Gupta, N.: A concept analysis inspired greedy algorithm for test suite minimization. In: Proceedings of the 6th ACM SIGPLAN-SIGSOFT workshop on Program analysis for software tools and engineering. ACM, Lisbon (2005)
8. Leon, D., Podgurski, A.: A Comparison of Coverage-Based and Distribution-Based Techniques for Filtering and Prioritizing Test Cases. In: Proceedings of the 14th International Symposium on Software Reliability Engineering. IEEE Computer Society, Los Alamitos (2003)
9. Chen, Z., Xu, B., Zhang, X., Nie, C.: A novel approach for test suite reduction based on requirement relation contraction. In: Proceedings of the 2008 ACM symposium on applied computing. ACM, Fortaleza (2008)
10. Zhong, H., Zhang, L., Mei, H.: An experimental study of four typical test suite reduction techniques. Inf. Softw. Technol. 50, 534–546 (2008)
11. Chen, T.Y., Lau, M.: A new heuristic for test suite reduction. Information and Software Technology 40(5-6) (1998)
12. Wong, W.E., Horgan, J.R., London, S., Mathur, A.P.: Effect of test set minimization on fault detection effectiveness. Softw. Pract. Exper. 28, 347–369 (1998)
13. Mansour, N., El-Fakih, K.: Simulated annealing and genetic algorithms for optimal regression testing. Journal of Software Maintenance 11, 19–34 (1999)
14. Black, J., Melachrinoudis, E., Kaeli, D.: Bi-Criteria Models for All-Uses Test Suite Re-

{mlbernar,dilucca}@unisannio.it

Abstract. In Object Oriented (OO) systems super-imposition is a way to implement crosscutting concerns that introduce scattering and tangling of code components among the Types implemented along Type Hierarchies. This paper presents the results of the analysis of a set of existing Java systems to confirm and verify this assumption. The analysis was carried out exploiting a method to automatically analyse and identify the Type Fragments implementing static crosscutting concerns in OO systems.

Keywords: Reverse Engineering, Aspect Mining, Code Analysis, Aspect Oriented Programming, Software Evolution, MOF.

1   Introduction

In Object Oriented (OO) systems, the usage of Types Hierarchies (and mainly the ones rooted in Abstract Classes or Interfaces) is a main cause introducing scattering and tangling in the modules implementing a Type along the hierarchy. As an example, a method declared by an Interface (i.e., a Type root of a hierarchy) and implemented by more than one class will have its behaviour scattered in all the classes implementing it and tangled with the behaviour of the other methods implemented in each class along the hierarchy. A main reason for that is that usually inheritance, interfaces' implementations and type nesting, are used as a way to implement crosscutting behaviours (i.e., concerns) by super-imposition [11]: each type in the system that need to contribute to a certain concern is forced to implement an interface, to inherit or to contain another type. This is because in OO systems just hierarchical decomposition is allowed as modularization mechanism.

To confirm and verify this assumption a set of existing Java systems have been analysed. This paper presents the results of this analysis together with the method used to identify the crosscutting among the concerns introduced by Type Hierarchies. The method allows to identify the Types Fragments (i.e., a

y   g   g/   g ca   be perf
this paper and it is not dealt with. Our focus is just to verify that Types in Hierarchies are seeds for crosscutting concerns and thus they can be considered as a starting point to mine aspects in existing systems.

The paper is structured as follows. Section 2 describes the meta-model exploited to represent concerns at class level. Section 3 presents the approach to identify the crosscutting concerns due to Seeds in a Java system. Section 4 illustrates the results of the analysis carried out on several Java systems. In Section 5 some relevant related works are discussed. Section 6 contains conclusive remarks and briefly discusses future work.

2   A Model to Represent the Relationships among Types and Concerns in OO Systems

The Figure 1 shows, as a UML class diagram, the model defined in [1] exploited to represent the static structure of an OO system in terms of its Concerns, Types, and the relationships among such Concerns with the portion of Types implementing them. Since the focus is on the static crosscutting, the grain of model is the class, i.e. a method is seen as a whole black-box (just its declaration

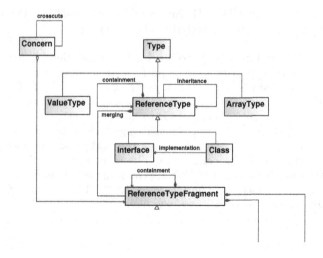

Type ragme   mp   y Fi
is represented by mean of a set of Reference Type Fragments (in the paper, for brevity, we refer to them also as Type Fragments or just Fragments). A ReferenceType can inherit from another ReferenceType as well as can contain another ReferenceType (e.g. an inner class). In model instances, relationships on types are mapped to the Type Fragments associated to one of the concerns. The meta-model has been defined as a MOF model and implemented by means of the EMF (Eclipse Modeling Framework) framework. In model instances, each Type Fragment is identified by the fully qualified name of the code component implementing it (e.g., the fully qualified name of a class method).

The model allows to represent different concerns separately depicting the complete system as the composition of all the concerns. The crosscutting relationships among the concerns can be identified by analysing their internal structure in terms of the Type Fragments associated to each concern: concerns whose fragments generate tangling and scattering are considered as crosscutting. A merge operation has been defined on the model to join concerns into a more abstract one. The merge of two concerns C_x and C_y creates a new concern C_z in place of C_x and C_y by merging their type fragments.

3 Type Hierarchy Analysis to Identify Concerns

The analysis of the system's Type Hierarchy exploits the method defined in [1], whose main steps are shortly illustrated in the following;

1) Analysis of Type Hierarchy to find Concerns' Seeds. A static code analysis of the system Type Hierarchy is performed, looking at inheritance, implementation and containment relationships. In particular any Reference Type that introduces, in all paths from a root to a leaf of the type hierarchy graph, the declaration of a new set of members is to be identified.

The Figure 2-(a) shows an example consisting of three hierarchies rooted in the Interfaces "I1", "I2" and "I3". Following the paths from the roots down to leaves, all the Types are to be considered. The three root Interfaces introduce basic behaviour (i.e. methods) for their abstractions and hence are considered Seeds of as many as Concerns. The Classes C1,C2,C3,C4,C5, and C6 are not seeds since they doesn't introduce any new member

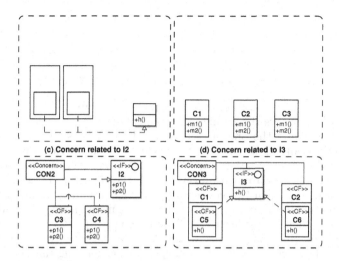

Fig. 2. A simple Type Hierarchy, the detected Concerns' Seeds and the Type Fragments composing the Concerns

made regardless of any semantic meaning about them. Just the structural information, extracted by the traversal of the type hierarchy, is exploited. At the end of the traversal, each concern will be associated to the Fragments of all Types that implement the corresponding single Seed.

The traversal of the hierarchy type graph starts from the leaves and goes up to the roots. Each type t encountered during the traversal is analysed to detect what seeds it implements. For each seed r, implemented by t, a type fragment tf is created and added to the concern c associated to the seed r.

The sub-figures 2-(b), 2-(c), and 2-(d) show the results of the traversal on the example of Figure 2-(a) for the three Concerns associated to the Seeds "I1", "I2" and "I3". In the figure the UML stereo-types "IF" and "CF" are, respectively, for "Interface Fragment" and "Class Fragment". For each Seed, starting from the leaves, the Fragments are created for each method that is substitutable with the considered seed. For example, from the classes "C1" and "C2" result the two fragments "C1" and "C2" including just the implementation of the methods declared by the seeds "I1" and "I3".

3) Clustering of Concerns. The resulting model instance contains a Concern for each identified Seed. This model may be too detailed because the identified Concerns are strictly connected to their implementation and the richness of detail ld "hide" the m re abstract actual C . Whe thi is the case

g a   g g at fragme   1,   up
trix value F_{ij} represents the number of fragments that are tangled between the
Concern in row i and the one in column j. The matrix is symmetrical as the
definition of crosscutting we consider (equivalent to that provided by Kiczales [7]
and its equivalent formalization provided by Ostermann [8]). Given such definition, scattered concerns are, within our model, the concerns containing at least
two type fragments. Then two concerns C_x and C_y are crosscutting if and only
if: (i) they both contain more than one Type Fragment (hence generating scattering) and (ii) there are at least two Type Fragments $f \in C_x$ and $g \in C_y$, with
the same fully qualified name (this means that the two concerns are introducing
members or relationships on the same Type, thus generating tangling).

In order to support the process, a prototype tool called "Concern Analyser"
(ConAN) was developed, on top of the Eclipse platform [2].

4   Case Study

Several open source java software systems were analysed to verify and validate
the assumption that Type Hierarchies are one of the cause of the introduction of
crossscutting concerns, and the effectiveness of the method to identify the seeds
and the Type Fragments involved in the concerns implementation. The Table 1
reports the list of the largest analysed systems. For each system, it is provided
the name, the version number, the LOC size, the number of Types (classes and
interfaces), the number of methods implemented in the system, the number of
the identified seeds (distiguishing between Class and Interface seeds), the total
number of fragments in the concern meta-model instance, and the number of the
Concerns resulting after the seeds' clustering step.

The table 1 highlights that, in all the systems, all the Interfaces were found
to be actually Seeds of Concerns while just few classes (with respect to the
total number of classes) were found as Seeds. This indicate us that interfaces
are more prone to be associated to Concern (as we expected, being them root

Table 1. Summary of the analyzed systems

Concern	#Seeds	Fragments #C	#I	#Valid Seeds
MindMap Model Actions	50	102	59	50
Types	43	167	92	44
Event Handling	11	265	8	11
Utils	11	14	8	8
MindMap GUI Action Menus	10	11	10	10
Hooks	7	29	5	5
Windows Configuration Storages	6	8	7	6
Edges	5	8	5	5
Persistence	4	123	3	4
Adaptability	4	35	0	4
MindMap Registry	4	1	4	5
Action Entities	2	34	2	2
Elements Linking	2	4	2	2
MindMap GUI Actions	2	4	2	2
Unmarshallable Entities	1	121	1	1
Action Validation	1	121	1	1
XML Representable Actions	1	12	1	1
Views	1	8	0	2
Mode Control	1	5	1	1
MindMap	1	5	1	1
Modes Handling	1	4	1	1
XML Elements	1	4	0	1
MindMap Node	1	3	1	1
Action Filtering	1	2	1	1
System Entry Points	1	2	1	1
MindMap Clouds	1	2	1	1
Undo Redo	1	2	0	1
Node Creation	1	1	1	1
Single Node Operations	1	1	1	1

Concern	#Seeds	Fragments #C	#I	#Valid Seeds
Figures	14	34	5	14
Tooling	9	33	1	9
EventHandling	7	27	10	8
EntitiesHandles	5	15	1	5
Editors	4	11	1	3
ContentProducers	4	4	0	4
UndoRedo	3	42	1	2
Views	3	12	1	3
EntitiesHolders	3	8	3	3
Connectors	3	8	1	3
Commands	2	15	1	2
EntityEnumerations	2	6	2	2
Layouting	2	4	2	2
Desktop	2	5	1	2
Animation	2	3	2	1
StorageFormats	2	3	1	2
DrawableElements	2	2	1	2
Palette Buttons	2	2	0	2
Persistence	1	41	11	1
Painting	1	7	1	1
VersionRequester	1	2	1	1
FigureTraversing	1	2	1	1
FigureHelpers	1	3	0	1
Factories	1	3	0	1
Constrainers	1	1	1	1
DragNDrop	1	1	1	1
DrawApplication	1	2	0	1
Strategies	1	1	1	1
ResourceManager	1	1	1	1
Locators	1	1	0	1

	0	1	2	3	4	5	6	7	8	9	10	11	12	13	14	15	16	17	18	19	20	21	22	23	24	25	Number of Fragment
0 Action Entities	*	0	0	0	0	6	0	0	0	0	0	0	13	0	0	0	0	0	0	0	0	0	0	0	0	19	36
1 Action Filtering	0	*	0	0	0	0	1	1	0	0	0	0	1	0	0	0	0	0	0	0	0	0	0	0	0	0	3
2 Action Validation	0	0	*	0	0	0	121	0	0	0	10	0	0	83	0	0	0	122	0	0	0	7	0	0	0	0	122
3 Adaptability	0	0	0	*	5	2	2	5	1	0	3	0	0	2	5	0	0	0	0	0	0	0	0	3	0	0	35
4 Edges	0	0	0	0	*	6	1	0	2	0	0	0	0	0	0	0	0	0	0	0	0	0	0	0	0	0	13
5 Elements Linking	0	0	0	2	6	*	0	0	0	0	0	0	0	0	0	0	6	0	0	0	0	0	0	0	0	0	6
6 Event Handling	6	1	121	2	1	0	*	7	0	0	11	1	0	89	0	1	0	121	0	167	121	3	0	8	0	3	273
7 Hooks Registration	0	1	0	2	0	7	*	0	0	0	0	0	0	0	0	0	1	0	0	0	0	0	0	0	0	0	34
8 MindMap	0	0	0	5	0	0	0	*	0	0	0	0	0	0	0	0	0	0	0	0	0	0	0	0	0	0	6
9 MindMap Clouds	0	0	0	1	2	0	0	0	*	0	0	0	0	0	0	0	0	0	0	0	0	0	0	0	0	0	3
10 MindMap GUI Action Menus	0	0	10	0	0	11	0	0	0	0	*	0	0	0	0	10	0	10	10	0	0	0	0	0	0	0	21
11 MindMap GUI Actions	0	0	0	3	0	0	1	0	0	0	0	*	0	0	4	0	0	0	0	0	0	0	0	0	0	0	6
12 MindMap Link Registry	0	0	0	0	0	0	0	0	0	0	0	0	*	0	0	0	0	0	0	0	0	0	0	0	0	0	5
13 MindMap Model Actions	13	0	83	0	0	89	0	0	0	0	0	0	0	*	0	0	0	93	0	118	83	2	0	7	0	12	161
14 MindMap Node	0	0	0	2	0	0	0	0	0	0	0	0	0	0	*	0	0	0	0	0	0	0	0	0	0	0	4
15 Mode Control	0	0	0	5	0	0	1	0	0	0	4	0	0	0	0	*	0	0	0	0	0	0	0	0	0	0	6
16 Modes Handling	0	0	0	0	0	0	0	0	0	0	0	0	0	0	0	0	*	0	0	0	0	0	0	0	0	0	5
17 Persistence	0	0	122	0	0	121	0	0	0	10	0	0	0	83	0	0	0	*	0	108	121	2	0	7	0	0	126
18 System Entry Points	0	0	0	0	0	0	0	0	0	0	0	0	0	0	0	0	0	0	*	0	0	0	0	0	0	0	3
19 Types	0	0	108	0	0	167	0	0	10	0	0	110	0	0	108	0	0	108	0	*	100	1	0	6	0	0	259
20 Unmarshallable Entities	0	0	121	0	0	121	0	0	18	0	0	63	0	0	121	0	108	0	0	121	*	2	0	7	0	0	122
21 Utils	0	0	2	0	0	3	1	0	6	0	1	2	0	0	2	0	1	2	*	4	0	0	0	0	0	0	22
22 Views	0	0	0	0	0	0	0	0	0	0	0	0	0	0	0	0	0	0	0	0	0	*	0	0	0	0	8
23 Windows Configuration Storages	0	0	7	0	0	8	0	0	0	0	0	7	0	0	7	0	6	7	4	0	*	0	0	0	0	0	15
24 XML Elements	0	0	0	3	0	0	0	0	0	0	0	0	0	0	0	0	0	0	0	0	0	0	0	*	0	0	4
25 XML Representable Actions	13	0	0	0	0	3	0	0	0	0	0	0	12	0	0	0	0	0	0	0	0	0	0	0	0	*	13

Fig. 3. Crosscutting Matrix of the FreeMind System

"Types   argest c   y   g a g
rithm. The former concern implemented all the kind of actions that users can
perform in the system while the latter was devoted to the definition of all types
of mind-map nodes.

The Figure 3 reports the Crosscutting matrix. The matrix allows to make an
evaluation of the degree of crosscutting of each concern with respect to the number of tangled and scattered fragments. For instance, the "Event Handling" concern is crosscutting with 16 other concerns (of the 29 total) and has a very high
number of fragments tangled with many of these concerns (121 fragments with
"Action Validation", 121 with "Persistence" and 167 with "Types"). The same
holds for concerns like "Unmarshallable Entities" and the "MindMap Model
Actions". These concerns would be the most critical ones in re-engineering or
migration approaches, requiring an effort to migrate them into aspects greater
than the one for concerns with lower values in the table. A validation to assess
the quality of the results was done performing the identification of seeds and fragments and all the other method's activities "by hand" by an expert (i.e., the "gold
standard"). In some cases the automatic clustering step grouped together concerns that were clustered in a different way by the manual analysis, producing
a different set of concerns or some difference in the concerns' composition. For
FreeMind, the last column of Table 2 highlights the clusters of seeds that differs
from those identified by the expert. One of the major difference was reported
for the Hooks concern. The clustering algorithm clustered together the concerns
Hooks (made up of 5 class Seeds) and Hooks Registration (made up of 1 interface seed and 1 abstract class seed) into a single concern named "Hooks". The
manual clustering, considered them as separate concerns introducing a separate
concern for "Hooks Registration" (not shown in the table). This however had a
little impact on the model since the introduced concern was only 2 fragments
in size. Other differences from the expert choices were related to some types
wrongly clustered in the Utils concern, because of suffixes closer to other seeds
in Utils. This was for 1 seed in Types (TimeWindowConfigurationStorageType),
1 seed in MindMap Registry (MindMapLinkRegistry seed) and 1 seed in Views
(EdgeView). In this case the changes in terms of number of fragments were very
small for the first two cases (3 fragments from Utils passed to Types and 2 to
MindMap Registry) while more relevant for the EdgeView seed (12 fragments
passed from Utils to View). Summarizing, we note that we had 8 seeds wrongly
clustered, on 176 (less than 5%), and the addition of 1 concern on a total of

5   Related Work

Marin et. al., in [4], propose a technique that combines together a metric based approach [6], a token-based one (exploiting identifier lexical analysis), and the dynamic based approach proposed in [10].

The approach proposed in [11] by Tonella and Ceccato focuses on crosscutting concerns produced by the scattered implementation of methods declared by interfaces that do not belong to the principal decomposition. Such interfaces, called "aspectizable" are identified and automatically migrated to aspects. This work shares with our approach the considerations that in OO systems, the interfaces can be used to model both main abstraction and secondary properties (i.e. they are Seeds for concerns). The main difference between the two approaches is the kind of elements analysed and the main goals.

An approach to model concerns in source code that influenced the definition of our model was proposed in [9]. Our model is much more dependent on language constructs of object-oriented single inheritance languages than the approach proposed in [9]. While this can restrict the range of applicability of our model it allows to reason about the complete structure of the system.

6   Conclusions and Future Work

The hypothesis that Type Hierarchies are one of the cause allowing the introduction of seeds for concerns that are crosscutting was verified to be valid. The method used to identify the Seeds, the Type Fragments composing the Concerns and their clustering into more general system's concerns has been verified to have a good effectiveness and to be efficient. Indeed it allowed to find seeds and concerns with a good precision with respect the ones resulted by the 'manual' analysis carried out by an expert and to sensibly reduce the needed effort.

Future work will be mainly addressed to consider fragments of code inside methods in order to identify also dynamic crosscutting. Empirical validation of the approach will be carried out too.

tive comparison of three aspect mining techniques. In: 13th International Workshop on Program Comprehension, IWPC (2005)

5. Kiczales, G., Mezini, M.: Aspect-oriented programming and modular reasoning. In:Proceedings of the 27th international Conference on Software Engineering, ICSE 2005, St. Louis, MO, USA, May 15 - 21, pp. 49–58. ACM, New York (2005)

6. Marin, M., van Deursen, A., Moonen, L.: Identifying Aspects Using Fan-In Analysis. In: Proceedings of the 11th Working Conference on Reverse Engineering, WCRE, November 08 - 12, pp. 132–141. IEEE Computer Society, Washington (2004)

7. Masuhara, H., Kiczales, G.: Modeling Crosscutting in Aspect-Oriented Mechanisms. In: Cardelli, L. (ed.) ECOOP 2003. LNCS, vol. 2743, pp. 2–8. Springer, Heidelberg (2003)

8. Mezini, M., Ostermann, K.: Modules for crosscutting models. In: Rosen, J.-P., Strohmeier, A. (eds.) Ada-Europe 2003. LNCS, vol. 2655, pp. 24–44. Springer, Heidelberg (2003)

9. Robillard, M.P., Murphy, G.C.: Representing concerns in source code. ACM Trans. Softw. 16(1), 3 (2007)

10. Tonella, P., Ceccato, M.: Aspect Mining through the Formal Concept Analysis of Execution Traces. In: Proc. of the 11th Working Conference on Reverse Engineering, WCRE, November 08 - 12, pp. 112–121. IEEE Computer Society, Washington (2004)

11. Tonella, P., Ceccato, M.: Refactoring the Aspectizable Interfaces: An Empirical Assessment. IEEE Trans. Softw. Eng. 31(10), 819–832 (2005)

Hiroshima University, 1–4–1 Kagamiyama, Higashi-Hiroshima 739-8527, Japan
dohi@rel.hiroshima-u.ac.jp
http://www.rel.hiroshima-u.ac.jp/

Abstract. In this paper, we concern a sampling method for Markov chain Monte Carlo (MCMC) in estimating software reliability, and propose a unified MCMC algorithm based on the Metropolis-Hasting method regardless of model on data structures. The resulting MCMC algorithm is implemented as a Java-based tool. Using the Java-based Bayesian inference tool, we illustrate how to assess the software reliability in actual software development processes.

1 Introduction

Software reliability is one of the most significant attributes of software quality. During the last four decades, many software reliability models (SRMs) have been proposed. In particular, SRMs based on non-homogeneous Poisson processes (NHPPs) have gained much popularity for describing stochastic behavior of the number of failures experienced over time.

In general, the reliability assessment consists of three phases: (i) data collection, (ii) model fitting and evaluation, and (iii) model application. At the first phase, we observe and collect software metrics of a target software development project to estimate the software reliability. Software metrics can be classified to design and testing metrics. Typical examples of design metrics are lines of code, the number of branches, and code complexity. On the other hand, testing metrics indicate testing effort, the number of software reviews and the number of experienced software failures. When we wish to estimate quantitative software reliability, it requires software failure data, i.e., time-series data for the number of failures. At the model fitting and evaluation phase, the observed failure data are applied to statistical estimation of model parameters and model selection. At the third phase, a selected model can be employed to estimate several relia-

we cannot obtain a sufficient number of observations to reduce the errors completely, because the number of software failures observed during software testing is limited. In other words, since software reliability estimation essentially involve the risk of large estimation errors, point estimation often fails to compute accurate software reliability measures.

One approach to estimate the software reliability is based on Bayesian statistics [21,10,16,17]. It requires prior knowledge about the model parameters in terms of a joint probability distribution. The prior information is then updated by using the likelihood of the observed data, generating a posterior distribution. Interval estimation, so-called credible intervals in the Bayesian context, can be performed based on quantile of this posterior distribution. However, posterior distributions which play a central role in Bayesian estimation are usually difficult to compute, except for a few cases. They cannot be derived as closed-form solutions. Hence approximate or numerical methods to compute posterior distributions are needed when we implement the Bayesian estimation.

Meinhold and Singpurwalla [10] presented an explicit form of the posterior distribution for Jelinski-Moranda SRM [6]. Yin and Trivedi [21] exhibited the direct numerical integral to Goel-Okumoto SRM [4] and delayed S-shaped SRM [18]. Recently, Okamura et al. [15,14] proposed variational Bayesian approaches for Goel-Okumoto SRM and delayed S-shaped SRM. Since the direct numerical integration and the variational approximation can be applied only in specific NHPP-based SRMs, they are not general methods for arbitrary NHPP-based SRMs.

The most popular and versatile approach would be Markov chain Monte Carlo (MCMC), which uses samples via pseudo-random variates instead of the analytical distribution. The MCMC has the advantage of applicability over many kinds of SRMs, but needs concrete sampling algorithms to evaluate posterior distributions. The concrete forms of MCMC should follow ad-hoc manners, namely, they have different forms with different types of SRMs. Kuo and Yang [7,8] proposed the MCMC approach to compute posterior distributions, where the resulting MCMC can be regarded as a versatile method by sampling from posterior distributions and can be effectively applied to NHPP-based SRMs. In fact, Kuo and Y   [7 8]   e the Gibbs al   ithms in   ratin Metr   oli -Hastin   (MH)

sampling for NHPP-based SRMs, and discuss a unified sampling algorithm based on the MH method. Section 5 is devoted to the implementation of the proposed MCMC algorithm. Here, we develop a Java-based tool to perform the Bayesian inference for NHPP-based SRMs.

2 Software Reliability Modeling

The NHPP-based SRMs are used to assess software reliability in testing and operational phases. Most of NHPP-based SRMs are defined on the following model assumptions:

Assumption A: Software failure times are independent and identically distributed (i.i.d.) random variables.

Assumption B: The total number of software failures over a whole software life cycle, N, is given by a Poisson distributed random variable with mean $\omega\ (>0)$.

Suppose that the cumulative distribution function (c.d.f.) of software failure time is given by $F(t)$, $t \geq 0$. From Assumption A, given the total number of failures, $N = n$, the number of software failures experienced before time t, $\{N(t), t \geq 0\}$, is given by

$$\Pr\{N(t) = x | N = n\} = \binom{n}{x} F(t)^x \left(1 - F(t)\right)^{n-x}. \tag{1}$$

Moreover, from Assumption B, we have the following probability mass function:

$$\Pr\{N(t) = x\} = \frac{(\omega F(t))^x}{x!} \exp\left(-\omega F(t)\right). \tag{2}$$

Since Eq. (2) implies that the number of software failures experienced before time t, $N(t)$, obeys an NHPP with a mean value function $\omega F(t)$, the stochastic process $N(t)$ can be characterized only by the failure time distribution $F(t)$.

In general, all of NHPP-based SRMs can be classified to finite and infinite fail   del   hich are defi ed in terms f the as mpt ti   pert f mea

3   Bayesian Estimation

Bayesian estimation is the well-established framework for parameter estimation based on prior information. The key idea is to regard model parameters as random variates. Let $\boldsymbol{\theta}$ and D be a parameter vector to be estimated and an observed data vector, respectively. From the well-known Bayes theorem, the posterior information on parameters is given by

$$p(\boldsymbol{\theta}|D) = \frac{p(D|\boldsymbol{\theta})p(\boldsymbol{\theta})}{\int p(D|\boldsymbol{\theta})p(\boldsymbol{\theta})d\boldsymbol{\theta}}, \tag{5}$$

where $p(\cdot)$ is an appropriate density or mass function. In Eq. (5), $p(\boldsymbol{\theta})$ and $p(\boldsymbol{\theta}|D)$ are called prior and posterior distributions (density or mass functions), respectively, and $p(D|\boldsymbol{\theta})$ corresponds to a likelihood function. Equation (5) can also be expressed without the normalizing constant $\int p(D|\boldsymbol{\theta})p(\boldsymbol{\theta})d\boldsymbol{\theta}$ in the following:

$$p(\boldsymbol{\theta}|D) \propto p(D|\boldsymbol{\theta})p(\boldsymbol{\theta}). \tag{6}$$

The computation of normalizing constant causes analytical or numerical integration over the domain of parameter vector $\boldsymbol{\theta}$. Except for a few specific cases, we cannot obtain the closed-form solution of the normalizing constant. Therefore any numerical technique must be applied to evaluate posterior distributions.

One straightforward approach is to utilize the general-purpose numerical integration such as trapezoidal rule, Simpson's rule and Gaussian quadrature. However, the numerical integration does not work for computing posterior distributions in the Bayesian estimation, because we often encounter the case where the posterior distribution has a large number of parameters. In such a situation, the general-purpose numerical integration may further impose rather computation costs on estimating normalizing constants. Moreover, even if the number of model parameters is small, the determination of integration range affects the resulting posterior distributions very sensitively.

On the other hand, several approximation methods have been proposed in the Bayesian context in order to avoid the difficulty of numerical integration

target posterior distributions. Thus it is important how to build an appropriate Markov chain. The fundamental MCMC algorithm is the Metropolis-Hastings (MH) algorithm. Moreover, as a special case of MH algorithm, the MCMC with Gibbs sampler is also one of the most famous MCMC algorithms.

The Gibbs sampling generates samples drawn from a target joint posterior distribution based on conditional posterior distributions. Let $p(\theta_1, \ldots, \theta_m | D)$ be a target joint posterior distribution of parameters $\theta_1, \ldots, \theta_m$. When one can generate samples drawn from the conditional posterior distribution:

$$p(\theta_i | \theta_1, \ldots, \theta_{i-1}, \theta_{i+1}, \ldots, \theta_m; D), \tag{7}$$

the Gibbs sampler is given by the following scheme:

$$\theta_1 \sim p(\theta_1 | \theta_2, \ldots, \theta_m; D), \tag{8}$$
$$\theta_2 \sim p(\theta_2 | \theta_1, \theta_3 \ldots, \theta_m; D), \tag{9}$$

$$\vdots$$

$$\theta_i \sim p(\theta_i | \theta_1, \ldots, \theta_{i-1}, \theta_{i+1}, \ldots, \theta_m; D), \tag{10}$$

$$\vdots$$

$$\theta_m \sim p(\theta_m | \theta_1, \ldots, \theta_{m-1}; D), \tag{11}$$

where $\theta_i \sim p(\theta_i | \cdot)$ indicates that a sample of θ_i is generated from the probability distribution $p(\theta_i | \cdots ; D)$. The above sampling can be regarded as a Markov chain with state space $(\theta_1, \ldots, \theta_m)$. In the Gibbs sampling, the stationary distribution of this Markov chain is exactly equivalent to the joint posterior distribution $p(\theta | D)$. In general, the sampling methods for conditional posterior distributions are simpler than those for the joint posterior distribution. Therefore, we obtain the samples from the joint posterior distribution by repeating the above sampling scheme.

The MH method is to generate samples drawn from posterior distributions according to the accept-rejection principle. Let $\pi(\cdot)$ be a probability density function of a target distribution, i.e the posterior distribution. Dissimilar to

problem in the MH method is how to choose an appropriate proposal distribu
tion. In the MH method, when the Markov transition kernel of proposal distri-
bution is symmetry i.e., $q(y|x) \equiv q(x|y)$, the acceptance probability is simply
given by

$$\alpha(x, y) = \min \left(1, \frac{\pi(y)}{\pi(x)} \right). \tag{13}$$

As a symmetric proposal distribution, the transition kernel based on a random
walk process is quite popular. If y is generated from

$$y = x + z, \quad z \sim f(z), \tag{14}$$

then the proposal distribution becomes $f(y - x)$. When z follows the normal
distribution with mean 0 and variance σ^2, the above proposal distribution indicates a random walk and $f(y - x)$ is obviously symmetric. Moreover, when the
proposal distribution is the conditional posterior distribution, the MH method
is reduced to the Gibbs sampling.

4   Bayesian Computation of NHPP-Based SRMs

4.1   Data Structure and Likelihood Function

Parameter estimation, i.e., finding model parameters fitted to observed software
failure data, is one of the most important steps in model-based software reliability evaluation. One of the popular techniques for the fitting is the maximum
likelihood (ML) estimation. The principle of ML estimation is to find model parameters so that a likelihood (or logarithmic likelihood) can be maximized. The
likelihood is defined as the probability that the observed data are drawn from
the model. In the Bayesian estimation, as seen in Eq.(5), the likelihood function
is required to compute the posterior distribution. Here we formulate a likelihood
function of model parameters for given observations. Since the formulation of
likelihood functions depends on data structure of the observations, we have to
define the data structures used in the estimation. Traditionally, two types of data

s a parameter $f(\;;\;)$ is a p
corresponding to the c.d.f. $F(\cdot;\boldsymbol{\theta})$.

Another data structure, a grouped (failure) data form, consists of the number of failures for fixed time intervals. Each record of the grouped data form is given by a pair of an observed time and the cumulative number of failures experienced before the observed time, i.e., $\mathcal{G} = \{(t_1, x_1), \ldots, (t_n, x_n)\}$, where x_i are the cumulative number of failures in time interval $[0, t_i)$. Then the likelihood function of NHPP-based SRMs [11] is given by

$$p(\mathcal{G}|\omega, \boldsymbol{\theta}) = \prod_{i=1}^{n} \frac{\{\omega\,(F(t_i;\boldsymbol{\theta}) - F(t_{i-1};\boldsymbol{\theta}))\}^{(x_i - x_{i-1})}}{(x_i - x_{i-1})!} \exp\left(-\omega F(t_n;\boldsymbol{\theta})\right), \quad (16)$$

where $t_0 = 0$ and $x_0 = 0$. Furthermore, if all the time intervals $t_i - t_{i-1}$, $i = 1, \ldots, n$, are identically constant, one obtains discrete NHPP-based SRMs which are specifically formulated on discrete time domain [19].

As seen in Eqs. (15) and (16), different data forms lead to different likelihood functions, and at the same time lead to different MCMC schemes depending on data structure. Hence, failure time data and grouped data were separately discussed in the traditional software reliability estimation. To improve the applicability of NHPP-based SRMs, it is necessary to consider an integrated data which contain both failure time and grouped failure data. This paper defines the integrated data, and attempts to develop unified MCMC algorithms which can handle both failure time and grouped data. In what follows, we present an integrated data structure and the corresponding likelihood function which are needed for the Bayesian computation of NHPP-based SRMs.

Let $\mathcal{I} = \{(t_1, u_1, z_1), \ldots, (t_n, u_n, z_n)\}$ be an integrated data form, where u_i is the number of failures experienced in the interval (t_{i-1}, t_i) and z_i is an indicator variable which means that a failure occurs at time t_i. If $z_i = 0$ for all $i = 1, \ldots, n$, the resulting data form is reduced to grouped failure data. If $u_i = 0$ for all i, $z_i = 1$, $i = 1, \ldots, n - 1$ and $z_n = 0$, the corresponding data exactly equal the failure time data. In addition, an integrated data form also deals with both failure time and grouped failure data at the same time. Based on integrated data the LLF of NHPP-based SRM   be f   lated as follow

one parameter, i.e., $p(\omega, \boldsymbol{\theta}) = p(\omega) \prod_{i=1} p(\theta_i)$. The prior distribution of ω is given by a gamma distribution with parameter vector (m_ω, ϕ_ω):

$$p(\omega) = \frac{\phi_\omega^{m_\omega} \omega^{m_\omega - 1} e^{-\phi_\omega \omega}}{\Gamma(m_\omega)}. \qquad (18)$$

According to Gibbs sampling and MH method in the Bayesian estimation, we provide the following sampling scheme as an MCMC algorithm for NHPP-based SRMs:

- S-1: Generate a new sample of ω drawn from the conditional posterior:

$$\omega \sim \text{Gamma}\left(m_\omega + \sum_{i=1}^{n}(u_i + z_i), \phi_\omega + F(t_n; \boldsymbol{\theta})\right), \qquad (19)$$

  where $\text{Gamma}(m, \phi)$ means the gamma distribution with parameter vector (m, ϕ).
- S-2: For $l = 1, \ldots, m$, execute S-2-1 through S-2-3.
- S-2-1: Generate a candidate $\tilde{\theta}_l$ using the following proposal distribution:

$$\tilde{\theta}_l = \theta_l + z_l, \qquad (20)$$

  where z_l is a random variable having a normal distribution truncated at both points L_l and U_l. Concretely, $\tilde{\theta}_l$ is generated from the following truncated normal density defined on $[L_l, U_l]$:

$$f_{\text{trunc}}(\tilde{\theta}_l; L_l, U_l, \theta_l, \sigma_l) = \frac{1}{\sqrt{2\pi}\sigma_l} e^{-\frac{(\tilde{\theta}_l - \theta_l)^2}{2\sigma_l^2}} / \Psi(L_l, U_l, \theta_l, \sigma_l), \qquad (21)$$

$$\Psi(L_l, U_l, \theta_l, \sigma_l) = \int_{L_l}^{U_l} \frac{1}{\sqrt{2\pi}\sigma_l} e^{-\frac{(s - \theta_l)^2}{2\sigma_l^2}} ds. \qquad (22)$$

- S-2-2: Compute the following acceptance probability $\alpha(\tilde{\theta}_l, \theta_l)$:

When the set of parameter vectors is given by $(\omega^{(1)}, \boldsymbol{\theta}^{(1)}), \ldots, (\omega^{(B)}, \boldsymbol{\theta}^{(B)})$, the predictive values of software reliability measures can be estimated as follows.

Mean value of cumulative number of faults:

$$\hat{E}[N(t)] = \frac{1}{B} \sum_{i=1}^{B} \omega^{(i)} F(t; \boldsymbol{\theta}^{(i)}), \tag{24}$$

Software reliability function:

$$\hat{R}(t|s) = \frac{1}{B} \sum_{i=1}^{B} \exp\{-\omega^{(i)}(F(t+s; \boldsymbol{\theta}^{(i)}) - F(s; \boldsymbol{\theta}^{(i)}))\}. \tag{25}$$

5 Tool Development

5.1 A Java-Based Tool

A Java-based prototype tool for Bayesian estimation in NHPP-based SRMs is developed to evaluate the software reliability. The models implemented on the tool are 11 usual NHPP-based SRMs presented in Table 1. The input is integrated data mentioned in Section 4, and MCMC algorithms described in Section 4 are performed. The outputs of tool are the graphs of predictive mean value functions, predictive software reliability functions and predictive failure-free probability and so on.

5.2 A Numerical Example

We give an example of software reliability assessment based on the developed tool. In this example, we use the failure data collection opened in DACS (Data & Analysis Center for Software), and particularly choose the System 40 data collected during the system testing of a military application. The System 40 data include both failure time and grouped data. Since our tool deals with grouped data, we present here an illustrative example for the grouped data consisting of

log-normal distribution [2]
truncated logistic distribution [12]
log-logistic distribution [5]
truncated extreme-value maximum distribution [13]
logarithmic extreme-value maximum distribution [13]
truncated extreme-value minimum distribution [13]
logarithmic extreme-value minimum distribution [3,13]

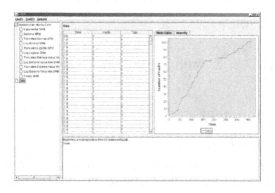

Fig. 1. Software failure data

The performance of the proposed MCMC algorithm depends on the variances of MH method. We set three kinds of standard deviations for the random walk on the parameter β; $\sigma_\beta = 0.01, 0.001, 0.0001$. Moreover, we take 100 burn-in samples which are discarded to avoid effects of initial values, and 1000 parameter samples are collected to compute the predictive mean value function. These design parameters like the standard deviation and the number of burn-in samples can be set on the developed tool.

Figure 2 depicts time-series graphs of the parameter β in the MCMC algorithm with $\sigma_\beta = 0.01, 0.001, 0.0001$. In general, since it is well known that there is no effective method to check whether or not the samples converge to station-

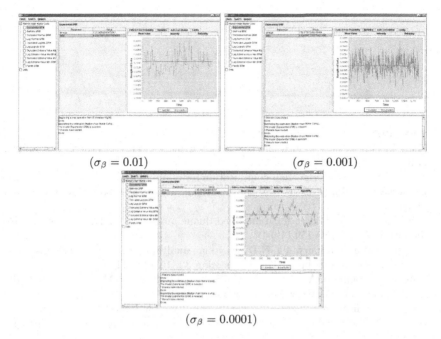

$(\sigma_\beta = 0.01)$ $(\sigma_\beta = 0.001)$

$(\sigma_\beta = 0.0001)$

Fig. 2. MCMC samples of parameter β

6 Conclusions

This paper has implemented a unified MCMC algorithm of Bayesian estimation for NHPP-based SRMs, which can be applied to estimate any kind of NHPP-based SRMs with both failure time and grouped data by using the MH method. Moreover, we develop a prototype tool written by Java language to estimate the software reliability measures.

In future, we will enhance the functionality of the tool; for example, estimating a Bayes factor for software release problem. In addition, the MCMC algorithm based on Gibbs sampling [8] will be also integrated on our Java-based tool.

References

1. Abdel-Ghaly, A.A., Chan, P.Y., Littlewood, B.: Evaluation of competing software reliability predictions. IEEE Transactions on Software Engineering SE-12, 950–967

York (1972)

7. Kuo, L., Yang, T.Y.: Bayesian computation of software reliability. J. Comput. Graphical Statist. 4, 65–82 (1995)

8. Kuo, L., Yang, T.Y.: Bayesian computation for nonhomogeneous Poisson processes in software reliability. Journal of the American Statistical Association 91, 763–773 (1996)

9. Littlewood, B.: Rationale for a modified duane model. IEEE Transactions on Reliability R-33(2), 157–159 (1984)

10. Meinhold, R.J., Singpurwalla, N.D.: Bayesian analysis of commonly used model for describing software failures. The Statistician 32, 168–173 (1983)

11. Musa, J.D., Iannino, A., Okumoto, K.: Software Reliability, Measurement, Prediction, Application. McGraw-Hill, New York (1987)

12. Ohba, M.: Inflection S-shaped software reliability growth model. In: Osaki, S., Hatoyama, Y. (eds.) Stochastic Models in Reliability Theory, pp. 144–165. Springer, Berlin (1984)

13. Ohishi, K., Okamura, H., Dohi, T.: Gompertz software reliability model: estimation algorithm and empirical validation. Journal of Systems and Software 82(3), 535–543 (2009)

14. Okamura, H., Grottke, M., Dohi, T., Trivedi, K.S.: Variational Bayesian approach for interval estimation of NHPP-based software reliability models. Working Paper (2007)

15. Okamura, H., Sakoh, T., Dohi, T.: Variational Bayesian approach for exponential software reliability model. In: Proc. 10th IASTED Int'l. Conf. on Software Eng. and Applications, pp. 82–87 (2006)

16. Singpurwalla, N.D., Soyer, R.: Assessing (Software) reliability growth using a random coefficient autoregressive process and its ramifications. IEEE Transactions on Software Engineering SE-11, 1456–1464 (1985)

17. Singpurwalla, N.D., Wilson, S.P.: Statistical Methods in Software Engineering. Springer, New York (1997)

18. Yamada, S., Ohba, M., Osaki, S.: S-shaped reliability growth modeling for software error detection. IEEE Transactions on Reliability R-32, 475–478 (1983)

19. Yamada, S., Osaki, S.: Discrete software reliability growth models. Journal of Applied Stochastic Models and Data Analysis 1(1), 65–77 (1985)

20. Yamada, S., Osaki, S.: Software reliability growth modeling: Models and applications. IEEE Transactions on Software Engineering SE-11, 1431–1437 (1985)

School of Electrical Engineering & INMC, Seoul National University, Korea
⁴ Multimedia Communications & Networking Lab., HP Labs, Palo Alto, CA 94304
{lochan.verma,seong.kim}@samsung.com, schoi@snu.ac.kr, sjlee@hp.com

Abstract. We present a transmission rate adaptation algorithm called
AGILE (ACK-Guided Immediate Link rate Estimation) for IEEE 802.11
networks. The key idea of AGILE is that the transmitter adjusts the transmission rate by means of measuring the SNR (Signal-to-Noise Ratio) during any frame reception including the ACK (Acknowledgment) frame, and
estimating the corresponding maximum achievable throughput using a
profile, which is materialized by extensive off-line measurement. AGILE
is equipped with an advanced RTS (Request-To-Send)/CTS (Clear-To-
Send) activation algorithm, *eRTS filter* that intelligently switches on/off
RTS frame transmission to enhance the achievable throughput depending
upon the existence of multiple contending (or even hidden) stations. The
effectiveness of AGILE is evaluated in our MadWifi-based testbed implementation and we compare its performance with different rate adaptation
schemes in various scenarios.

1   Introduction

The transmission rate optimization over the medium quality variation is a well-
known algorithmic issue. Ideally, a rate adaptation algorithm should downgrade
or upgrade to a suitable rate with wireless channel dynamics in a timely manner.
Most of today's algorithms suffer in agility as they monitor the channel quality
over predefined time period and/or threshold number of frame transmissions. It
is also important that rate adaptation decisions are not influenced by increased
wireless medium contention or the presence of a hidden station.

Rate adaptation algorithms can be classified as: (i) *Close Loop*, which requires
feedback from the receiver to make a rate selection, and (ii) *Open Loop*, which is
not dependent on receiver feedback. Current 802.11 standard does not support
any feedback from the receiver to the transmitter, which makes algorithms like
RBAR (Receiver-Based AutoRate) [4] and OAR (Opportunistic Auto-Rate) [11]

supported by a threshold table.

We present a transmission rate adaptation algorithm called *AGILE* (ACK-Guided Immediate Link rate Estimation) for IEEE 802.11 networks. The strength of AGILE lies in precise and timely rate adaptation, which is driven by the SNR measurement of any frame reception including ACK frames, and a predetermined look-up table. This table named as *profile* represents the relation between delivery ratio and SNR for a given transmission rate, and has been materialized by extensive field-testing experiments. AGILE also utilizes an advanced collision resolution technique, *eRTS filter* that enhances achievable throughput when there exist multiple contending (or even hidden) stations.

The rest of the paper is organized as follows. In Section 2, the design rules and implementation procedure of AGILE are described. In Section 3, the solution for collision awareness is presented. Section 4 presents the comparative performance evaluation based on testbed measurements, and the paper concludes with Section 5.

2   AGILE

Design Overview. In order to promptly respond to the channel dynamics, AGILE utilizes SNR of any frame received. Initially, the first frame on a link is sent at the lowest transmission rate and after receiving an ACK or any other frame, the most suitable rate is selected from the profile look-up. Our idea is that the SNR of a frame represents the quality of the wireless medium at that time. This is in line with the reciprocity theorem that states *the characteristics of the wireless medium remain unchanged if the roles of transmitter and receiver are interchanged at a particular instant* [12].

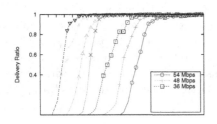

Profile shown in Fig. 1 has been generated through extensive off-line experiment using two NICs (Network Interface Cards) for different 802.11a rates. Note that profile is dependent on vendor and chipset. We use Atheros/MadWifi NIC/driver

retransmission.

Table 1. AGILE rate adjustment for retransmissions with 802.11a

Attempt	Initial	Retry1	Retry2	Retry3	Retry4	Retry5	Retry6	Retry7
Rate	Current	Current	18 (6)*	18 (6)*	6	6	6	6

* (6) denotes that the lowest transmission rate is used when 'Current' is less than or equal to 18 Mbps.

AGILE Algorithm. Assume an L-byte frame is to be transmitted using a transmission rate index i out of the 802.11a data rate set. The probability of a successful frame transmission is given by $P_s^i(L) = (1 - P_{e\_data}^i(L)) \cdot (1 - P_{e\_ack}^i(14))$, where $P_{e\_data}^i(L)$ and $P_{e\_ack}^i(14)$ represent the error probabilities for an L-byte data frame and the 14-byte ACK frame, respectively. $P_s^i(L)$ is determined through a profile look-up according to the SNR of a received frame.

Let $s^i(k)$ be the probability that a data frame is successfully transmitted at rate index i after k transmission attempts. $s^i(k) = (1 - P_s^i(L))^{k-1} \cdot P_s^i(L)$. The transmission time for a frame with rate index i can be determined by

$$T_{frame}^i(L) = \sum_{k=1}^{Max\_Try} s^i(k) \cdot \sum_{j=0}^{k-1} \left[DIFS + \overline{T}_{Backoff}(j) + T_{data}^i(L) + SIFS + T_{ack}^i \right],$$

(1)

where Max_Try is the maximum frame transmission attempts, $DIFS$, $SIFS$, $CWmin$, $CWmax$, and $SlotTime$ hold the same meaning as in IEEE 802.11 standard [5], and $\overline{T}_{Backoff}(j)$ is the average backoff interval in μsec, after j consecutive unsuccessful attempts:

$$\overline{T}_{Backoff}(j) = \begin{cases} \frac{(CWmin+1)^j - 1}{2} \cdot SlotTime & 0 \leq j < 6, \\ \frac{CWmax}{2} \cdot SlotTime & j \geq 6, \end{cases}$$

(2)

$$\left(\begin{array}{cc} L & 8 \end{array} \right)$$

algorithm:

ALGORITHM 1. *AGILE rate control algorithm*
1. $\forall\ i$, *Ä looks up the profile to calculate* $P_s^i(L)$ *using SNR of a received frame.*
2. $\forall\ i$, *Ä executes Eq. (1) to calculate* $T_{frame}^i(L)$ *using* $P_s^i(L)$ *in Step 1.*
3. *Ä selects rate index i with the minimum* $T_{frame}^i(L)$ *as the rate index.*

3   Collision Awareness

High wireless medium contention or the presence of hidden stations results in many transmission failures due to frame collisions; triggering the algorithms based on frame loss estimation to unnecessarily downgrade the transmission rate. The usage of RTS/CTS is an effective solution to tackle the problem of increased frame collisions. However, it costs precious bandwidth consumption.

AGILE and other SNR-based rate control algorithms have intrinsic collision awareness since rate adaptation decisions are driven by SNR measurements and not by the currently-experienced frame loss levels. Nevertheless, they do require intelligence to protect transmissions from suffering collisions to further boost the performance. In the absence of such a protection mechanism, the achievable throughput of a station can be reduced due to increased retransmissions.

eRTS filter. Inspired by A-RTS (Adaptive RTS) filter proposed in [14], we develop eRTS (enhanced RTS) filter to protect the transmissions from collisions. eRTS design makes it implementation friendly into the current open source drivers. The key parameter in A-RTS is *RTSWnd*, which specifies the window size, in terms of the number of frames, within which all data frames are sent with a preceding RTS frame. Another parameter *RTSCounter* depends upon RTSWnd and represents the actual number of data frames sent with a preceding RTS frame. Initially, RTSWnd and RTSCounter are set as zero, meaning that the RTS/CTS exchange is disabled. A data frame is preceded by an RTS frame as long as RTSCounter is larger than zero. RTSWnd is incremented by one if the last data frame tra   i ion w   successful   d RTS w   t used   d

old) retries for a successful transmission triggers RTSWnd control. We also modify the A-RTS filter to perform a linear decrease of RTSWnd if RTSWnd exceeds the *LThresh* (Linear Threshold); otherwise, it follows multiplicative decrease. RThresh and LThresh values are experimentally determined and fixed as 1 and 3, respectively. The A-RTS filter incorporating the above changes is called *eRTS* filter. Algorithm 2 depicts its complete operation. A station, say $\ddot{A}$, which has a data frame to transmit runs the following algorithm:

ALGORITHM 2. *eRTS filter*
1. $\ddot{A}$ increases retry_count for each frame retransmission.
2. If RTS is disabled and retry_count $\geq$ RThresh then $\ddot{A}$ increments RTSWnd by 1, and sets RTSCounter equal to RTSWnd.
3. If step 2 conditions are not satisfied, $\ddot{A}$ checks if RTS is enabled XOR retry_count $\equiv$ 0, if it is true step 4 is executed otherwise it jumps to step 5.
4. If RTSWnd > LThresh, decrement RTSWnd by 1, otherwise reduce RTSWnd by a half. Set RTSCounter equal to RTSWnd.
5. Finally $\ddot{A}$ checks if RTSCounter > 0, and if true, $\ddot{A}$ enables RTS transmission to precede the current data frame and decrements RTSCounter by 1. Otherwise RTS transmission is disabled for the current data frame.

4   Testbed Results

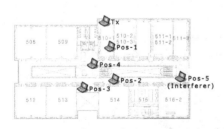

Fig. 2 shows the floor plan of our indoor Linux based testbed. Each laptop is equipped with a Cisco aironet 350 802.11a/b/g PCMCIA card. All experiments are performed using the 802.11a at channel 157 with the center frequency of 5.785 GHz. Using Iperf traffic generator tool the transmitter generates UDP packets of size 1003 bytes as fast as it can so that it always has a packet to trans-

decisions either after predefined time period or threshold number of frame transmission. This criterion makes them less responsive to channel variations. The experiment to study the effect of increasing wireless medium contention is performed with the receiver at Pos-1. The transmitters are placed next to each other at Tx in Fig. 2. As seen in Fig. 3(b), AGILE achieves a throughput gain of 20.8%, 50.4%, and 76% over the worst performer (AMRR) with 3, 4, and 5 contending nodes, respectively. With increasing contention levels, each station experiences an increase in the frame losses, thus triggering rate decrement decisions in SAMPLE, ONOE, and AMRR.

Through the experiment to verify the responsiveness to varying link quality, we explore the agility of different rate adaptation algorithms. In order to create variation in channel quality, we block the transmitter NIC card every 5 seconds for 5 seconds with a thick book forming a canopy around the card. This reduces

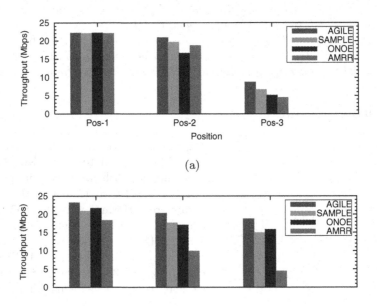

Fig. 4. Throughput performance comparison of AGILE with other algorithms considering the varying medium quality scenario and the transmitter mobility scenario

the SNR of the transmitted and the received frames. The receiver is located at Pos-2 in this experiment. AGILE provides 20.5%, 9.6%, and 20.7% throughput gain over SAMPLE, ONOE, and AMRR as seen in Fig. 4.

4.2 Transmitter Mobility

We perform this experiment by placing the receiver at Pos-2 and transmitter moves back and forth between Tx and Pos-1 at roughly 1 m/sec, which is normal human walking speed. As shown in Fig. 4, AMRR has a throughput gain of 9.3% over SAMPLE, which is consistent with the results reported in [14].

AGILE has throughput gain of 13.6%, 14%, and 4.7% over SAMPLE, ONOE, and AMRR, respectively. AGILE shows the performance superior to other algorithms by quickly reacting to the channel dynamics and selecting accurate rates.

4.3 Effect of Hidden Stations

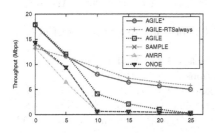

To generate a hidden station topology, we place a receiver at Pos-4 while two transmitters are located at Tx and Pos-5. The transmitter at Pos-5 is named as the hidden interferer, and generates broadcast UDP packets of 1003 bytes at various traffic generation rates to expose the transmissions from Tx to Pos-4 to mild, moderate, and intense interference from the hidden interferer. Transmitter at Tx fol-

throughput. However, AGILE-RTSalways outperforms all other schemes for 5–25 Mbps rate of hidden interference.

AGILE* represents the most suitable algorithm across mild, moderate, and intense interference conditions. Overall, AGILE is a very responsive rate adaptation algorithm and the supplementary eRTS filter further boosts its performance.

5 Conclusion

In this paper, we propose an SNR-based rate adaptation algorithm called AGILE and provide collision awareness with eRTS filter. We have implemented both AGILE and eRTS into MadWifi driver and performed extensive experiments to compare the performance with existing algorithms. In all scenarios, AGILE provides the best performance. As a future work, we plan to introduce on-line compensation into the profile, which is obtained through off-line experimentation. This will enable each station to have a profile for each individual wireless link enabling AGILE to perform even better.

References

1. Onoe Rate Control Algorithm,
   http://madwifi.org/browser/madwifi/trunk/ath_rate/onoe/
2. Bicket, J.: Bit-rate selection in wireless networks. Master's thesis. MIT (2005)
3. del Prado Pavon, J., Choi, S.: Link Adaptation Strategy for IEEE 802.11 WLAN via Received Signal Strength Measurement. In: Proc. IEEE ICC 2003, Anchorage, AK, USA, May 2003, pp. 1108–1113 (2003)
4. Holland, G., et al.: A Rate-Adaptive MAC Protocol for Multi-Hop Wireless Networks. In: Proc. ACM MobiCom 2001 (2001)
5. IEEE Std. IEEE 802.11-1999, Part 11: Wireless LAN Medium Access Control (MAC) and Physical Layer (PHY) specifications (August 1999)
6. Judd, G., et al.: Efficient Channel-aware Rate Adaptation in Dynamic Enviroments. In: Proc. ACM MobiSys 2008, Breckenridge, Colorado, USA (June 2008)
7. Kamerman, A., Monteban, L.: WaveLAN-II: A High-Performance Wireless LAN

14. Wong, S., et al.: Robust Rate Adaptation for 802.11 Wireless Networks. In: Proc. ACM MobiCom 2006 (2006)
15. Zhang, J., et al.: A Practical SNR-Guided Rate Adaptation. In: Proc. IEEE INFOCOM 2008, Las Vegas, Nevada, USA (April 2008)

1 Seocheon, Kihung, Yongin, Gyeonggi, 449-701, Korea
`rakibultowhid@yahoo.com`

Abstract. A new encoding technique for low density parity check (LDPC) code at the uplink of 3rd Generation Partnership Project Long Term Evolution (3GPP LTE) is proposed. The concept of approximate lower triangulation (ALT) is used where the parity check matrix is pre-processed and encoded in $O(n)$ complexity. This encoding technique is applied in the uplink of LTE system where single carrier frequency division multiple access (SC-FDMA) is used as the multiple access scheme. As the encoding is performed in a $O(n)$ complexity, it will outperform the existing LDPC encoding which is not used in LTE uplink due to its high encoding complexity. The proposed encoding is simulated in the SCFDMA scenario and the BER curve is shown.

Keywords: SC-FDMA, LTE, LDPC, ALT, low complexity.

1 Introduction

Orthogonal frequency division multiplexing (OFDM) has become widely accepted primarily because of its robustness against frequency selective fading channels which are common in broadband mobile wireless communications [1]. Orthogonal frequency division multiple access (OFDMA) is a multiple access scheme used to accommodate multiple simultaneous users. Despite the benefits of OFDM and OFDMA, they suffer the drawback of high peak to average power ratio (PAPR) and hence the single carrier frequency division multiple access (SC-FDMA) is introduced which utilizes single carrier modulation and frequency domain equalization. SC-FDMA has similar performance and essentially the same overall complexity as those of OFDMA system and has been adopted as the uplink multiple access scheme for the 3rd Generation Partnership Project Long Term Evolution (3GPP LTE) [2]. Turbo code is used in the SCFDMA system as a tool for channel coding. But the turbo code suffers from the high decoding

considered as a less complex operation than decoding. Therefore, major efforts have been given to reduce the decoding complexity and very little attention is given to the encoding side. But the sparse structure of parity check matrix in LDPC codes helps the belief propagation algorithm to estimate the transmitted codeword with relatively small number of iterations which make the decoding almost linear. Therefore encoding becomes more complicated operations than decoding and hence, the encoding of LDPC gains the attention of recent researchers. For the application of LDPC code in SCFDMA also encourages low complexity encoding. The encoder implementation for an LDPC code has complexity quadratic in the block length and to encode it in linear time remains the challenging issue. It was suggested in [11] and [12] to use cascaded graphs rather than bipartite graphs. To construct a code which can be encodable and decodable in linear time, one has to choose the number of stages and the relative size of each stage carefully. One weakness of this approach is that each stage has considerably smaller length than the length of the overall code and results in some performance loss compared to the standard LDPC code. It was suggested in [13] to force the parity-check matrix to have almost lower triangular form. It states that the ensemble of codes is restricted by the degree constraints as well as by the constraint that the parity-check matrix has lower triangular shape. This restriction confirms the encoding complexity in a linear time but, in general, could not prevent some loss of performance. An LDPC encoding scheme with a complexity $O(n + g^2)$ was proposed in [14] where the authors developed a special structure for the parity check matrix using approximate lower triangulation (ALT). This makes the encoding almost linear when the associated coefficient g can be kept quite small. But the larger gap makes the encoding complexity far from linear.

The aim of this paper is to construct an LDPC code which can be encoded with a $O(n)$ complexity linear encoding by converting the parity check matrix into an ALT form with some post processing steps. The rows of the parity check matrix forming the ALT part are kept unchanged while deleting the other rows. In this way the resultant H matrix will have same number of columns but reduced number of rows and the codeword length remains same. In the de rd l gth will v depe din the l gth f the parit bits

3GPP LTE is a driving force in the mobile communication industry. For high data rate wireless communications, multiuser transmission is achieved through OFDMA and SC-FDMA. OFDMA has been chosen on the LTE downlink because of the spectral efficiency and robustness it offers in the presence of multipath propagation [16]. SC-FDMA has been chosen on the LTE uplink due to its improved performance regarding PAPR. OFDMA waveforms are characterized by a high dynamic range, which results from the IDFT and translates to a high PAPR. Signals with a high PAPR require the power amplifier to operate with a large backoff from the compression point. This effectively reduces both the mean power output level and the overall power efficiency.

2.1 Transceiver Structure in SC-FDMA Used at the Uplink of 3GPP LTE

A block diagram of a SC-FDMA transceiver system is shown in Fig. 1. SC-FDMA can be regarded as discrete Fourier transform (DFT)-spread OFDMA, where time domain data symbols are transformed to frequency domain by DFT before going through OFDMA modulation. The orthogonality of the users stems from the fact that each user occupies different subcarriers in the frequency domain, similar to the case of OFDMA. Because the overall transmit signal is a single carrier signal, PAPR is inherently low compared to the case of OFDMA which produces a multicarrier signal.

The transmitter of an SC-FDMA system first modulate and encode the symbols and then groups the symbols into blocks each containing N symbols. Next it performs an N-point DFT to produce a frequency domain representation of the input symbols. It then maps each of the N-DFT outputs to one of the $M(> N)$ orthogonal subcarriers that can be transmitted. The collection of N subcarriers assigned to the DFT output is referred to as a chunk. An M-point inverse DFT (IDFT) transforms the subcarrier amplitudes to a complex time domain signal. The transmitter performs two other signal processing operations prior to transmission. It inserts a set of symbols referred to as a cyclic prefix (CP) in order to provide a guard time to prevent inter-block interference due to multi-path propagation. Insertion of CP i   t shown in the tra   iver block t   reduce drawin

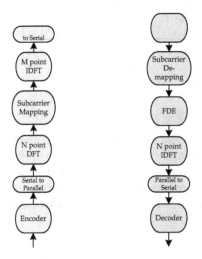

Fig. 1. Transceiver structure using SC-FDMA

2.2 LDPC as a Channel Coding Technique in SC-FDMA

Turbo code is currently used at the SC-FDMA system as a tool for channel coding. But the turbo code suffers from the high decoding complexity and relatively high latency, which make them unsuitable for some applications. At the uplink of 3GPP LTE, a cell phone is sending the message to the base station. As the complexity and latency is the prime issue in communicating from a cellular phone to a base station, turbo code application may not be suitable in this scenario. As the LDPC code doesn't suffer from latency problem, it can offer a potential candidacy in this regard. But the problem lies in the fact that LDPC code has a high encoding complexity and $O(n)$ complexity encoding for LDPC is yet to be proposed. The opportunity for the inclusion of LDPC code as a channel coding technique depends on a successful proposal of $O(n)$ complexity LDPC encoding scheme. In this paper, we propose such encoding scheme which will be suitable for the uplink of LTE system. In the next section, we discuss the theoretical

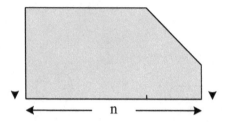

Fig. 2. Representation of a parity check matrix in an approximate lower triangular form

nodes and m is the number of check nodes. Assume that by performing row and column permutations only we can bring the parity-check matrix H into the form indicated in Fig. 2 and it brings H into approximate lower triangular form. Since this transformation is accomplished solely by permutations, the matrix is still sparse. More precisely, it is assumed that the matrix is brought in the form

$$H = \begin{bmatrix} M & T \\ N & P \end{bmatrix},$$ (1)

where M is $t \times (n-t)$, N is $(m-t) \times (n-t)$, T is $t \times t$ and P is $t \times (m-t)$. Further, all these matrices are sparse and T is lower triangular with ones along the diagonal. The dimension of the matrix M is variable since the dimension of matrix T can vary depending on the randomly generated H matrix. Therefore the message and parity bit lengths vary depending on the randomly generated parity check matrix H.

Let $x = (s, p)$ where s denotes the systematic part and p denotes the parity part, s has length $(n-t)$, and p has length t. From $Hx^T = 0^T$, the following equations can be obtained

$$Ms^T + Tp^T = 0,$$ (2)

$$Ns^T + Pp^T = 0.$$ (3)

From the above equations we get

the submatrix P from the original matrix H, the resulting matrix $-PT^{-1}M +$
N contributes to generate the required matrix $PT^{-1}M$ which will be used to
construct the modified N matrix. We denote it as N_n. So the newly developed
H matrix can be written from the Eq. 6 as

$$H = \begin{bmatrix} M & T \\ N_n & P \end{bmatrix}.$$

Hence, once the $T^{-1}M$ matrix with dimension $t \times (n-t)$ has been precomputed,
the determination of p can be accomplished in complexity $O(t \times (n-t))$ without
considering the sparsity of these matrices. Rather than precomputing $T^{-1}M$
and then multiplying with s^T, we can determine p by breaking the computation
into two smaller steps, each of which is efficiently computable. We first determine
Ms^T, which has complexity $O(n)$ since M is sparse. Next, we multiply the result
by T^{-1}. Since $T^{-1}[Ms^T] = y^T$ is equivalent to the system $[Ms^T] = Ty^T$, this can
also be accomplished in $O(n)$ by back-substitution, since T is lower triangular
and also sparse. It follows that the overall complexity of determining p is $O(n)$.
The computational complexity for p is summarized in Table.1.

The combination of M and T submatrices contribute the required check equations which are necessary to calculate $p_1, ..., p_t$ parity bits. Therefore, we can
delete the N_n and P submatrices from developed H_n matrix to reduce complexity further at the encoding stage. After this step, the resultant matrix become

$$H_p = \begin{bmatrix} M & T \end{bmatrix}$$

The proposed scheme is simulated in 3GPP LTE uplink scenario. The simulation parameters used here are listed in the Table 2. As the BER performance of
LDPC and Turbo codes are similar, the proposed code is only compared with the
well known Richardson scheme which is used to encode LDPC code. The simulation result in Fig. 3 shows that the proposed LDPC scheme exhibits almost
similar performance with the Richardson scheme. There is a little performance
degradation due to the increase in code rate.

Equalizer	MMSE	Pulse shaping	RRC filter

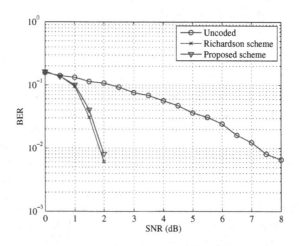

Fig. 3. BER plot for uncoded and LDPC encoded SC-FDMA system

4 Conclusion

A new encoding technique for LDPC code at the uplink of 3GPP LTE is proposed. The concept of ALT is used where the parity check matrix is preprocessed and encoded in $O(n)$ complexity. This encoding technique is applied in the uplink of LTE system where SC-FDMA is used as the multiple access scheme. As the encoding is performed in a $O(n)$ complexity, it outperforms the existing LDPC encoding technique. With the proposed encoding technique, LDPC code can be a potential candidate to be placed at the 3GPP LTE uplink. The proposed encoding is simulated in the SC-FDMA scenario and the BER curve is shown. The results show that the proposed encoding offers similar bit error rate with linear encoding complexity. Our future work is to combine LDPC and Turbo codes to

mun. Mag. 44(3), 38–45 (2006)

3. Gallager, R.G.: Low Density Parity Check Codes. IRE transactions on Information Theory IT-8, 21–28 (1962)
4. Gallager, R.G.: Low-Density Parity-Check Codes. MIT Press, MA (1963)
5. Mackay, D.J.C., Neal, R.M.: Near Shannon limit performance of low density parity check codes. IEE Electron Letter 32(18), 1645–1646 (1996)
6. Mackay, D.J.C.: Good error-correcting codes based on very sparse matrices. IEEE Trans. Inform. Theory IT-45(2), 399–431 (1999)
7. Wiberg, N.: Codes and decoding on general graphs. Linkoeping studies in science and technology (440) (1996)
8. Richardson, T.J., Shokrollahi, A., Urbanke, R.: Design of capacity approaching low-density parity-check codes. IEEE Trans. Inform. Theory 47, 619–637 (2001)
9. Luby, M., Mitzenmacher, M., Shokrollahi, A., Spielman, D.: Analysis of low density codes and improved designs using irregular graphs. In: Proc. 30th Annu. ACM Symp. Theory of computing, pp. 249–258 (1998)
10. Kschischang, F.R.: Codes defined of graphs. IEEE Commun. Mag. 41(8), 118–125 (2003)
11. Luby, M., Mitzenmacher, M., Shokrollahi, A., Spielman, D., Stemann, V.: Practical loss-resilient codes. In: Proc. 29th Annual ACM Symp. Theory of Computing, pp. 150–159 (1997)
12. Sipser, M., Spielman, D.: Expander codes. IEEE Trans. Inform. Theory 42, 1710–1722 (1996)
13. MacKay, D.J.C., Wilson, S.T., Davey, M.C.: Comparison of constructions of irregular Gallager codes. In: Proc. 36th Allerton Conf. Communication, Control, and Computing (September 1998)
14. Richardson, T.J., Urbanke, R.: Efficient encoding of low-density parity-check codes. IEEE Trans. Inform. Theory 47(2), 638–656 (2001)
15. Lin, S., Costello, D.J.: Error control coding. Pearson prentice hall, London (2004)
16. Nee, R.V., Prasad, R.: OFDM for wireless multimedia communications. Artech House (2000)
17. Luby, M., Mitzenmacher, M., Shokrollahi, A., Spielman, D.: Improved low-density parity-check codes using irregular graphs. IEEE Trans. Inf. Theory 47(2), 585–598 (2001)

Ryouhei Kawano and Toshiaki Miyazaki

Graduate School of Computer Science and Engineering, The University of Aizu,
Aizu-Wakamatsu, Fukushima 965-8580, Japan

Abstract. This paper proposes a method for dual optimization of sensor function allocation and effective data aggregation in wireless sensor networks. This method realizes dynamic allocation of sensor functions so as to balance the distribution of each sensor function in a target monitoring area. In addition, effective data aggregation is performed by using a tree network topology and time division multiple access (TDMA), which is a collision-free communication scheme. By comparing the results from the proposed method with the results from non-optimized methods, it can be validated that the proposed method is more effective. The proposed method is 1.7 times more efficient than non-optimized methods in distributing sensor functions. With this method, the network lifetime is doubled, and the number of data packets received at a base station (BS) is considerably increased by avoiding packet collisions.

1 Introduction

Recently, wireless sensor networks (WSNs) have attracted considerable attention. However, some problems must be addressed in order to meet real-world demands. These include higher instability, higher uncertainty, and lower power capacity of WSNs when compared to conventional networks. Furthermore, in the case of a WSN, resource allocation problems need to be solved [1]. For example, dynamic sensor function allocation is required in order to realize a data-centric concept [2] that enables users to access the required sensed data from the WSN without having to know about individual sensor nodes. An effective data aggregation method is also required for effectively observing the target field.

This paper proposes a method for the dual optimization of dynamic sensor function allocation and effective data aggregation. In this method, the distribution of each sensor function in the target monitoring area can be balanced by dynamic sensor func-

sion probability are achieved; however, overheads in TRAMA are too high to permit communication between nodes without packet collisions. Graph coloring algorithms are often used to solve resource allocation problems [5][6][7]. They provide effective solutions, but are not suitable for WSNs. This is because WSNs are often controlled in a decentralized or distributed manner. The graph coloring algorithms are unfortunately centralized ones and do not take any environmental changes into account.

Compared to the related works, the proposed method has the following features:

- *Sensor function distribution balancing*
Sensor function allocation is carried out so as to balance the distribution of each sensor function in a target monitoring field. Although the sensing accuracy depends on the total number of sensor nodes deployed in the target field, we can monitor the target field regardless of the number of sensor nodes.

- *Extension of network lifetime*
Power consumption in a WSN can be reduced by providing a dynamic sleep state in addition to a static sleep state; this helps increase the lifetime of the WSN. The dynamic sleep state also helps in reducing packet collisions and sensing and transmission of redundant data.

- *Robustness*
Since the sensor function allocation is dynamically performed using the currently available sensor nodes, the proposed method is robust to failures and the disappearance of a node.

- *High scalability*
To establish a network, it is necessary to ensure that each node communicates only with its neighbors. The proposed method has high scalability for network construction.

2 Wireless Sensor Network Model

In this paper, we consider a WSN that is organized autonomously as follows: first, multiple sensor nodes are scattered across the target field. Next, each sensor node negotiates with its neighboring sensor nodes and determines its sensing task. Then, depending on the sensing task, the node starts transmitting the sensed data to a BS via

sensor node allocates its own sensor function and time slot for TDMA by using a graph coloring algorithm and constructs a tree network structure, whose root is the BS, for effective aggregation of the sensed data. Subsequently, each sensor node exchanges information with its neighboring nodes. Next, in the active period, each sensor node receives the sensed data by using the allocated sensor function and buffers the data in a data forwarding list. In addition, the sensed data received from the child nodes in the communication tree are also buffered in the data forwarding list. These buffered data are then transmitted to the parent node selected in the previous control period. Here, a parent node refers to a directly connected neighboring node in the vicinity of the root of the communication tree. Every node repeats the abovementioned process, and an observer can obtain all the sensed data from the deployed sensor nodes. Finally, in the sleep period, the sensor node goes into a sleep state and remains inactive for a given time.

We assume that all the sensor nodes are synchronized and their state transitions are carried out simultaneously. In practice, to realize the proposed method, we use a traditional sensor network synchronization method such as reference broadcast synchronization (RBS) or flooding time synchronization protocol (FTSP) [8][9]. With these methods, it is possible to achieve millisecond-order synchronization. In addition, if a packet arrives, the main procedure shown in Fig. 1 is interrupted and the packet information is immediately added to the packet list P. Here, if a node does not receive any packet from a neighboring node for a given period of time, the node removes the ID of the corresponding neighboring node from the neighboring node list.

3.1 Control Period

The control period is very important in our method and performs the following two tasks.

Task 1: Dual optimization using a distributed graph coloring algorithm
To perform sensor function allocation and the time slot allocation in TDMA, we use a distributed graph coloring algorithm called dynamic probability-function or DP algorithm, which we have had proposed in a previous study [10]. In the coloring algorithm, each color refers to an integer number, starting from zero. The color allocated to a node should be different from the colors of its neighboring nodes. The maximum number of

```
self->sensorID = 0;
self->timeslot = 0;
P = {}; //cleared

// If a packet arrives, this main procedure is interrupted and the
// packet information is added to list P.
setupPacketReceiveHandler();

// Main process
repeat{
    runCtrlPeriod();
    runActiveAndSleepPeriod();
}
}

procedure runCtrlPeriod(){
    start = random(ctrlPeriodTime);
    wait until start time;

    // Task1: Coloring process
    // Sensor function allocation
    oneHopColoring();
    // Timeslot allocation
    twoHopColoring();

    // Task2: Tree construction/update
    treeConstruction();

    // Notify/Update
    broadcast own new information to the neighboring nodes;

    wait until the end of the control period, ctrlPeriodTime;
}
```

Fig. 1. Outline of the proposed method

• *Sensor function allocation*

In order to balance the distribution of each sensor function, each sensor node uses the DP algorithm to allocate to itself a sensor function that is different from that of its neighboring nodes; this process is referred to as "oneHopColoring()" and is shown in Fig. 1.

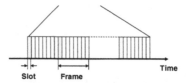

Fig. 2. Processing periods and their corresponding time slots in the proposed method

control is realized in a centralized manner; that is, the BS allocates a time slot to each node. However, it is difficult to implement this approach since our target is a decentralized WSN. Therefore, we apply our coloring algorithm to time slot allocation in TDMA. This enables autonomous and dynamic time slot allocation.

For time slot allocation, each node should be assigned a time slot that is different from that of the two-hop reachable nodes. This is because for realizing a multihop wireless network, it is necessary to avoid the packet collisions that result from hidden terminals or nodes. An example of time slot allocation is shown in Fig. 3. Here, each number indicates the allocated time slot number for the corresponding sensor node. In this example, stable communication is realized because each node has a time slot that is different from the time slot of the two-hop reachable nodes, and packet collisions do not occur even if nodes with the same time slot number send packets simultaneously.

We modified the DP coloring algorithm to solve the time slot allocation problem as follows: each sensor node should be allocated a color without any color conflict with the two-hop reachable nodes. This modification is relatively simple and can be applied to the WSNs studied herein. This modified coloring algorithm is called "two-HopColoring()" and is shown in Fig. 1.

Task 2: Tree construction
For realizing a data aggregation path to a BS, a tree structure whose nodes comprise the deployed sensor nodes is considered. The BS is the top or root node of the tree. Actual data aggregation is performed using the TDMA scheme, and the sensed data are transferred toward the BS from a node to its neighboring node in an appropriate time slot through a multihop path in the tree topology. Thus, for effective transfer of the sensed data to the BS, the tree topology should be balanced such that each multi-

Communication area

Fig. 3. Example of an acceptable time slot allocation. The number on each node represents the time slot number.

Capability for multisink sensor networks

A multisink WSN is a robust system in terms of data aggregation since the sensed data can be aggregated via other BSs in the event of damage to even a single BS. Moreover, the loads and power consumption of the BSs and the relay nodes are balanced, because of which the lifetime of the WSN is increased. In our algorithm, Task 1, which allocates sensor functions and time slots to each sensor node, does not depend on the number of BSs. Furthermore, each sensor node constructs the shortest path to the nearest BS in Task 2. Thus, the proposed method can be directly applied to multisink sensor networks without any modifications.

3.2 Active Period and Sleep Period

The active period has multiple data aggregate spans, and each data aggregate span consists of time frames and time slots, as shown in Fig. 2. Thus, for one active period, each sensor node can send multiple packets using the TDMA communication method. In other words, the number of packets transmitted by a node in each active period can be regarded as the number of assigned time frames.

Remaining battery power	Active period				Time
0.75 ~ 1.00	Data aggregate	Data aggregate	Data aggregate	Data aggregate	
0.50 ~ 0.75	Data aggregate	Data aggregate	Data aggregate	Sleep	
0.25 ~ 0.50	Data	Data	Sleep	Sleep	

sleeps during the remaining span of the active period. Here, a sensor node must perform the data aggregation at least once in each active period.

In the sleep period, each sensor node simply changes to the sleep state for a given time so that power consumption is reduced.

4 Evaluations

In order to evaluate the effectiveness of the proposed algorithm, the following simulation-based experiments were conducted. First, we created four network topologies with different number of nodes—50, 100, 150, and 200—in a field of area 100 m × 100 m. Here, the location of each node was defined by using x- and y-coordinates whose values range from 0 to 100 m. In addition, the communication radius between the sensor nodes was assumed to be 20 m. In these networks, the average degree of each node, i.e., the average number of neighboring nodes, for the 50-, 100-, 150-, and 200-node topologies was 5.2, 10.3, 13.1, and 14.7, respectively; and the number of sensor functions in each sensor node was set to 4. The proposed algorithm was applied 10 times to each network under the abovementioned conditions, and the average of the 10 times trails was used for evaluating the effectiveness of the proposed algorithm. The energy consumption model was based on the Crossbow MICAz model, which is one of the most commonly used sensor network nodes [11]. To reduce the simulation time and verify the behavior of the WSN under low-power conditions, the battery power of each sensor node was initially set to 0.4 mAh.

For comparison, five other methods were also examined. In the first method, a tree structure was constructed, but communication among the sensor nodes was performed in a random manner. This method was referred to as "Random."

In the second method, called "Sensor only," the sensor function allocation task was invoked, but the transfer of packets among the sensor nodes was random; this method did not have a tree structure. Thus, packet collisions often occurred in this method.

In the third method, called "TDMA only," a time slot was allocated to each sensor node; however, the sensor function allocation was not carried out with the use of our graph coloring algorithm.

In the fourth method, called "Ideal," data aggregation in each cycle was constantly

4.1 Balance in the Distribution of Each Sensor Function and the Number of Aggregated Packets

In order to show the effect of sensor function allocation and time slot allocation, "Proposed," "Sensor only," "TDMA only," and "Random" were evaluated from the viewpoint of the distribution of various types of sensor functions and the number of aggregated packets. In order to evaluate the effectiveness of these methods, we introduced a measure. This measure was calculated by using the following procedure: first, the field in which the sensor nodes were scattered was divided into small areas. Next, in each small area, the variance of frequency distributions of the colors that were mapped to the nodes was calculated. Finally, the measure was defined as the sum of the variances of all the divided areas. A small calculated measure implied that the colors were relatively uniformly mapped, and this was a favorable condition.

Fig. 5 shows the experimental results. The x-axis represents the number of nodes scattered in the WSN, and the bar graphs represent the newly introduced evaluation values. The evaluation values obtained for the "Proposed" and "Sensor only" methods indicated that these methods were approximately 60% (1/0.6 = 1.7 times) more efficient than the "TDMA only" and "Random" methods. Since our distributed coloring algorithm was employed in these two methods, the results show that this algorithm is effective at balancing the distribution of sensor functions.

The line graphs in Fig. 5 provide a summary of the results obtained for the simulation of the total number of packets received at the BS. The number of packets received at the BS in the "Proposed" and "TDMA only" methods was considerably larger than that in the "Random" and "Sensor only" methods. For 50-node and 100-node deployments, the number of packets received at the BS in the "Proposed" and "TDMA only" methods increased 14.3 times. This was because packet collisions were prevented to a considerable extent. Generally, in the TDMA scheme, if many sensor nodes are deployed in the target field, it is difficult to completely avoid packet collisions because of the lack of time slots. The ratio of the number of packets received at the BS in the "Proposed" and "TDMA only" methods to that in the "Random" and "Sensor only" methods was smaller in the 150-node and 200-node deployments than in the 50-node and 100-node deployments. However, the ratio was still more than 4.3. This result indicated that in the TDMA scheme, the "Proposed" and "TDMA only"

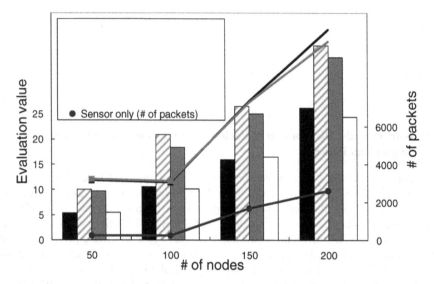

Fig. 5. Variance of the number of sensor functions deployed and the number of packets. The x-axis represents the number of nodes scattered in the field, the left y-axis represents the evaluation value, and the right y-axis represents the number of packets received by the BS. (Note that the bar graphs of the "Random only" and "Sensor only" methods overlap.).

4.2 Network Lifetime vs. the Number of Aggregated Packets

Fig. 6 plots the number of packets received at a BS during one cycle over time when 50 nodes are deployed in the target field. In this figure, the x-axis represents time, and the y-axis represents the number of packets received at the BS. The lines in the plot differ with the method applied and the location of the BS. Two different cases were considered for the location of the BS. In the first case, the BS is located at a corner of the field, i.e., BS = (0,0). In the second case, the BS is located at the center of the field, i.e., BS = (50,50). From the figure, it can be observed that the BS received many packets from the WSN in one cycle in the "Greedy" method; however, the network lifetime in this method was shorter when compared to the network lifetime in the other methods. On the other hand, although the network lifetime of the "Ideal" method was longer than that of the network in the other methods, the number of packets received at the BS in one cycle was smaller in the "Ideal" method than in the other methods. In the proposed method, the number of packets received at the BS was initially identical to that in the "Greedy" method. The number of aggregated packets received at the BS in one cycle decreased with a decrease in the power remaining in the node battery. For exam-

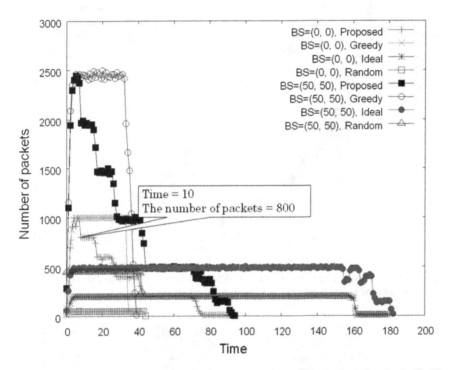

Fig. 6. The number of packets received at the BS in one cycle. The number of nodes is 50. The x-axis represents time, and the y-axis represents the number of packets received at the BS in one cycle.

Fig. 7 shows the average power remaining in the batteries of all the nodes that are deployed in the WSN, where in 50 nodes are scattered in the target field. The x-axis shows the simulation time, and the y-axis shows the initial power of the battery (0.4 mAh). The lines in the plot differ with the method applied and the location of the BS. Each dot in the figure corresponds to the average number of active nodes at a given time, and the vertical error bar associated with the dot corresponds to its variance. As is evident from the figure, battery power consumption was reduced in the proposed method; further, the node lifetime in the proposed method was almost double the node

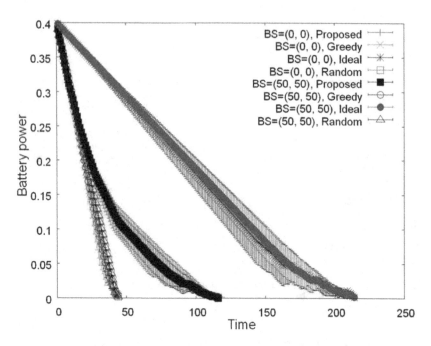

Fig. 7. Battery power. The number of nodes deployed in the network is 50. The x-axis represents time, and the y-axis represents the average battery power.

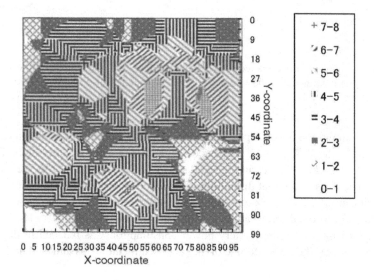

Proposed	150	0.54	0.54	0.55	0.54	0.54
Proposed	200	0.72	0.72	0.72	0.73	0.72
Greedy	50	0.58	0.57	0.58	0.54	0.57
Greedy	100	0.86	0.83	0.86	0.87	0.86
Greedy	150	0.73	0.72	0.73	0.73	0.73
Greedy	200	0.78	0.79	0.79	0.79	0.78
Ideal	50	0.36	0.33	0.32	0.31	0.33
Ideal	100	0.38	0.39	0.36	0.38	0.38
Ideal	150	0.54	0.54	0.55	0.55	0.55
Ideal	200	0.74	0.74	0.74	0.74	0.74
Random	50	0.10	0.10	0.13	0.11	0.11
Random	100	0.12	0.12	0.12	0.12	0.12
Random	150	0.36	0.33	0.39	0.30	0.35
Random	200	0.48	0.49	0.49	0.48	0.48
BS location: center of the field, (50,50)						
Proposed	50	0.67	0.63	0.66	0.69	0.66
Proposed	100	0.83	0.84	0.83	0.85	0.84
Proposed	150	0.90	0.91	0.90	0.91	0.90
Proposed	200	0.87	0.87	0.87	0.87	0.87
Greedy	50	0.74	0.62	0.63	0.64	0.66
Greedy	100	0.84	0.84	0.85	0.81	0.84
Greedy	150	0.89	0.90	0.89	0.90	0.89
Greedy	200	0.88	0.88	0.88	0.88	0.88
Ideal	50	0.74	0.65	0.67	0.69	0.69
Ideal	100	0.88	0.90	0.89	0.87	0.89
Ideal	150	0.93	0.93	0.93	0.93	0.93
Ideal	200	0.91	0.91	0.91	0.91	0.91
Random	50	0.48	0.44	0.45	0.50	0.47
Random	100	0.65	0.65	0.65	0.68	0.66
Random	150	0.72	0.79	0.75	0.75	0.75
Random	200	0.86	0.85	0.86	0.85	0.85

From Figs. 6 and 7, it can be seen that with the proposed method, the network lifetime and the number of packets received at a BS are optimized and effective data aggregation is realized. The evaluation results are similar in all the other cases where 100, 150, and 200 nodes were scattered in the target field.

4.3 Area Coverage of Each Sensor Function

coverage.　　　　　　refers to the location of the BS,　　　　represents the sensor function, "# of nodes" refers to the sum of the nodes deployed in the WSN, "Sensor function" refers to the function allocated to each sensor, and "Avg." refers to the average value of the area coverage of the sensor function. From Table 1, it can be seen that a high area coverage can be achieved with the proposed method. In particular, the area coverage is as high as 90% when the number of scattered nodes is 150 and BS = (50,50). On the other hand, the area coverage in the "Random" method is relatively low in almost all the cases. Contrary to our expectations, the area coverage in the "Greedy" method was low since the network lifetime in this case was short. We could realize a long lifetime in the "Ideal" method by sacrificing on area coverage. This means that a long network lifetime and a high area coverage cannot be simultaneously achieved in the "Greedy" and "Ideal" methods. The area coverage and network lifetime in the proposed method are better than the area coverage and network lifetime in the other methods.

5   Conclusions

We proposed a method for the simultaneous optimization of sensor function allocation and time slot allocation in TDMA. This method was based on a distributed graph coloring algorithm and realized dynamic sensor function allocation while taking into consideration the balance between the distribution of the sensor functions in the target monitoring area. In addition, by using the TDMA scheme, wherein time slots were dynamically assigned to the appropriate sensor nodes, packet collisions were avoided. A tree network structure was introduced for effective data aggregation. The tree topology was autonomously generated and maintained so as to shorten the data transfer paths between the sensor nodes and the BS. The experimental results showed that sensor function allocation was more balanced in the proposed method than in non-optimized methods. In addition, as a result of collision-free communications, the number of data packets received at the BS in the proposed method increased from 4.3 to 14.3 times the number of data packets received at the BS in non-optimized methods. Furthermore, the network lifetime in the proposed method was double that in other individual optimization or non-optimized methods; further, high area overage could be

3. Zhang, X., Hong, J., Zhang, L., Shan, X., Li, V.O.K.: CP-TDMA: Coloring and Probability-Based TDMA Scheduling for Wireless Ad Hoc Networks. IEICE Tran. on Communications E91-B(1), 322–326 (2008)
4. Rajendran, V., Obraczka, K., Garcia-Luna-Aceves, J.J.: Energy-Efficient, Collision-FreeMedium Access Control for Wireless Sensor Networks. In: First ACM Conference on Embedded Networked Systems, SenSys 2003 (2003)
5. Jensen, T.R., Toft, B.: Graph Coloring Problems. Wiley-Interscience, Readings (1994)
6. Gandham, S., Dawande, M., Prakash, R.: Link Scheduling in Sensor Networks: Distributed Edge Coloring Revisited. In: INFOCOM 2005, vol. 4, pp. 2492–2501 (2005)
7. Hirayama, K., Yokoo, M.: The Distributed Breakout Algorithm. Artificial Intelligence Journal 161(1-2), 89–116 (2005)
8. Elson, J., Girod, L., Estrin, D.: Fine-Grained Network Time Synchronization using Reference Broadcasts. In: Proceedings of the 5th Symposium on Operating Systems Design and Implementation (OSDI 2002), Boston, Massachusetts (2002)
9. Romer, K.: Time Synchronization in Ad Hoc Networks. In: Proc. the 2nd ACM International Symposium on Mobile Ad Hoc Networking & Computing (MobiHoc 2001) Long Beach, California, pp. 173–182 (2001)
10. Kawano, R., Miyazaki, T.: Distributed Coloring Algorithm for Wireless Sensor Networks and Its Applications. In: Proc. IEEE 7th International Conference on Computer and Information Technology (CIT 2007), Fukushima, Japan, October 2007, pp. 997–1002 (2007)
11. MICAz data sheet, Crossbow,
http://www.xbow.com/Products/
Product_ pdf_files/Wirless_pdf/M ICAz_Datasheet.pdf

[1] Faculty of Information Science and Engineering, Ningbo University,
315211, Ningbo, P.R.China
[2] Institute of Computing Technology, Chinese Academic of Sciences,
100080, Beijing, P.R.China
zhangyun_8851@163.com, {jianggangyi,yumei,chenken}@nbu.edu.cn

Abstract. Three-dimensional video (3DV) consists of multi-view video and multi-view depth video, which provides three-dimensional perception and makes people more interested in depth contrast and pop-out regions. Meanwhile, 3DV is with both high temporal and inter-view correlation. In this paper, we define a novel depth perceptual region of interest (ROI) for 3DV and propose two joint extraction schemes according to correlation types of 3DV. Then, depth based ROI extraction is proposed by jointly using depth, motion and texture information. Furthermore, we also present a novel inter-view tracking method for 3DV, in which inter-view correlation among views and extracted ROI of neighboring views are utilized to facilitate ROI extraction among different views. Experimental results show that the proposed ROI extraction and tracking algorithms maintain high extraction accuracy and low complexity.

Keywords: Three-dimensional video; region of interest; inter-view correlation.

1 Introduction

Three dimensional video (3DV) can be used for new interactive multimedia applications, such as 3D television, and free-viewpoint video communications [1]. They not only provide 3D perception, but also provide interactive functionalities, such as content-based video edit and view switching that allowing users freely to change viewpoints. These interactive functionalities call for low complex and semantic region-of-interest (ROI) extraction to facilitate video processing.

On the other hand, the 3DV data consists of multi-view video and multiple

contours [6]. However, it is with high complexity because previously extracted ROIs have not been used for ROI extraction among neighboring views although there are intrinsic inter-view correlation among views.

2 Depth Perceptual ROI Definition and Extraction for 3DV

In mono-view video, ROI is often related to moving regions and textural regions. However, ROI in 3DV is additionally related to the 3D perception, i.e. depth or disparity. People are often more likely interested in regions with small depth value, such as pop-out region and depth contrast regions.

Let 2D-GOP denote a two dimensional picture array of 3DV. Obviously, the simplest ROI extraction scheme for 3DV is expanding ROI extraction from conventional single view video. That is T0 frames are extracted firstly, then, the rest frames of the 2D-GOP track the extracted ROIs of temporal preceding frames. As multi-view video data originate from the same scene, the inherent dependencies include inter-view ones among neighboring views and temporal ones among successive images. Thus, it is with high complexity because of inter-view correlation are not efficiently used.

Based on these analyses, we present two joint extraction schemes in which previously extracted ROIs of time preceding or inter-view neighboring frames are utilized to improve robustness and reduce computational complexity, shown as Figs.1~2. Fig.1 shows temporal based joint extraction scheme (TBJES), in which each rectangle indicates a frame and arrow indicates reference direction. In a 2D-GOP, there is only a frame of the center view, i.e. S2T0 shown as the white rectangle in Fig.1, extracting ROI independently. Then, neighboring frames adopt the inter-view correlation with S2 and the extracted ROIs of S2T0 to extract ROI. Finally, the

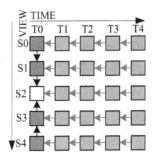 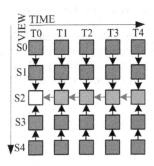

3 Depth-Spatio-Temporal Joint ROI Extraction and Tracking

3.1 Depth Based ROI Extraction

In this paper, depth based ROI extraction is proposed to extract ROI for a frame by jointly using motion, texture and depth information of 3DV.

Step1. Let vectors $\mathbf{F}$ and $\mathbf{D}$ be the color video and depth video, respectively. Motion mask $\mathbf{M}^m$ is extracted from the differences among temporally successive frames. We segment foreground regions $\mathbf{M}^f$ from the background regions by using a threshold, and the background regions are set as non-interested regions. Then, contours mask of color video, $\mathbf{M}^c$, and depth discontinuous regions, $\mathbf{M}^d$, are extracted by using edge detection algorithm.

Step2. Because moving object and depth discontinuous regions are usually ROI, we construct characteristic region, $\mathbf{M}^f \cap [\mathbf{M}^m \cup \mathbf{M}^d]$, as seeds of ROI depth plane. According to histogram of depth values in $\mathbf{M}^f \cap [\mathbf{M}^m \cup \mathbf{M}^d]$ regions, the depth image $\mathbf{D}$ is divided into different depth planes $\mathbf{D}^z$ according to the mean and variance of the histogram, where z is the ordinal number of the depth plane.

Step3. ROI contours are constructed by integrating foreground motion region, depth contour and color contour as $\mathbf{M}^f \cap [\mathbf{M}^m \cup \mathbf{M}^d \cup \mathbf{M}^c]$. Morphological process, contour recovery and noise elimination operations are performed on $\mathbf{M}^f \cap [\mathbf{M}^m \cup \mathbf{M}^d \cup \mathbf{M}^c]$ to build a closed and more reliable ROI contours, $\mathbf{M}^l$.

Step4. To exclude the background regions in $\mathbf{D}^z$, a boundary scanning process guided by $\mathbf{M}^l$ is conducted on depth planes $\mathbf{D}^z$ by supposing image boundaries are background.

3.2 Inter-view ROI Tracking and Extraction

Multi-view video is captured from the same scene by a camera array. There is intrinsic geometry correlation among the ROIs of different views. Therefore, we can generate the corresponding ROI in other views by using the neighboring extracted ROI information. Let $\mathbf{M}=(X, Y, Z)$ be a point of ROI in the world coordinate system,

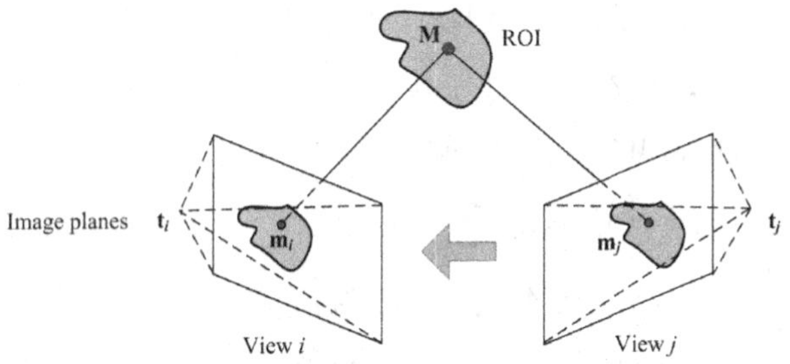

Fig. 3. Relation between ROI point in 3D world coordinate and its points on 2D image planes

Fig. 3 shows the relation between ROI point in 3D world coordinate and the ROI points on 2D image planes. The ROI points on different 2D image planes are projected from the same ROI point in 3D world coordinate. Thus, if ROI of the jth view has been extracted, the ROI points in i^{th} view can be generated as

$$Z_i \bar{\mathbf{m}}_i = Z_j \mathbf{A}_i \mathbf{R}_i \mathbf{R}_j^{-1} \mathbf{A}_j^{-1} \bar{\mathbf{m}}_j - \mathbf{A}_i \mathbf{R}_i \mathbf{R}_j^{-1} \mathbf{t}_j + \mathbf{A}_j \mathbf{t}_i \tag{2}$$

where Z_j and Z_i is the depth value. According to (2), $\mathbf{m}_i$ is determined by $\mathbf{m}_j$ and depth value Z_j, and it is denoted as $\bar{\mathbf{m}}_i = f(\bar{\mathbf{m}}_j, Z_j)$ for short, where f is the mapping function. Let $\bar{\mathbf{m}}_j^+ = (x_j + \sigma_x, y_j + \sigma_y, \mathbf{I}_j^+)$, $\bar{\mathbf{m}}_i^+ = (x_i + \sigma_x, y_i + \sigma_y, \mathbf{I}_i^+)$ be a neighboring point of $\bar{\mathbf{m}}_j$ and $\bar{\mathbf{m}}_i$, where σ_x and σ_y are offsets in the x-axis and y-axis, $\mathbf{I}_j^+$ and $\mathbf{I}_i^+$ are pixel values. Let Z_j^+ be the neighboring depth value of Z_j. Thus, the pixel corresponding to $\bar{\mathbf{m}}_j^+$ on i^{th} image plane is calculated as

$$\hat{\bar{\mathbf{m}}}_i^+ = f(\bar{\mathbf{m}}_j^+, Z_j^+). \tag{3}$$

Because depth map is smooth and with high spatial correlation in ROI, $\hat{\bar{\mathbf{m}}}_i^+$ is approximate to $^{-+}$ when | | and | | is smaller than T and T . So we can get

The center of $W_{k,t}$ is calculated by

$$\begin{cases} x'_{k,t} = \sum_{i=1}^{p} \xi_{k,t-i} \left(x_{k,t-i} - x_{k,t-i-1} \right) + x_{k,t-1} \\ y'_{k,t} = \sum_{i=1}^{p} \varsigma_{k,t-i} \left(y_{k,t-i} - y_{k,t-i-1} \right) + y_{k,t-1} \end{cases}. \tag{5}$$

The width and height of $W'_{k,t}$ is predicted as

$$\begin{cases} w'_{k,t} = \lambda_w \cdot \sum_{i=1}^{p} \alpha_{k,t-i} w_{k,t-i} \\ h'_{k,t} = \lambda_h \cdot \sum_{i=1}^{p} \beta_{k,t-i} h_{k,t-i} \end{cases}, \tag{6}$$

where $\alpha_{k,t}$, $\beta_{k,t}$, $\xi_{k,t}$ and $\varsigma_{k,t}$ are weight coefficients, λ_ϕ is window size scaling coefficient correlated with motion magnitude and it is calculated as

$$\lambda_\phi = 1 + \max \left(0, \theta \times \left(\phi_{k,t-1} - \phi_{k,t-2} \right) \right) / \phi_{k,t-1}, \quad \phi \in \{w, h\}, \tag{7}$$

where θ is a scaling coefficient. Finally, depth based ROI extraction is adopted to extract the accurate ROI within the predictive windows.

4 Experimental Results and Analyses

In order to testify the effectiveness of our ROI extraction algorithm, simulations are implemented with multi-view video sequences provided by Microsoft, Ballet and Breakdancers [7]. They have both fast motion and slow motion. Fig.4 show eight views the two 3DV sequences.

(a) Ballet (1st frame of eight views, up: multi-view video, down: multi-view depth video)

other two men are in regions with large depth, which don't belong to the defined ROI. In the video coding process, MB is the minimal unit of bit allocation and computational power allocation. Thus, only MB size ROI extraction accuracy is required. Fig.5 (d) shows MB level ROI mask.

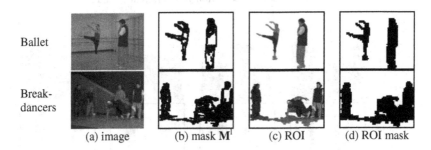

Ballet · Break-dancers · (a) image · (b) mask $\mathbf{M}^I$ · (c) ROI · (d) ROI mask

Fig. 5. Results of Depth based ROI Extraction

4.2 Inter-view ROI Tracking and Extraction

Only partial pixels of ROIs (i.e. $1/[(T_x+1) \times (T_y+1)]$) in 5th view are calculated as Eq.(2) point by point. The rest pixels are calculated as Eq.(4) which directly gets the value of surrounding tracked pixels. Then, the extracted ROIs are blocklized into MB. As T_x and T_y increase, the ROI extraction accuracy will decrease, meanwhile, the computational complexity will decrease significantly. Fig.6 shows an example that ROIs of a neighboring view (the 5th view) are tracked from ROIs of the 4th view with different T_x and T_y. The first row shows the extracted ROI, the second row show the ROI masks. It is clear that almost identical MB level ROI masks can be generated when T_x and T_y are smaller than 3.

In the extraction experiments, T_x and T_y are set as 1 so that almost 75% complexity are saved, meanwhile, ROI can be extracted precisely. Figs.7 show extracted ROIs of four neighboring views with time T0 (denoted by 'S0T0' as Figs. 1 ~ 2. They are with high accuracy for different views. ROIs with different depth projected to neighboring

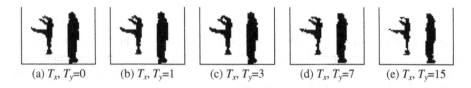

(a) T_x, T_y=0   (b) T_x, T_y=1   (c) T_x, T_y=3   (d) T_x, T_y=7   (e) T_x, T_y=15

Fig. 6. Inter-view ROI extraction with different T_x and T_y

Ballet

Break-
dancers

(a)S0T0   (b)S1T0   (c)S3T0   (d)S4T0

Fig. 7. ROI of neighboring views of 10th time instant

4.3 Temporal ROI Tracking and Extraction

Fig.8 shows ROI extraction results of temporal four successive frames, 11th to 14th frames of S2 view of the multi-view video sequences, denoted by 'S2T1', 'S2T2', 'S2T3' and 'S2T4' corresponding to Figs.1~2, respectively. Here, θ is set as 3. For

Break-
dancers

(a)S2T1   (b)S2T2   (c)S2T3   (d)S2T4

Fig. 8. ROI of successive four frames of view S2

5 Conclusion

Three dimensional video (3DV) is with both temporal and inter-view correlation. We presented two depth-spatio-temporal ROI extraction schemes in which depth, motion and texture information of 3DV data are jointly utilized to extract semantic ROIs. With the help of previously extracted ROIs, temporal and inter-view ROI tracking algorithms are proposed to improve ROI extraction efficiency and reduce computational complexity. The advantages of the proposed schemes are high extraction accuracy and low complexity, which are of great importance to content based multi-view video processing.

Acknowledgments. This work was supported by the Natural Science Foundation of China (60672073, 60832003) and the Innovation Fund Project for Graduate Student of Zhejiang province (YK2008044).

References

1. Tanimoto, M.: Overview of free viewpoint television. Signal Proc.: Image Comm. 21(6), 454–461 (2006)

layered representation. In: ACM SIGGRAPH and ACM Trans. Graphics, Los Angeles, CA, August 2004, pp. 600–608 (2004)

[1] Dept. of Computer Science Engineering, Inha University
[2] School of Information & Media, Kyungin Women's College
[3] School of Management & Tourism, Kimpo College
[4] Dept. of Computer and Information Science, Sunmoon University, South Korea
choisymail@gmail.com, kjspace@inha.ac.kr, softman@kic.ac.kr,
jhchoi@kimpo.ac.kr, rim@sunmoon.ac.kr, jhlee@inha.ac.kr

Abstract. What are important in wireless sensor networks are energy efficiency, reliable data transmission, and topological adaptation to the change of external environment. This study proposes dynamic routing algorithm that satisfies the above-mentioned conditions at the same time using a dynamic single path in wireless sensor networks. In our proposed algorithm, each node transmits data through the optimal single path using hop count to the sink and node average energy according to the change of external environment. For reliable data transmission, each node monitors its own transmission process. If a node detects a damaged path, it switches from the damaged path to the optimal path and, by doing so, enhances network reliability. In case of a topological change, only the changed part is reconstructed instead of the whole network, and this enhances the energy efficiency of the network.

Keywords: Wireless Sensor Networks, Reliability, Energy efficiency, Topology adaptation, dynamic routing algorithm.

1 Introduction

Wireless sensor networks, which are composed of tiny and resource constrained wireless devices, have been widely deployed for monitoring a specific phenomenon or recognizing surrounding situations throughout a wide area. In those systems, real-time information on events happening within a specific area can be collected. With decrease in the size and cost of sensor nodes, sensor networks can be utilized in various areas including environmental monitoring, ecological studies, national defense, medicine, transportation, disaster prevention, and intrusion detection [1,2].

other sensor nodes as relay nodes. Because the number of hops can be large in a large-scale sensor network, the reliability of network can be enhanced by applying a broadcast-based data transmission method [4,5]. However, because such a method increases nodes' energy consumption, it may result in the problem that the network is divided or stopped. To solve this problem, existing methods improved network reliability by transmitting data through multiple paths [6]. However, the use of multiple paths causes additional energy consumption, so not desirable in terms of energy efficiency. Furthermore, in a sensor network using limited resources, its topology is changed frequently, and such changes require the modification of network structure. For this, network is updated periodically or when changes are detected by an algorithm for detecting network changes. However, as network reconstruction involves all the nodes in the network, it increases energy consumption, and delays data transmission during the period of update.

Aiming at reliable data transmission, energy efficiency, and topological adaptability to the change of external environment, this study proposes a routing algorithm that chooses the optimal single path dynamically in wireless sensor networks. The proposed method transmits data after searching for the optimal path using hop count (HC) and node average energy (NAE). In response to the change of external environment, each node monitors the transmission process. If a node detects a damaged path, it changes the optimal path dynamically in a way of distributing energy consumption evenly over nodes and, by doing so, it enhances network reliability and energy efficiency of the network. In addition, on the change of network topology, only the changed part is reconstructed instead of the whole network and this minimizes unnecessary energy consumption.

Chapter 2 reviewed related studies, and Chapter 3 described the method proposed in this study. Chapter 4 presented the results of experiment in comparison with existing methods, and Chapter 5 analyzed the results of experiment.

2 Related Studies

Flooding is the most reliable one among the methods for a source node that detects events in surrounding environment using sensors to transmit its collected data to a sink [3,5]. In Flooding, a source node transmits its collected data to neighbor nodes that are

the packet but without designating the next node to which data will be transmitted. A node that has received the packet determines independently whether to transmit the packet by comparing its COST with the received COST. Consequently, data detected by a source node is transmitted in a direction that decreases COST. GRAB uses multiple paths for reliable data transmission, and uses credit for adjusting the width of multiple paths. As the width of multiple paths is controlled using credit in GRAB, the reliability of data transmission increase.

3 Dynamic Routing Algorithm

The process of dynamic routing algorithm is composed of three processes as follows: initialization process as the initial step of network construction; transmission process as the data transmission step; and reconfiguration process for coping with the deletion or move of sensor nodes and the change of external environment. Table 1 defines the types and functions of packets used in dynamic routing algorithm.

Table 1. Types and functions of packets used in dynamic routing algorithm

Packet type	Function
INIT	Packet broadcasted by a sink to the network at the beginning of sensor network construction.
TRN	Packet broadcasted when data has occurred in a source node or is transmitted to a neighbor node.
ACK	Packet broadcasted by a sink that has received a TRN packet for preventing looping.
HELLO	Packet for a newly added node or a moved node to advertise its existence to its neighbor nodes.

3.1 Initialization Process

At the beginning of network construction, a sink transmits an INIT packet. On the transmission of an INIT packet, the sink sets the transmission node ID to its ID, and HC and NAE to 0. Here, HC is the number of hops between the sink and the receiving

$$\text{COST}_n = \frac{(HC_{n-1}+1)^2}{NAE_{n-1} \cdot HC_{n-1} + NRE_n}, \qquad (4)$$

where

NRE_n : Normalized residual energy of Node N.
HC_{n-1} : HC of the node that has sent an INIT packet to Node N.
NAE_{n-1} : NAE of the node that has sent an INIT packet to Node N.

If COST calculated from a received INIT packet is smaller than the existing value, the path becomes the optimal path to the sink. The receiving node updates its entry in the COST table that stores updated HC, NAE and COST. And then it changes the INIT packet by replacing the transmission node ID to its own ID, and HC and NAE with the updated HC and NAE and sends it to its neighbor nodes. This process is continued until all the nodes receive the INIT packet at least once and set the minimum COST between them and the sink. INIT packet transmission by the sink is required only once at the beginning of network construction. In addition, in order to maintain the optimal path to the sink, all the nodes should know the minimum COST set by its neighbor nodes and HC, NAE on the setting.

When a node transmits an INIT packet, HC and NAE contained in the packet are values when the transmission node set the minimum COST. That is, although a node that has received an INIT packet cannot set its minimum COST from the received information, it can know the minimum COST, HC and NAE set by the neighbor node that has transmitted the packet. Each node in dynamic routing algorithm records HC, NAE and COST which set the optimal path to the sink by its neighbor nodes.

3.2 Transmission Process

A group of nodes that have detected the same data selects a source node, a representative node that will transmit the data for the group in order to prevent data redundancy and the waste of resources. Among the nodes that have detected the same data, the one with the minimum COST becomes the source node. The source node or the transmission node that delivers receiving data from the source node to the sink broadcasts data to all of its neighbor nodes at a distance of one hop rather than to a

However, because there may happen a situation where data cannot be transmitted to the sink due to an unexpected change of external environment or the breakdown of a transmission node, data monitoring process is required. After the source node has sent the TRN packet, if the node with the minimum COST chosen as the transmission node is in a normal state, it will receive a TRN packet with decreased COST from the transmission node, which is one of the neighbor nodes. And as this means that the TRN packet has been transmitted properly, and the source node ends its monitoring process. However, if the source node has not received a TRN packet with decreased COST within a specific length of time, the path is considered to have been damaged. If a damaged path is detected, the source node deletes the record of the damaged node's information from its COST table, and modifies the TRN packet as described above and sends it again. Lastly, the sink that has received the TRN packet ends the transmission process by sending an ACK packet in order to prevent looping.

3.3 Reconfiguration Process

In network operation, power consumption is not equal among the nodes. In dynamic routing algorithm, in order to maintain the optimal path, each node should maintain the latest minimum COST according to the change of external environment and inform its neighbor nodes of it. A decrease in a node's residual energy may affect other nodes' setting of the minimum COST. However, if residual energy has to be reported to the neighbor nodes whenever it changes, it will increase the energy consumption of the whole network and shorten network lifetime. For this, dynamic routing algorithm updates the COST table only when a packet has to be sent. In addition, when a node dies out due to breakdown or battery discharge, the problem can be solved by the monitoring process.

When a new node is added, the new node has only its own node ID and residual energy. In order to participate in the network, the added node builds a COST table and sends a HELLO packet. Its neighbor nodes who have received the HELLO packet reply with an ACK packet that contains their HC, NAE in their COST table and does not require a reply. The node receiving the ACK packet is the new node that sent the HELLO packet or a neighbor node of the node that has sent the ACK packet. The new node that sent the HELLO packet calculates HC, NAE and COST from HC, NAE received from its neighbor nodes by equation (1), (2), (3) and (4). Only when the

has been added, it is processed in the same way as that for the addition of a new node.

4 Experiment and Performance Evaluation

For the simulation, we built a 300x300 square sensor field. In a sensor field, 100 sensor nodes including a sink were deployed at random. The sink was positioned at the left bottom part of the sensor field. The sink was assumed to be a large-capacity system without a limitation in power like an ordinary PC, and all the nodes were assumed to consume 0.021J for sending 128 bytes of data and 0.014J for receiving the same amount of data respectively, for sending and receiving a bit at a transmission rate of 10kbps in WIN NG [7]. Power consumption in the standby mode was not counted. Table 2 shows parameters and its values used in simulation.

Table 2. Simulation parameters and values

Parameters	Values
Number of nodes	100
Range of radio Transmission in each node	30m
Energy consumption for transmission	0.021J
Energy consumption for receiving	0.014J
Initial energy	10J
Packet size	128 Bytes
Simulation time	400 sec

For the simulation, we chose a source node at random and generated a sensing event at each second. During a total of 400 seconds' simulation, the radio transmission range was set to 30m uniformly for all the nodes including the sink. In order to evaluate the performance of the proposed dynamic routing algorithm, we executed the simulation as above 10 times and compared the results with Flooding and GRAB.

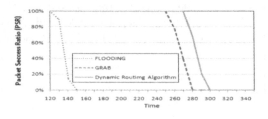

comparison show that network lifetime increased in dynamic routing algorithm.

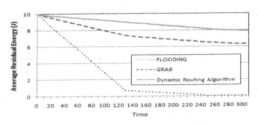

Fig. 2. Comparison with the Average Residual Energy over time

Figure 2 shows the change of the average residual energy of all the sensor nodes except the sink measured at every 10 seconds. In Flooding, the nodes showed rapid consumption of energy until 130 seconds and then a slow consumption rate because nodes near the sink exhausted their energy first and fell in a disabled state. In GRAB and dynamic routing algorithm, on the contrary, not all the nodes participated in data transmission to the sink as in Flooding, but only selected nodes on the path participated, so energy consumption was not rapid. In the experiment, GRAB performed ADV packet transmission involving all the nodes at every 50 seconds in order to cope with the change of network topology, and used multiple paths for reliability. In the results of comparison, dynamic routing algorithm showed energy efficiency around 16.5% higher than GRAB.

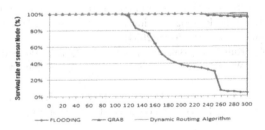

Fig. 3. Comparison with the Survival rate of sensor node over time

requirements of high energy efficiency and network reliability at the same time. In addition, when the network topology is changed, only the changed part is reconstructed instead of the whole network, and this minimizes unnecessary energy consumption in each node and enhances the energy efficiency of the whole network. Because sensor nodes around the sink consume energy more than other sensor nodes, however, network lifetime is dependent on nodes around the sink.

In order to solve this problem, research is going on for enhancing reliability and energy efficiency and, at the same time, increasing the lifetime of the whole network through moving the sink or adjusting the optimal transmission distance according to the change of external environment.

Acknowledgement

"This research was supported by the MKE(Ministry of Knowledge Economy), Korea, under the ITRC(Information Technology Research Center) Support program supervised by the IITA(Institute of Information Technology Advancement)" (IITA-2009-C1090-0902-0020).

References

1. Akyildiz, I.F., Su, W., Sankarasubramaniam, Y., Cayirci, E.: A Survey on Sensor Networks. IEEE Communications Magazine 40(8), 102–114 (2002)
2. Szewczyk, R., Osterwil, E., Polastre, J., Hamilton, M.: A Mainwaring Habitat Monitoring With Sensor Networks. Communications of the ACM 47(6), 34–40 (2004)
3. Al-Karaki, N., Kamal, E.: Routing techniques in wireless sensor networks: A survey. IEEE Wireless Communications 11(6), 6–28 (2004)
4. Heinzelman, W., Kulik, J., Balakrishnan, H.: Adaptive Protocols for Information Dissemination in Wireless Sensor Networks. In: Proc. 5th ACM/IEEE Mobicom Conference, pp. 174–185 (1999)
5. Intanagonwiwat, C., Govindan, R., Estrin, D.: Directed diffusion: a scalable and robust communication paradigm for sensor networks. In: Proc. of ACM MobiCom, pp. 56–67 (2000)
6. Ye, F., Zhong, G., Lu, S., Zhang, L.: Gradient Broadcast: A Robust Data Delivery Protocol for Large Scale Sensor Networks. Wireless Networks 11, 285–298 (2005)

Department of Electrical, Computer & IT, Islamic Azad University,
Qazvin Branch, Qazvin, Iran
ma.armaghan@gmail.com, haghighat@qazviniau.ac.ir

Abstract. Many multimedia network applications require multicast routing with certain Quality-of-Service (QoS) constraints. As constrained minimum Steiner tree problem, QoS multicast routing problem is known to be NP-Complete. The bandwidth constraint and the end-to-end delay constraint are two important QoS constraints. In this paper, we propose algorithms to solve the bandwidth-delay constrained least-cost multicast routing problem based on Tabu Search (TS) with an efficient candidate list strategy, which produces a good solution faster than the traditional simple TS-based algorithms. In addition, we use a simple form of systematic dynamic tabu tenure. Computational results for various random generated networks show that the proposed algorithms in comparison with the other existing short-term memory version of TS-based algorithms and heuristics are faster, more effective, and more suitable for large scale networks.

Keywords: Multicast Routing, Quality-of-Service, Tabu Search, Candidate list strategy, Dynamic tabu tenure.

1 Introduction

The development of high-speed communication networks has increased demand for numerous applications especially in the areas of telecommunication, distribution and transportation systems. In many of these applications, a source is required to send information to multiple destinations with varying QoS constraints through a communication network. To support such communication efficiently, one of the key issues that needs to be addressed is QoS multicast routing. An efficient QoS multicast routing algorithm should construct a multicast routing tree, by which the data can be transmitted from the source to all the destinations with guaranteed QoS, which typically enforce a restriction on the admissible multicast routing tree. Multicast routing

Hence computational intelligence methods such as genetic algorithm (GA), simulated annealing (SA), and tabu search (TS) become more suitable. These methods are a type of promising technique to solve combinatorial optimization problems [6] including the constrained Steiner tree problem. Several GA-based algorithms have been proposed to solve the constrained Steiner tree problem [7-9]. In addition some algorithms have been proposed to construct the constrained Steiner tree with tabu search techniques [10-14]. In most of the TS-based algorithms [10,12,13], at each iteration some random moves are examined. In tabu search randomization is de-emphasized on the assumption that intelligent search should be based on more systematic forms of guidance [15]. Therefore, Ghaboosi and Haghighat [14] explored the entire neighborhood on a given iteration, and illustrated how evaluating all feasible moves instead of examining some random moves will result in a better solution considering average tree cost. But it takes a long time special for situations where neighborhood space is large or its elements are expensive to evaluate.

In this study, we propose algorithms to solve the bandwidth-delay constrained least-cost multicast routing problem based on Tabu Search with an effective candidate list (CL) strategy named Hybrid candidate list. We generate the candidate moves by the intelligent process, CL strategy, rather than by a random or simple process, for example, to evaluate all possible moves in a current neighborhood. Such a CL strategy can be useful to produce optimal results in a relatively short amount of time specially when the network has large number of nodes. We demonstrate that by the use of Hybrid candidate list not only search speed but also solution quality will be improved. In addition instead previous TS-based multicast routing algorithms, we use a simple dynamic tenure structure, in which the tabu tenure can be varied dynamically during the search. It provides a dynamic and robust form of search [15].

The rest of this paper is organized as follows. The problem definition and formulation is given in section 2. Section 3 provides a brief introduction to the tabu search method. In section 4 we describe proposed short-term TS-based algorithms. Section 5 introduces the time complexity of the proposed algorithms. Section 6 gives the performance evaluation of the proposed algorithms. Conclusions and recommendations for further work follow in Section 7.

2 Problem Definition and Formulation

not to the multicast group. Assume $P_T(s,d)$ represents a unique path in the multicast tree from the source node s to the destination node $d \in M$. The total cost of the multicast tree $T(s,M)$ is defined as $C(T(s,M)) = \sum_{e \in T(s,M)} C(e)$, the total delay of the path $P_T(s,d)$ in the multicast tree $T(s,M)$ is defined as $D(P_T(s,d)) = \sum_{e \in P_T(s,d)} D(e)$, and the bottleneck bandwidth of the path $P_T(s,d)$ is simply defined as $B(P_T(s,d)) = \min\{ B(e), e \in P_T(s,d) \}$. Assume Δ_b represents the end-to-end delay constraint and $(_b$ the bandwidth constraint of each destination node. The bandwidth-delay-constrained least-cost multicast problem is defined as minimizing $C(T(s,M))$ while $D(P_T(s,d)) \leq \Delta_b$ and $B(P_T(s,d)) \geq (_b$. Fig. 1 illustrates an example of a network graph, a multicast group, and a Steiner tree.

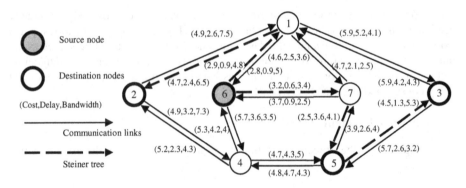

Fig. 1. An example of a network graph, a multicast group, and a Steiner tree

3   Tabu Search Method

Tabu search was introduced by Glover [15,16] as a meta-heuristic for solving combi-

4 The Proposed Short-Term TS-Based Algorithms

4.1 Pre-processing Phase

The pre-processing phase is the start point of all proposed algorithms. In this phase all the links from the network graph whose residual bandwidths are less than the bandwidth constraint are deleted. If in the refined graph the multicast group nodes are not in a connected sub-graph, then this topology does not satisfy the bandwidth constraint which causes the source node to negotiate with the corresponding application to relax the bandwidth threshold. In addition, this phase can further reduce the size of the network graph by removing all degree-one nodes which do not belong to the multicast group.

4.2 Initial Solution

The initial feasible solution is a shortest path tree, which is constructed in a greedy fashion by using Dijkstra's shortest path algorithm. The resulting set of shortest paths from the source node to each of the destination nodes defines a tree that serves as the initial solution. According to the parameters that are used as distances in Dijkstra's algorithm, initial solutions can be named as least-delay tree (LD tree) and least-cost delay-constrained tree (LC delay-constrained tree) [14].

4.3 Objective Function

In our algorithms, the objective function is the total cost of the multicast tree which has to be minimized.

4.4 Move

In this study, we use four types of move by the names of Steiner node move, Path move, K-Path move, and Complete move which are used in [14]. They are described briefly in the following. The Steiner node move has been proposed by Skorin-Kapov and Kos [11]. This move is an elementary move which adds or removes a single Steiner node. After each move, to construct the delay-constrained least-cost spanning

In Complete move which has been proposed by Ghaboosi and Haghighat [14], a solution is encoded with a two-dimensional matrix, each element of it represents a path associated to the edge in a directed complete graph over the multicast group nodes. To initialize the associated path of each edge, Dijkstra's shortest path algorithm is used. This move is an edge switching move. First, it removes an edge from the complete graph, and next it replaces it with a new edge where its associated path is an alternative least-cost delay-constrained path in the original network graph which is constructed with the Kth shortest path algorithm proposed by Jimenez and Marzal. After each move, complete graph is transformed to its associated delay-constrained minimum Steiner tree in two steps. First, the modified version of Prim's algorithm is used to obtain the minimum spanning tree of the original network graph. Finally each edge of the obtained minimum spanning tree is replaced with its associated path to convert it to a Steiner tree.

4.5 Penalty

Whereas it is likely that an infeasible solution can be found during the search, an extra penalty is assigned by increasing the cost so that these would be less likely to be accepted.

4.6 Backup-Set

A Backup-set is generated after the pre-processing phase and all feasible replace paths, which are used in compound moves, are stored in it in order to prevent them from being regenerated during the search at different iterations.

4.7 Hybrid Candidate List

Some candidate list strategies have been described by Glover and Laguna [15] such as Aspiration Plus and Elite Candidate List. We usefully combine these two strategies and develop the new candidate list strategy named Hybrid candidate list. In Hybrid candidate list, a Master List is built by recording the best K moves, which encountered in the examination of all possible moves on a given iteration. Then at each subsequent iteration, not only moves inside the Master List have to be examined, but also

To avoid reversal of moves and cycling, a tabu list is constructed where forbidden moves are listed. In our approach, we store a single added node or a single dropped node for the Steiner node move in tabu list. For the other proposed moves, we store a block of edges constructing an added path or a deleted path in tabu list. In addition, we use a simple form of systematic dynamic tabu tenure consists of creating a sequence of tabu tenure values in the range determined by t_{min} and t_{max}, which these values alternately increase and decrease. We define t_{max} to be equal of multicast group size, and t_{min} to be half of it. For example, if multicast group size is equal to 6, then the following sequence can be used for the range defined above is (3,5,4,6). This sequence is then used, to assign the current tabu tenure value, and may be repeated as many times as necessary until the end of the search. Systematically varying the tabu tenure in this way results in a balance between intensification and diversification, since short tabu tenures allow fine-tuning of neighborhood search and close examination of regions around a local optimum, while long tenures tend to direct the search to different parts of the solution space [15].

4.9 Aspiration Criteria

We employ a simple type of aspiration criterion which overrides the tabu status of a move when it yields a solution better than the best obtained so far.

4.10 Termination Rule

A fixed number of iterations have been used as the stopping criterion. In addition, the proposed algorithms stop when the objective function value dose not improve for a certain number of subsequent iterations.

5 Time Complexity

Let $n = |V|$ be the number of network nodes, $l = |E|$ be the number of network links, $m = |M \cup \{s\}|$ be the number of multicast group nodes, and q be the number of iterations. Table 1 shows the total time complexity of the proposed short-term TS-

Table 1. Time complexity of the proposed short-term TS-based algorithms

Move	Total time complexity
Steiner node move	$l + n^2 + q'(l(n - m)\log n) + (q - q')(lK \log n)$
Path move	$l + n^2 + mn^2 + q'm^2 + (q - q')K$
K-path move	$l + n^2 + m(l + kn \log \dfrac{l}{n}) + q'km^2 + (q - q')K$
Complete move	$l + n^2 + m(l + kn \log \dfrac{l}{n}) + q'km^4 \log m + (q - q')Km^2 \log m$

6 Performance Evaluation

In this section, we have performed comprehensive simulation studies on various random generated networks with 10–100 nodes to evaluate the performance of the proposed TS-based algorithms. To generate random networks, we have used a random graph generator based on the Salama graph generator [5]. In all of these networks, the size of the multicast group is equal to 30% of the number of network nodes.

Table 2 shows the average of the simulation results regarding total tree cost for the proposed short-term TS-based algorithms which use Hybrid candidate list and dynamic tabu tenure. Also it shows the average tree cost obtained using KPP1, KPP2, and BSMA heuristics and some existing short-term TS-based algorithms in order to compare the proposed algorithms with them. We conclude from these values that using Hybrid candidate list and dynamic tabu tenure make a notable impact on the performance of the algorithms. It indicates that most of the proposed algorithms achieve better outcomes than their similar short-term TS-based algorithms without these strategies which are proposed in [14].

Table 3 indicates the degree of improvement made by the Hybrid candidate list and dynamic tabu tenure on the short-term TS-based algorithms in connection with total tree cost and execution time. The outcomes from this table confirm that the most effect of using the Hybrid candidate list related to total tree cost is on the performance of the algorithms with the Steiner node move. In addition, the maximum effect of using these strategies related to execution time is on the performance of the algo-

			LC delay-constrained tree	832.432
		K-path move	LD tree	905.594
			LC delay-constrained tree	849.310
		Complete move	LD tree	762.149
			LC delay-constrained tree	771.521
	Ghaboosi and Haghighat algorithms	Steiner node move	LD tree	994.804
			LC delay-constrained tree	974.716
		Path move	LD tree	898.996
			LC delay-constrained tree	838.697
		K-path move	LD tree	918.415
			LC delay-constrained tree	875.352
		Complete move	LD tree	770.486
			LC delay-constrained tree	781.802
	Skorin-Kapov and Kos algorithm	Steiner node move	Least-cost delay-constrained spanning tree	942.769
	Youssef et al. algorithm	Based on path switching operation	LC delay-constrained tree	897.581
	TSDLMRA	Based on path switching operation	Shortest path tree	912.755
Heuristics algorithms	KPP1	-------	-------	950.860
	KPP2	-------	-------	957.268
	BSMA	-------	-------	915.315

Table 3. Degree of improvement that Hybrid candidate list and dynamic tabu tenure can cause

Move	Initial solution	Degree of cost improvement	Degree of time improvement
Steiner node move	LD tree	9.526 %	56.71 %
	LC delay-constrained tree	5.947 %	59.425 %
Path move	LD tree	1.929 %	30.41 %
	LC delay-constrained tree	0.747 %	31.925 %
K-path move	LD tree	1.396 %	3.51 %
	LC delay-constrained tree	2.975 %	4.033 %
Complete move	LD tree	1.082 %	57.468 %
	LC delay-constrained tree	1.315 %	52.121 %

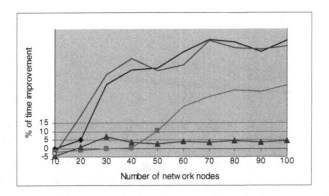

Fig. 2. Time improvement percentage that the Hybrid candidate list can cause

performance of the proposed short-term TS-based algorithms. By growing the network size, the impact of the Hybrid candidate list is more apparent.

7 Conclusion

In this paper, various short-term TS-based algorithms are proposed to construct a bandwidth-delay-constrained least-cost multicast tree. An efficient CL strategy named Hybrid candidate list and a simple dynamic tenure structure are employed in these algorithms. Simulation results show that such a CL strategy can be useful to produce optimal results in a relatively short amount of time specially when the network has large number of nodes. In our future work, we will consider both a more comprehensive computational study that examines additional CL strategies and the impact of one of the less frequently used parts in tabu search, the strategic oscillation approach, on the performance of the TS-based QoS multicast routing algorithms.

Acknowledgments. The authors would like to thank Nejla Ghaboosi for her profitable guidance.

References

1. Hakimi, S.L.: Steiner problem in graphs and its implications. Networks 1(2), 113–133 (1971)
2. Garey, M., Johnson, D.: Computers and intractability: a guide to the theory of NP-completeness. Freeman, San Francisco (1971)
3. Kompella, V.P., Pasquale, J.C., Polyzos, G.C.: Multicast routing for multimedia commu-

9. Haghighat, A.T., Faez, K., Dehghan, M., Mowlaei, A., Ghahremani, Y.: GA-based heuristic algorithms for bandwidth-delay-constrained least-cost multicast routing. Computer Communications 27(1), 111–127 (2004)
10. Youssef, H., Al-Mulhem, A., Sait, S.M., Tahir, M.A.: QoS-driven multicast tree generation using tabu search. Computer Communications 25(11–12), 1140–1149 (2002)
11. Skorin-Kapov, N., Kos, M.: The application of Steiner trees to delay constrained multicast routing: a tabu search approach. In: ConTEL 2003: Proc. seventh international conference on telecommunications, vol. 2, pp. 443–448 (2003)
12. Wang, H., Wang, J., Wang, H., Sun, Y.M.: TSDLMRA: an efficient multicast routing algorithm based on tabu search. Journal of Network and Computer Applications 27(2), 77–90 (2004)
13. Wang, X., Cao, J., Cheng, H., Huang, M.: QoS multicast routing for multimedia group communications using intelligent computational methods. Computer Communications 29, 2217–2229 (2006)
14. Ghaboosi, N., Haghighat, A.T.: Tabu search based algorithms for bandwidth-delay-constrained least-cost multicast routing. Telecommunication Systems 34(3–4), 147–166 (2007)
15. Glover, F., Laguna, M.: Tabu search. Kluwer Academic, Dordrecht (1997)
16. Glover, F.: Tabu search—part I. INFORMS Journal on Computing 1(3), 190–206 (1989)
17. Prim, R.: Shortest Connection Networks and Some Generalizations. Bell System Technical Journal 36, 1389–1401 (1957)
18. Dijkstra, E.W.: A note on two problems in connection with graphs. Numerische Mathematik 1, 269–271 (1959)
19. Jimenez, V.M., Marzal, A.: Computing the K-shortest paths: a new algorithm and an experimental comparison. In: Vitter, J.S., Zaroliagis, C.D. (eds.) WAE 1999, vol. 1668, pp. 15–29. Springer, Heidelberg (1999)

[1] Dept. of Comp. Sc. & Engg, Dr. B. C. Roy Engineering College, Durgapur, India
[2] Dept. of Comp. Sc. & Tech., Bengal Engineering and Science University, Shibpur, India
subir_ece@rediffmail.com, ghosal_amrita@yahoo.com,
{sanjib.sur11,avishekdan}@gmail.com, siprad@hotmail.com

Abstract. Wireless sensor networks (WSNs) consist of a large number of small, battery-powered wireless sensor nodes and thereby constrained with energy resource. The network as a whole must minimize the energy usage in order to enable untethered and unattended operation for an extended period of time. One fundamental way of reducing such energy usage and enhancing lifetime is judicial placement of sensor nodes within the network area. The present work proposes a lifetime-enhancing node-deployment strategy. Primarily more nodes are deployed towards the sink exploiting the fact that more energy is drained out from the nodes close to the sink. Further, locations which are approximately equi-distant from the sink are assigned different classes of priorities according to their responsibility of forwarding data of nodes located in the neighbouring cells. The principle of this strategy is justified by Lemma and corresponding proof. Exhaustive simulation is conducted to observe the impact of node distribution on network lifetime. The result is compared with one of the existing deployment strategies, which shows our scheme outperforms the existing one in terms of network lifetime.

Keywords: node deployment, network lifetime, coverage, connectivity.

1 Introduction

A wireless sensor network (WSN) [1] is a collection of sensor nodes which are deployed in a given area of interest. A sensor node is made up of components such as sensing unit, processing unit, a transceiver unit and a power unit [1], [2]. The sensor nodes collect data from their surroundings and send the collected data to their neighbouring nodes in single hop [3], [4]. The neighbouring nodes in turn send the data to the nodes which are located in single hop distance from them. In this way the data is

copter in random manner [5]. In pre-determined deployment, the locations of the nodes are specified. It is mainly used in indoor applications. For example, manual placing of sensor nodes in pre-determined locations is done to monitor manufacturing plants, detection of corrosions and overstressed beams [5] in large old buildings etc.

Several works have been carried out to increase the network lifetime of the network. In one such work, M. Esseghir *et al.* [6] have proposed a near-optimal heuristic algorithm for placing the nodes in sensor network targeting to enhance network lifetime. Node-deployment is done in two phases. In the first phase, nodes are placed to ensure coverage whereas in the second phase it is done in such a manner that each point of the network area is served by two distinct sensor nodes.

In another work [7], the authors have proposed a node deployment strategy solving an optimization problem to find out minimum number of deployed sensors under the constraints of quality of monitoring and network lifetime. The scheme assigns different energy levels to sensor nodes as a function of distance from the sink. Based on such energy levels of the nodes, node density is determined.

Sze-Chu Liu has proposed [8] a lifetime-extending deployment strategy based on load balancing concept. In this strategy, communication load among sensors are analyzed first and a node distribution algorithm is thereby proposed to balance the load and extend lifetime. Unlike [7], node density is determined by the location and not by the energy level of the node.

Liu Yunhuai, Ni Hoilun, and L. M. Ngan have proposed a non-uniform, power-aware distribution scheme in [9] to overcome the problem of sink routing hole. Sink routing hole is a phenomenon caused by fast failure of nodes near the sink due to higher relay workload on such nodes compared to that of farther nodes. It results in loss of connectivity. The sink routing hole typically occurs in case of uniform distribution. Simulation results [9] show that the power-aware deployment scheme can significantly improve the long-termed network connectivity and service quality.

Bin Li *et al.* in their work [10] have proposed an optimal distribution for deploying the nodes with a target to prolong network lifetime. They have also analyzed the effect of node deployment strategies on network lifetime following various distributions (optimal, uniform and poisson). They claim that network lifetime has been prolonged greatly using the optimal distribution proposed by them compared to uniform and Poisson distribution.

In most of these works the proposed deployment stategies have guaranteed the

2 Regular Hexagonal Cell Architecture

We consider regular hexagonal cell (RHC) [10] architecture where the network coverage area is divided into regular hexagonal cells as shown in Figure 1. A cell indicated by C_i^j denotes the jth number cell of the ith layer. For example, cell C_2^6 is located in layer 2 and the cell number within this layer is 6. The sink node is located at the centre cell of the regular hexagonal cell architecture. The sensor nodes are placed in cells of different layers surrounding the centre cell. The cells of the layers are further categorized into two groups- primary and secondary. Primary cells (C_p) in a layer are those cells where the layer takes a turn of 60^0 and share a common boundary with more number of cells of the adjacent layer. Primary cells in the arcitecture are shown as shaded hexagonal cells. Secondary cells (C_s) are those which share a common boundary with relatively less number of cells of the adjacent layer. Secondary cells are shown as non-shaded hexagonal cells. The number of cells in each layer is 6 * i, where i=1, 2, ..., N and N is the number of the farthest layer from the sink. We designate the locations on the boundary of two consecutive layers with different classes of priority based on their responsibility of forwarding data of the neighbour nodes located at the adjacent cells and their distances from the sink. The minimum-distant vertices associated with the C_p cells of ith layer on the boundary between i^{th} & $(i+1)^{th}$ layers are categorized as priority-1 vertices ($V_{prior-1}$). For example in Figure 1, on the boundary line between layer 2 & 3 there are two minimum-distant vertices associated with a C_p cell (C_2^5). These two vertices are priority-1 vertices. Similarly the minimum-distant vertices associated with the C_s cell on the same boundary are categorized as priority-2 vertices ($V_{prior-2}$). There is only one minimum-distant vertex with priority-2 associated with a C_s cell (C_2^4) on this boundary. The rest of the vertices (if any) on the boundary are with priority-3 ($V_{prior-3}$).

The following relevant notations are used to describe the architecture:

- r – radius of a cell
- R_s – sensing range of a sensor node
- R_c – communication range of a sensor node

The relationship between cell radius r and node's sensing range R_s must satisfy

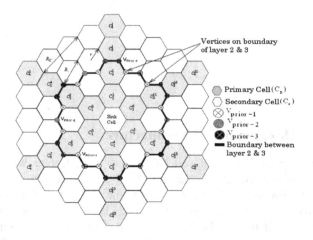

Fig. 1. Regular Hexagonal Cell Architecture

Definition of Coverage: A unit area is said to be covered if every point in the area is within the sensing range of an active node [11].

Definition of Connectivity: A network is connected if any active node can communicate with any other active node either in single hop or in multiple hops [11].

3 Energy Efficient Distribution of Nodes

The nodes are deployed in two phases. In the first phase, nodes are deployed at the centre of each cell ensuring the coverage of the network. If any of the nodes are unable to take part in data routing and/or data sensing, the coverage of the network is broken. Therefore in the second phase redundant nodes are placed throughout the entire network area with a target to enhance network lifetime.

Lemma 1: For a given network area A×A, the number of layers (N) should follow the relationship $N \geq \sqrt{\dfrac{13}{3} \dfrac{R}{R_c}}$, where $R = \dfrac{1}{2} \times A$ in order to maintain connectivity of the network.

Proof: If the radius of each cell of the multi-layered architecture is r, then the distance between the centre of the sink cell and the farthest edge of a cell of any other layer is

$$or, N \geq \frac{2}{\sqrt{3}r}$$

replacing, $r \leq \dfrac{R_C}{\sqrt{13}}$ in above equation, we have

$$or, N \geq \sqrt{\frac{13}{3}} \frac{R}{R_c}$$

Corollary 1: For a given network area A×A the number of layers (N) must follow the relationship $N \geq \dfrac{2}{\sqrt{3}} \dfrac{R}{R_s}$, in order to maintain the coverage of the network.

Proof: From lemma 1, the relationship between R and N is evaluated as,

$$\sqrt{3}rN + \frac{\sqrt{3}}{2}r \geq R$$

replacing, $r \leq \dfrac{R_s}{2}$ in the above equation, we have

$$N \geq \frac{2}{\sqrt{3}} \frac{R}{R_s}$$

3.1 Deployment Scheme

In the first phase, the scheme requires $\displaystyle\sum_{i=1}^{N} 6*i$ number of nodes whereas the second phase needs at most N*(6N) number of nodes. The deployment scheme is pre-determined in nature and the location (x, y) where the nodes are to be placed can be computed as follows-

π π π π

$$m = \begin{cases} 2 & \text{for} \quad C_i^{2i+1}, C_i^{2i+2}, \ldots, C_i^{3i} \\ 3 & \text{for} \quad C_i^{3i+1}, C_i^{3i+2}, \cdots, C_i^{4i} \\ 4 & \text{for} \quad C_i^{4i+1}, C_i^{4i+2}, \cdots, C_i^{5i} \\ 5 & \text{for} \quad C_i^{5i+1}, C_i^{5i+2}, \cdots, C_i^{6i} \end{cases}$$

where $i = 1, 2, \ldots, N$

For example, the value of m can be found out for determining the centre location of the cell C_2^5: as i=2, the cell can be mapped with C_i^{2i+1}; so m=2.

$$a = \begin{cases} i & \text{for } V_{prior-1} \text{ of } C_i^{i*(k-1)+1} \text{ cell} \\ 1, 2, \ldots, i & \begin{array}{l} \text{for } V_{prior-2}, V_{prior-3} \text{ and centre location of cell } C_a^k, C_{a+1}^{k+1*(m+1)}, C_{a+2}^{k+2*(m+1)}, \\ \ldots, C_N^{k+(N-a)*(m+1)} \end{array} \end{cases}$$

where k= m*a + 1

For example, the value of a can be found out for determining the centre location of the cell C_2^5: as i=2 and m=2 (as shown earlier), the cell can be mapped with C_a^k where k = m*a+1 = 2*a + 1 = 5; so a=2.

$$S = \begin{cases} 0 & \text{for } V_{prior-2}, V_{prior-3} \text{ and centre location of each cell} \\ r & \text{for } V_{prior-1} \end{cases}$$

$$Q = \begin{cases} 0 & \text{for } V_{prior-1} \text{ and centre location of each cell} \\ r & \text{for } V_{prior-2} \text{ and } V_{prior-3} \end{cases}$$

coordinate, putting the same values in equation (2) we get the value of y-coordinate as 6. So (x, y) coordinate of the centre of C_3^2 cell is $(10\sqrt{3}, 6)$. Similarly the coordinates of the centre of other cells can be obtained using the above two equations.

3.1.2 Redundant Node Distribution

To ensure that each cell of each layer gets at least one redundant node, the number of redundant nodes at the farthest (i=4 in example architecture, Figure 2) layer is 6N. The present scheme considers 6N number of nodes to be distributed at each layer. In layer 1 (Refer Figure 2) all the cells are primary and the vertices on the boundary between sink cell and layer-1 have prority-1 ($V_{prior-1}$). So these 6*4 (N=4) redundent nodes are first distributed in the vertices located on this boundary. There are 6 such vertices with priority-1 ($V_{prior-1}$). The remaining (24-6) redundant nodes are distributed equally within each cell area in random manner. The locations for random deployment are found by using equations (3) & (4) as follows-

$$X_{rand} = X_c + \frac{\sqrt{3}}{2} r * rand(0,1) * cos(2\pi * rand(0,1)) \qquad (3)$$

$$Y_{rand} = Y_c + \frac{\sqrt{3}}{2} r * rand(0,1) * sin(2\pi * rand(0,1)) \qquad (4)$$

where X_c and Y_c are the x and y coordinates of the centre of a cell within which the nodes are randomly deployed, whereas the locations for deployment at pre-determined places can be found by using equations (1) & (2). Here the pre-detrermined places or vertices are located on the boundary between the layers. Any vertex located on the boundary between the layers can be identified by three adjacent cells (Refer Figure 2). Now the co-ordinate of each vertex can be found out by putting appropriate values of different parameters (i, r, m, S, Q, a and p) of any of the three adjacent cells of that vertex, though the cells belong to different layers. The coordinate of any vertex can be computed by any set of parameter values of a particular cell. For example in Figure 2, the (x, y) coordinates of one vertex associated with the sink cell, C_1^1 and C_1^2 cells is computed as $(2\sqrt{3}, 2)$. The corresponding

example, the co-ordinates of priority-2 vertices associated with C_1^1, C_2^1 and C_2^2 cells located on the same boundary are computed as ($6\sqrt{3}$, 2) by putting appropriate value of i, r, m, S and a in equations (1) & (2) for C_1^1 cell.

The vertices on the boundary between layer 2 & 3 and onwards are having any one of the three types of priorities. The redundant nodes are deployed at vertices with priority-1, priority-2 and priority-3. After placing nodes at the vertices in the order of their priorities, if excess redundant nodes remain, these are distributed within the cell randomly. On the boundary between layer 2 & 3, there are 12 vertices with priority-1 ($V_{prior-1}$), 6 vertices with priority-2 ($V_{prior-2}$) and remaining 12 vertices are with priority-3 ($V_{prior-3}$). In this case, out of the total redundant nodes 6*4 (N=4), 12 nodes are placed at vertices with priority-1 and 6 are placed at vertices with priority-2. So for the 12 vertices with priority-3, only 6 (24-(12+6)) nodes remain. These 6 nodes are placed uniformly i.e., one after another at the 12 vertices with priority-3. The vertex associated with C_2^4, C_3^5, and C_3^6 cells with priority-2 also lie on this boundary. As an example, the location can be found out as (0, 16) by putting i=2, r=4, m=1, S=0, Q=4, a=1and p=1 in equations (1) & (2). The location of another vertex associated with C_2^5, C_2^7 _and C_3^8 cells on the same boundary having priority-3 is ($-6\sqrt{3}$, 14) is obtained by putting parameters values i=2, r=4, m=2, S=0, Q=4, a=2 and p=2 in equations (1) and (2).

Lemma 2: Energy draining rate of the nodes located in C_p is higher than that of the nodes located in C_s.

Proof: Let E_p and E_s denote the energy consumption by the nodes inside the primary and secondary cell respectively for the additional task of forwarding the data of the nodes located in their respective neighbouring cells.

In addition to its own activity, a Primary cell (C_p) forwards data sent by 3 of its adjacent cells. On the contrary, a Secondary cell (C_s) forwards data sent by 2 adjacent cells. Therefore

$$E \ = 3* \ E \tag{5}$$

ployment, each cell gets a node in its centre (shown by 'O'). In the second phase, the numbers of redundant nodes to be deployed in a layer are 6*(N = 4) = 24. On the boundary between the sink and layer 1, all six vertices have priority-1. After placing nodes at all such six vertices (shown by '■'), 18 (24-6) redundant nodes remain. Now these 18 redundant nodes are equally distributed among the cells of layer 1 in random manner (shown by '□').

On the boundary between layer 1 and 2, there are 18 vertices. Out of these 18 vertices, 6 are with priority-1. Nodes are deployed first at priority-1 vertices (shown by '●'). The remaining 12 (18-6) vertices are with priority-2 and therefore nodes are deployed at these locations next (shown by '⊕'). Now remaining 6 (18-12) nodes are distributed randomly within the cell area of layer 2 (shown by '⊕').

On the boundary between layer 2 and 3, there are 30 vertices. There are 12 vertices with priority-1 located on this boundary. So nodes are deployed first at these locations (shown by '▲'). The remaining 12 redundant nodes are then placed at the 18 (30-12) vertices. Out of these 18 vertices, 6 vertices are with priority-2. So these priority-2 vertices are filled next (shown by '△'). After filling the locations at vertices with priority-1 and priority-2, 6 (24-(12+6)) redundant nodes remain. These 6 redundant nodes are placed at the 12 vertices with priority-3 one after another (shown by '△').

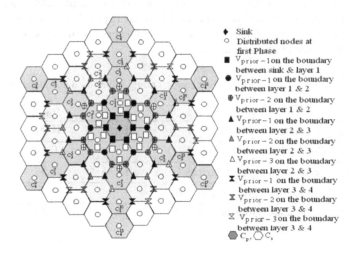

♦ Sink
○ Distributed nodes at first Phase
■ $V_{prior-1}$ on the boundary between sink & layer 1
● $V_{prior-1}$ on the boundary between layer 1 & 2
⊕ $V_{prior-2}$ on the boundary between layer 1 & 2
▲ $V_{prior-1}$ on the boundary between layer 2 & 3
△ $V_{prior-2}$ on the boundary between layer 2 & 3
△ $V_{prior-3}$ on the boundary between layer 2 & 3
✗ $V_{prior-1}$ on the boundary between layer 3 & 4
✗ $V_{prior-2}$ on the boundary between layer 3 & 4
✗ $V_{prior-3}$ on the boundary between layer 3 & 4
⬡ C_p, ○ C_r

are placed among the 24 vertices with priority-3 one after 3 vertices (shown by '   ').

4 Performance Evaluation

The effectiveness of the proposed life-time enhancing node deplyment strategy (LENDS), reported in the earlier section is evaluated through simulation. Here we have evaluated the effectiveness of our scheme by comparing with one of the existing schemes.

4.1 Simulation Environment

The simulation is performed using MATLAB (version 7.1). The performance of the scheme is evaluated considering network lifetime as a performance metric.

Network lifetime: It is defined as the number of turns that the network is running [10]. A turn is defined as the time when all sensor cells in the network finish collecting and returning their data to the sink cell once.

During the simulation we have considered that due to the battery consumption some sensor nodes become inoperative. When the amount of energy of a node is less than a particular threshold value, we consider that node as a dead node. In this work, a node is considered as a dead node if the amount of energy of that node is less than 5% of its initial energy. Table 1 lists the relevant parameters and their associated values [10], [12] considered in this simulation.

Table 1. Parameters and their corresponding values used in simulation

Parameters	Value
Initial Energy ($E_{initial}$)	1000 J
Constant sensing energy (E_m)	0.1 J
Constant transmission energy (E_s)	3.5 J
Constant reception energy (E_r)	3 J
Dead node's threshold energy	50 J

Table 2. Required number of nodes for different network size

Number of layers	Min^m number of nodes ensuring coverage	No. of nodes ensuring at least one redundant node at each cell
3	36	90
5	90	240
7	168	468

4.2 Simulation Results

The network running turns in terms of which network lifetime is defined is computed and plotted for varying number of redundant nodes. Three sets of results for three different network sizes are illustrated in Figure 3, 4 and 5 respectively. Figures show that network-running turns steadily rise with the increase of nodes for all sizes of the network. Results signify the fact that network lifetime prolongs with the increase of the number of redundant nodes.

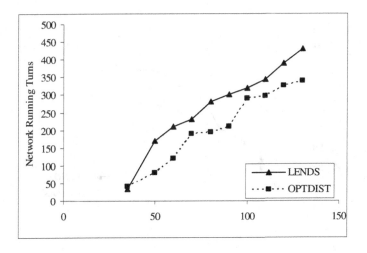

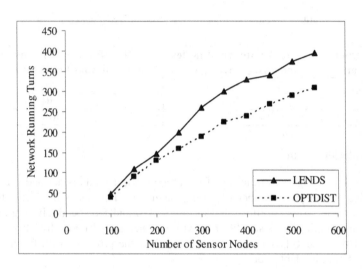

Fig. 4. Network lifetime for five layers of RHCs

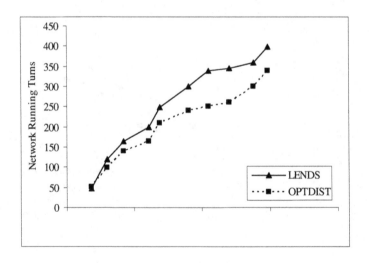

sink. To resist the shortening of network lifetime further, certain locations within a layer are identified as prioritized based on the importance of the locations in terms of sharing workload of neighbouring locations. Finally the scheme is simulated and the results are compared with one of the existing schemes [10], which follow optimal distribution of nodes. Network lifetime is greatly enhanced in the proposed predetermined node deployment scheme compared to the scheme following optimal distribution.

As a future extension, the present scheme may be made more realistic by considering 3-D environment. Moreover the scheme can be further analyzed using different QoS parameters.

References

1. Akyildiz, I.F., Su, W., Sankarasubramaniam, Y., Cayirci, E.: A survey on sensor networks. IEEE Communications Magazine 40(8), 102–114 (2002)
2. DasBit, S., Ragupathy, R.: Routing in MANET and Sensor Network- A 3D position based approach. Journal of Foundation of Computing and Decision Sciences 33(3), 211–239 (2008)
3. Ghosal, A., Halder, S., DasBit, S.: A Scheme to tolerate Jamming in multiple nodes in Wireless Sensor Networks. In: Proceedings of Wireless VITAE, pp. 948–951. IEEE press, Los Alamitos (2009)
4. Ghosal, A., Halder, S., Chatterjee, S., Sen, J., DasBit, S.: Estimating delay in a data forwarding scheme for defending jamming attack in wireless sensor network. In: Proceedings of 3rd International Conference NGMAST. IEEE CS press, Cardiff (to appear, 2009)
5. Younis, M., Akkaya, K.: Strategies and Techniques for Node Placement in Wireless Sensor Networks: A Survey. Elsevier Ad Hoc Network Journal 6(4), 621–655 (2008)
6. Esseghir, M., Bouabdallah, N., Pujolle, G.: Sensor placement for maximizing wireless sensor network lifetime. In: Proceedings of IEEE 62nd VTC, vol. 4, pp. 2347–2351 (2005)
7. Maleki, M., Pedram, M.: QoM and lifetime-constrained random deployment of sensor networks for minimum energy consumption. In: IEEE Proceedings Information Processing in Sensor Networks, pp. 293–300 (2005)
8. Sze-Chu Liu, A.: lifetime-extending deployment strategy for multi-hop wireless sensor networks. In: Proceedings of the 4th Annual CNSR Conference, pp. 53–60 (2006)
9. Liu, Y., Ngan, H., Ni, L.M.: Power-aware node deployment in wireless sensor networks. In: Proceedings of IEEE International Conference on Sensor Networks, Ubiquitous, and Trustworthy Computing, vol. 1, pp. 128–135 (2006)
10. Li, B., Wang, Q., Yang, Y., Wang, J.: Optimal Distribution of Redundant Sensor Nodes

¹ School of Information Technology and Mathematical Sciences,
University of Ballarat P.O. Box 663, Ballarat, Victoria 3353, Australia
{j.yearwood,a.kelarev}@ballarat.edu.au
² School of Computing and Information Systems, University of Tasmania, Private Bag 100,
Hobart, Tasmania 7001, Australia
BHKang@utas.edu.au

Abstract. The present article is devoted to experimental investigation of the performance of three machine learning algorithms for ITS dataset in their ability to achieve agreement with classes published in the biological literature before. The ITS dataset consists of nuclear ribosomal DNA sequences, where rather sophisticated alignment scores have to be used as a measure of distance. These scores do not form a Minkowski metric and the sequences cannot be regarded as points in a finite dimensional space. This is why it is necessary to develop novel machine learning approaches to the analysis of datasets of this sort. This paper introduces a k-committees classifier and compares it with the discrete k-means and Nearest Neighbour classifiers. It turns out that all three machine learning algorithms are efficient and can be used to automate future biologically significant classifications for datasets of this kind. A simplified version of a synthetic dataset, where the k-committees classifier outperforms k-means and Nearest Neighbour classifiers, is also presented.

1   Introduction and Motivation

Classification of data is very important in artificial intelligence, machine learning, knowledge acquisition and data mining. Many efficient classifiers have been implemented in the Waikato Environment for Knowledge Analysis, WEKA, see [14] and [16]. For additional relevant examples of recent results on classification methods let us also refer the readers to [1, 6, 8, 11, 12, 17].

It is especially important to devise machine learning algorithms automating the analysis of nucleotide and protein sequences. Indeed, the datasets of DNA, RNA and protein sequences are growing and becoming a huge resource in view of the rapid

clustering of a set of nuclear ribosomal DNA sequences were considered in [9].

Long DNA sequences cannot be regarded as points in a finite dimensional space. They cannot be accurately represented using short sequences of the values of numerical or nominal attributes. Besides, rather sophisticated and biologically significant local alignment scores have to be used as a measure of similarity or distance between DNA sequences. These scores do not possess properties of the standard Euclidean norm in a finite dimensional space. Moreover, they do not satisfy axioms of the more general Minkowski metrics, which include as special cases the well known Euclidean distance, Manhattan distance, and max distance. These circumstances make it impossible to utilise previous implementations of the machine learning algorithms. One has to develop novel algorithms and adjust familiar ones.

In order to achieve strong agreement between classifications produced by these machine learning algorithms and biological classifications, one must use measures of strong similarity between sequences which are biologically significant. We are using local alignment scores to develop novel classification algorithms and investigate their accuracy for a set of nuclear ribosomal DNA sequences. Our algorithms are using strong similarity measures based on local alignments, which have not been applied in this context before, and turn out to be highly efficient for DNA sequences of this kind.

Although datasets of DNA sequences cannot be regarded as sets of points in a finite dimensional space, typically the datasets used for classification are fairly small because of the relatively high cost of determining each sequence. It is possible to compare the task of classifying a set of DNA sequences with a number of optimization problems in graph theory. In particular, it can be formulated as a classification problem for the set of vertices of a finite connected undirected weighted graph. Notice that an alternative model for classifying DNA code based on analogy with neural networks and FSA was introduced in [6]. Some steps of our algorithms are analogous to the steps which occur in solutions to the minimum dominating set of vertices problem in graph theory. We refer to [15] for graph-based data mining.

2   Local Alignment Scores for Machine Learning Algorithms

This paper investigates and compares the efficiency of three machine learning algo-

These scores do not satisfy the axioms of Minkowski metrics, which include as special cases the standard Euclidean distance used in previous implementations, Manhattan distance, and max distance.

Long nucleotide sequences cannot be regarded as points in a finite dimensional space. Besides, it is impossible to calculate new sequences from the given ones. In particular, one cannot compute the arithmetical average, or mean, of several given sequences. Hence our methods are different from those considered before.

Hidden Markov Models, or HMMs, can also be applied to the analysis of DNA sequences. Originally Hidden Markov Models were developed for speech processing. When it comes to nucleotide or protein sequences, However, HMMs are usually used to distinguish between various types of subregions of the sequence. For example, they can be used to identify coding and non-coding regions of DNA. Originally, HMMs were developed in the context of speech and signal processing, and this research also continues: see, for example, [3–5].

The alignment scores in our algorithms provide a measure of similarity that is significant biologically. To illustrate let us suppose that we have a long DNA sequence L, and an identical copy S of a segment within the sequence L. Obviously, every correct biological classification should place both L and S in one and the same class. This may however be difficult to determine using other metrics. Indeed, L and S may have seriously different values of statistical parameters. Therefore traditional statistical approaches, mapping L and S into an n-dimensional space and using standard Euclidean norm there, may not notice their similarity at all. In contrast, sequence alignment will immediately show that there is a perfect match between S and a segment in the sequence L.

Our experiments used a dataset with sequences of a region of the nuclear ribosomal DNA (nrDNA) that is often used to work out evolutionary relationships between species and genera. The dataset includes many of different species from all subgenera and sections of Eucalyptus, as well as some other genera that are closely related to Eucalyptus. For a detailed description of the dataset we refer to [13].

In this dataset we looked at the following groupings, based on phylogeny represented in [13] (in the Figures 2, 3 and 5 of [13]):

1.   Stockwellia, Eucalyptopsis and Allosyncarpia (2 accessions);

and Frank (2005), see Section 6.4. Hence our algorithms had to be designed differently and have been encoded with the Bioinformatics Toolbox of Matlab. We used the

$$\text{swalign(Seq1, Seq2)}$$

function of the Bioinformatics Toolbox, which returns the optimal local alignment score. Higher alignment scores correspond to lower distances between closely associated sequences.

Thus, our paper deals with novel machine learning algorithms for DNA sequences based on alignment scores and suitable for analysis of highly variable regions of DNA.

3 The Discrete k-Means Classifier with Alignment Scores

The k-means algorithm and the Nearest Neighbour algorithms are classification techniques used most often and are implemented in the WEKA environment. Complete explanations of these methods are given, for example, by Witten and Frank [16], see Chapter 4.

It is explained in [16] that when the traditional k-means algorithm is used for classification, it simply computes the centroids of classes in the training set, and then uses the centroids to classify new elements as they become available. Traditional k-means algorithm uses standard Euclidean distances and computes the arithmetical average, or mean, of the points in each class. It is explained in Section 4.8 of [16] on p. 137 that the task of finding the centroid of a class C in the k-means algorithm is equivalent to finding a solution x to the following

$$\text{minimize} \sum_{y \in C} \|x - y\|^2 \text{ subject to } x \in \mathbb{R}^n \tag{1}$$

In other words, the centroid of a class C is the point of the n-dimensional space $\mathbb{R}^n$ with the minimum sum of squares of distances to all known points c in the class C. Every new point in the n-dimensional Euclidean space is then assigned to the class represented by its nearest centroid. The running time complexity of the k-means algo-

geometrical sense, and we had to modify them. In order to emphasize this property of our machine learning algorithm, here we call it a *discrete k-means classifier*.

Our algorithm operates on the set of given sequences only and does not create any new sequences as means of the given ones. As a centroid of the class C our algorithm uses a solution x to the following optimization problem:

$$\text{minimize} \left(\max_{y \in C} \|x - y\| \right) \text{ subject to } x \in C. \tag{2}$$

A solution to this problem is a sequence with minimum largest distance to all other sequences in the class. We can think of this approach as a way of approximating the class by a sphere centred at the centroid. Then the optimization problem minimizes the radius of the sphere. After the centroids have been found, each new sequence is then assigned to the class of its nearest centroid. The running time of this algorithm is O(k).

Every alignment score between each pair of the given sequences is found once during a pre-processing stage of the algorithm, and then these scores are looked up in a table during the search for centroids. The average success rates of this method for classifying new sequences in comparison with the classes obtained and published in [13] are represented in Figure 1.

Accuracy of Machine Learning Algorithms						
	Discrete k-means classifier	k-committees classifier				Nearest Neighbour classifier
		$r = 2$	$r = 3$	$r = 4$	$r = 5$	
Blossum30	64.75	70.69	74.66	78.00	78.98	85.26
Blossum40	72.87	76.04	77.85	79.05	80.70	85.11
Blossum50	76.80	79.07	79.70	80.26	81.12	85.37
Blossum60	71.87	75.50	77.07	79.52	80.39	86.94
Blossum70	70.41	74.82	77.53	79.06	79.11	86.22
Blossum80	76.86	77.99	78.75	80.96	82.74	86.97
Blossum90	76.64	77.98	78.64	79.78	81.77	85.94
Blossum100	72.78	76.10	77.71	79.31	81.02	86.90

Fig. 1. Tenfold cross validation

classes obtained in [13]. The results on the accuracy of this algorithm are presented in Figure 1. As we see, the Nearest Neighbour algorithm turns out to be substantially more accurate.

The Nearest Neighbour algorithm compares each new sequence with all previous sequences, and assigns it to the class of the nearest known sequence using the alignment scores. The running time of this algorithm is $O(n)$, where n is the number of all sequences in the dataset. Since $n>k$, we see that the process of applying the Nearest Neighbour algorithm to classify new sequences is slower.

5 The k-Committees Classifier with Alignment Scores

This section is devoted to a novel k-committees algorithm. The idea behind this algorithm is natural. However, we have not found it in the literature. In particular, this algorithm is not discussed in the monograph by Witten and Frank [16]. Thus, we are developing this algorithm independently as a new one.

Instead of using a single centroid to represent each class, we select a few representatives in each class. These representatives form a committee of the class. Let us denote the number of the representatives chosen in each class by r.

When the training stage is complete, during the classification stage every new sequence is then assigned to the class of its nearest committee member. If every class has the same number r of committee members and it is desirable to indicate this number explicitly, then we call our method the (k, r)-*committees* algorithm, or the *k-committees of r representatives* algorithm.

The set of representatives selected in a class will be called a committee of the class. As a committee of r representatives of the class C in our algorithm uses the points $x_1,...,x_r$ defined by

$$\text{minimize } \max_{y \in C} \min_{i=1,...,r} \|x_i - y\| \text{ subject to } x_1,...,x_r \in C,$$

i.e., the set X of r points from the finite set C such that the largest distance from any point y in C to the set X achieves a minimum.

Intui ively speaking, this means that the k-committees algorithm approxi

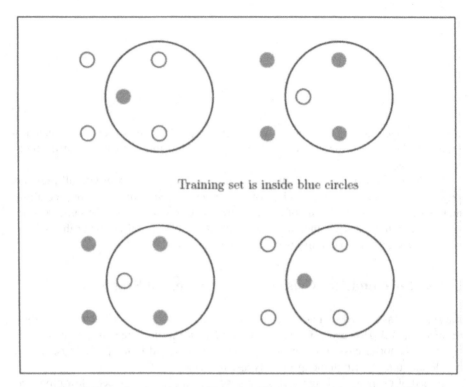

Training set is inside blue circles

Fig. 2. Example where k-committees classifier outperforms k-means and NN

For the ITS dataset our algorithm has to use only some of the given DNA sequences as new centroids and cannot compute new points, unlike other machine learning algorithms. Another serious difference is that the k-committees method concentrates on careful selection of a very small number of members for each committee. In contrast, various known modifications of the Nearest Neighbour algorithm deal with large sets of prototypes obtained by pruning or condensing the whole class by removing noise or outliers. It may be possible to compare the k-means and k-committees algorithms with elections of the presidents and state governments, and the Nearest Neighbour algorithm and its refinements with polls, statistical surveys and sampling processes.

We used the standard tenfold cross validation, explained in [16], Section 5.3, and investigated the efficiency of the classes produced by our algorithms for classifying new sequences that have not been included in the training set. With regard to the ITS dataset, the k-committees algorithm plays an intermediate role. To illustrate experi-

with r = 2.

6 Conclusions

The Nearest Neighbour, k-means, and k-committees classification algorithms based on alignment scores are suitable for practical analysis of datasets of this type, and have sufficiently high accuracy. These algorithms can be used for classifying new sequences not considered before as they become available.

Our algorithms use highly biologically significant local alignment scores as an indication of distance between sequences and achieve relatively high level of accuracy when compared with known biological classifications. The experimental results we have obtained demonstrate that the success rates of our algorithms are significantly higher than those of analogous methods using traditional Euclidean norms and presented, for example, on the WEKA web site (see [14]).

For ITS dataset the Nearest Neighbour classification algorithm with alignment scores has turned out to be more accurate but much slower than the k-means algorithm with these scores.

We have generated a synthesic data set where the k-committees classifier is substantially more accurate than both the discrete k-means method and the Nearest Neighbour classifier. This demonstrates that there exist 'noisy' datasets where the k-committees classifier outperforms two other algorithms considered in this paper. On the other hand, in the special case of the ITS dataset, the k-committees algorithm is intermediate in accuracy. Hence it can be used in situations where it is possible to spend CPU time on pre-processing data and prepare the committees of representatives in advance so that future classification questions are answered more quickly than by the Nearest Neighbour classifier, and more accurately than by the k-means classifier.

Acknowledgements

This research started during our joint work on IRGS grant K14313 of the University of Tasmania. The second author has been supported by several grants from the Asian Office of Aerospace Research and Development.

Annual IEEE/ACIS International Conference on Computer and Information Science, Melbourne, Australia, July 11-13, pp. 438–443 (2007)

5. Huda, S., Yearwood, J., Togneri, R.: A constraint based evolutionary learning approach to the expectation maximization for optiomal estimation of the Hidden Markov Model for speech signal modeling. IEEE Transactions on Systems, Man, Cybernetics, Part B 39(1), 182–197 (2009)

6. Kang, B.H., Kelarev, A.V., Sale, A.H.J., Williams, R.N.: A new model for classifying DNA code inspired by neural networks and FSA. In: Hoffmann, A., Kang, B.-h., Richards, D., Tsumoto, S. (eds.) PKAW 2006. LNCS (LNAI), vol. 4303, pp. 187–198. Springer, Heidelberg (2006)

7. Kaufman, L., Rousseeuw, P.J.: Finding Groups in Data: An Introduction to Cluster Analysis. John Wiley & Sons, New York (1990)

8. Kelarev, A.V., Kang, B.H., Sale, A.H.J., Williams, R.N.: Labeled directed graphs and FSA as classifiers of strings. In: 17th Australasian Workshop on Combinatorial Algorithms, AWOCA 2006, Uluru (Ayres Rock), Northern Territory, Australia, July 12–16, pp. 93–109 (2006)

9. Kelarev, A., Kang, B., Steane, D.: Clustering algorithms for ITS sequence data with alignment metrics. In: Sattar, A., Kang, B.-h. (eds.) AI 2006. LNCS (LNAI), vol. 4304, pp. 1027–1031. Springer, Heidelberg (2006)

10. Lee, K., Kay, J., Kang, B.H.: KAN and RinSCut: lazy linear classifier and rank-in-score threshold in similarity-based text categorization. In: Proc. ICML 2002 Workshop on Text Learning, University of New South Wales, Sydney, Australia, pp. 36–43 (2002)

11. Park, G.S., Park, S., Kim, Y., Kang, B.H.: Intelligent web document classification using incrementally changing training data set. J. Security Engineering 2, 186–191 (2005)

12. Sattar, A., Kang, B.H.: Advances in Artificial Intelligence. In: Proceedings of AI 2006, Hobart, Tasmania (2006)

13. Steane, D.A., Nicolle, D., Mckinnon, G.E., Vaillancourt, R.E., Potts, B.M.: High-level relationships among the eucalypts are resolved by ITS-sequence data. Australian Systematic Botany 15, 49–62 (2002)

14. WEKA, Waikato Environment for Knowledge Analysis,
http://www.cs.waikato.ac.nz/ml/weka

15. Washio, T., Motoda, H.: State of the art of graph-based data mining, SIGKDD Explorations. In: Dzeroski, S., De Raedt, L. (eds.) Editorial: Multi-Relational Data Mining: The Current Frontiers; SIGKDD Exploration 5(1), 59–68 (2003)

16. Witten, I.H., Frank, E.: Data Mining: Practical Machine Learning Tools and Techniques ith Java Implementati   Morgan Kaufmann, San Francisco (2005)